To my parents, Rocio Cruz and Felipe Gutierrez.

Introducing Spring Framework

A Primer

Felipe Gutierrez

Apress·

Introducing Spring Framework: A Primer

ISBN-13 (pbk): 978-1-4302-6532-0

ISBN-13 (electronic): 978-1-4302-6533-7

Publisher: Heinz Weinheimer
Lead Editor: Steve Anglin
Development Editor: Lori Bring
Technical Reviewer: Rohan Walia
Editorial Board: Steve Anglin, Mark Beckner, Ewan Buckingham, Gary Cornell, Louise Corrigan, James T. DeWolf, Jonathan Gennick, Jonathan Hassell, Robert Hutchinson, Michelle Lowman, James Markham, Matthew Moodie, Jeff Olson, Jeffrey Pepper, Douglas Pundick, Ben Renow-Clarke, Dominic Shakeshaft, Gwenan Spearing, Matt Wade, Steve Weiss
Coordinating Editor: Anamika Panchoo, Kevin Shea
Copy Editor: Mary Behr
Compositor: SPi Global
Indexer: SPi Global
Artist: SPi Global Cover Designer: Anna Ishchenko

Distributed to the book trade worldwide by Springer Science+Business Media New York, 233 Spring Street, 6th Floor, New York, NY 10013. Phone 1-800-SPRINGER, fax (201) 348-4505, e-mail orders-ny@springer-sbm.com, or visit www.springeronline.com. Apress Media, LLC is a California LLC and the sole member (owner) is Springer Science + Business Media Finance Inc (SSBM Finance Inc). SSBM Finance Inc is a Delaware corporation.

For information on translations, please e-mail rights@apress.com, or visit www.apress.com.

Apress and friends of ED books may be purchased in bulk for academic, corporate, or promotional use. eBook versions and licenses are also available for most titles. For more information, reference our Special Bulk Sales–eBook Licensing web page at www.apress.com/bulk-sales.

Any source code or other supplementary materials referenced by the author in this text is available to readers at www.apress.com. For detailed information about how to locate your book's source code, go to www.apress.com/source-code/.

Contents at a Glance

Contents

About the Author

Felipe Gutierrez is a software architect, with a bachelors and master degree in computer science from Instituto Tecnologico y de Estudios Superiores de Monterrey Campus Ciudad de Mexico. With over 20 years of IT experience, during which time he developed programs for companies in multiple vertical industries, such as government, retail, healthcare, education, and banking. Right now, he is currently working as a senior consultant for EMC/Pivotal, specializing in the Spring Framework, Groovy, and RabbitMQ, among other technologies. He works as a consultant for big companies like Nokia, Apple, Redbox, and Qualcomm, among others. He is also a technical reviewer for the upcoming book from Apress, *Spring Recipes, Third Edition.*

About the Technical Reviewer

Rohan Walia is a Senior Software Consultant with extensive experience in client-server, web-based, and enterprise application development. He is an Oracle Certified ADF Implementation Specialist and a Sun Certified Java Programmer. Rohan is responsible for designing and developing end-to-end applications consisting of various cutting-edge frameworks and utilities. His areas of expertise are Oracle ADF, Oracle WebCenter, Fusion, Spring, Hibernate, and Java/J2EE. When not working, Rohan loves to play tennis, hike, and travel. Rohan would like to thank his wife, Deepika Walia, for using all her experience and expertise to review this book.

Acknowledgments

I would like to express all my gratitude to the Apress team: to Steve Anglin for accepting my proposal; Anamika Panchoo for keeping me on track; Lori Bring and Mary Behr for their patience with me; Matthew Moodie, Kevin Shea, and Mark Powers for helping me out when I needed it; and the rest of the Apress team involved in this project. Thanks to everybody for making this possible.

Thanks to my technical reviewer, Rohan Walia, and the entire Spring team for making the Spring Framework the best programming and configuration model for modern Java-based enterprise applications.

Thanks to my parents, Rocio Cruz and Felipe Gutierrez, for all their love and support; and to my best friend, my brother Edgar Gerardo Gutierrez. Even though we live far away, we are closer than ever; thanks, "macnitous."

—Felipe Gutierrez

Introduction

This book is an introduction to the well-known Spring Framework that offers an inversion of control container for the Java platform. The Spring Framework is an open source application framework that can be used with any Java application.

After reading this book, you will know how to do the following:

- Use the Spring Framework efficiently.

- Add persistence through JDBC and NoSQL databases.

- Do unit and integration testing.

- Apply AOP (aspect-oriented programming) to separate concerns.

- Create web applications and expose RESTful APIs.

- Send messages via JMS and AMQP by using ActiveMQ and RabbitMQ.

- Use dynamic languages like Groovy, Ruby, and Bean Shell.

- Use Groovy with Spring.

- Use the new Spring Boot and Spring XD technologies.

Who This Book Is For

Introducing Spring Framework is a hands-on guide for any developer who is new to the Spring Framework and wants to learn how to build applications with it. Within this book you will find all the necessary elements to create enterprise-ready applications by using the Spring Framework and all its features and modules.

How This Book Is Organized

This book uses a simple **My Documents** application that you will develop incrementally over the course of the book. The book consists of the following four parts:

- Part I: Spring Framework Basic: You will learn about the dependency injection design pattern, and Spring's container implementation and how it will help you create a better design by programming towards interfaces. You'll learn the different configurations that you can apply to the Spring Framework. You will also learn how to use bean scopes, work with collections and resource files, and how to test your Spring applications.

- Part II: Spring Framework: You will learn how to use aspect-oriented programming by using different advices to separate concerns. Also, you'll learn to add persistence and integrate your Spring application with other systems. And you will be able to add your Spring application to the Web and expose some of the features of it by exposing the RESTful API. You'll also be able to send e-mails.

- Part III: Advance Techniques With Spring Framework: You will learn how to integrate existing applications with dynamic programming languages such as Groovy or Ruby. You'll learn how to use NoSQL databases with Spring and how to use RabbitMQ to send messages. Finally you will learn how to send tweets using Spring Social.

- Part IV: The New Spring I/O: You will learn how to integrate Spring and Groovy into your Spring application. You'll learn about two new technologies from the Spring team: Spring Boot, which simplifies your development by permitting zero configuration files, and Spring XD, a new technology for real-time analytics.

So let's go ahead and start with the Spring Framework!

PART I

Spring Framework Basics

The Spring Framework provides a programming and configuration model for creating Java-based enterprise applications. In Part I, you will learn all the basics of this framework.

You will begin by creating your very first Spring application and get a sneak peek at one of the newest technologies, Spring Boot. You'll see how Spring Boot will speed up your development. You will then start working with classes and their dependencies, and you'll see how they interact with each other. Then you will apply different configurations, find their differences and apply them to the Spring Framework.

After that you'll work with bean scopes and discover how the Spring container instantiates the classes depending on the scope of your choice. Also you will work with collections. You will find out how collections can interact with your Spring application. You'll be using resource files that will help you to have an external configuration without having to recompile your code.

Finally, you will use the Testing module from Spring to easily create unit and integration tests.

CHAPTER 1

■ ■ ■

Your First Spring Application

Most books start with a very long explanation about the technology they are using, the history of it, and often a small example that you can't run until you reach later chapters. In this book, I am going to take a different approach. I am going to start with some basic examples and I will explain in detail what they do and how to use them so that you get to know Spring quickly. The examples in this chapter will show you how easy it is to integrate the Spring Framework into any existing project or how to start one from scratch and modify it without any effort.

Figure 1-1 shows the Spring Framework web site, `http://spring.io`. In this web site, you can find all of the Spring Extensions, guides, and documentation to help you understand better the Spring ecosystem.

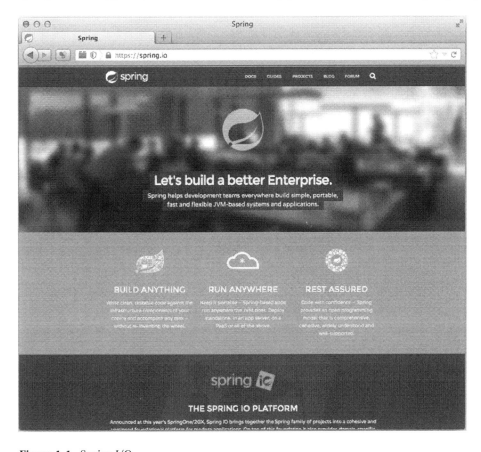

Figure 1-1. *Spring I/O*

Pre-Requirements

In order to start with the first example you need to have some tools installed.

- You need the Java JDK installed and configured. (The JVM must be accessible on the command line, either Windows or Unix). You can install the JDK 1.6 and above. Look for it at this link: www.oracle.com/technetwork/java/javase/downloads/index.html.

- Because you are going to use the latest version of Spring Framework, version 4.0.5.RELEASE, you are going to use Gradle to build and run your examples. So far Gradle is one of the best building tools available today that runs using Groovy as a primary language; it is extensible and robust; contains a better library management that can be extended; and is now the preferred way by the Spring core team to build the Spring Framework and its Extensions. If you want to know more about Gradle, take a look at their web site at www.gradle.org (see Figure 1-2).

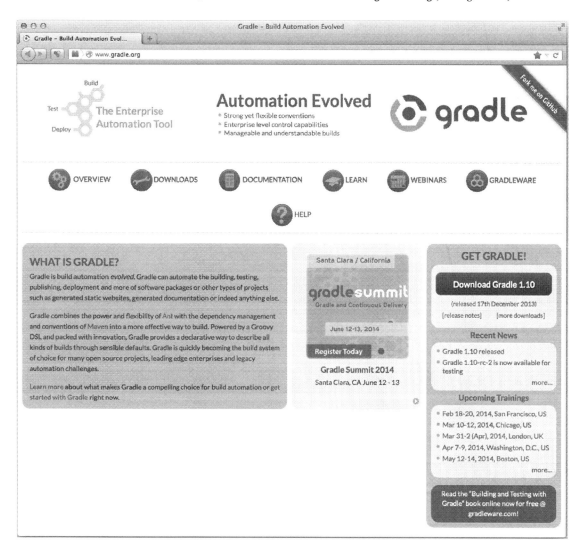

Figure 1-2. *Gradle Web Site*

░ **Note**   Appendix A shows you how to install Gradle.

Hello World Example

Let's start with the famous and well known "Hello World" example for your first Spring Application. You need to create the following folder structure (either in Windows or Unix).

- build.gradle
- ••• src
  - ••• main
    - ••• java
      - ••• com
        - ••• apress
          - ••• isf
            - ••• spring
              - Application.java
              - HelloWorldMessage.java
              - MessageService.java

Why do you need this folder structure? Gradle follows a community standard for creating Java applications, and primarily is based on Maven (an XML build tool that still is widely used) and a convention. So everything that belongs to the src/main/java folder will be compiled, and the result will be output to a build folder.

Listing 1-1 shows your build.gradle file. This file is the key for Gradle to run. In this file, you specify what plug-ins you are going to use. Every plug-in has its own tasks that you can run, such as compile, build, test, jar, etc. Also, you can specify what repositories to use in order to look for the dependencies you specified. In this example, you are going to use the spring-context module version 4.0.5.RELEASE that Gradle will download with all its dependencies. Furthermore, you are telling it that you are going to pass the name of the mainClass in order to run it.

Listing 1-1. build.gradle

```
apply plugin: 'java'
apply plugin: 'application'

mainClassName = System.getProperty("mainClass")

repositories {
    mavenCentral()
}

dependencies {
    compile 'org.springframework:spring-context:4.0.5.RELEASE'
}
```

Listing 1-2 shows a simple Interface with only one method.

Listing 1-2. MessageService.java

```
package com.apress.isf.spring;

public interface MessageService {
        public String getMessage();
}
```

Next, let's create the HelloWorldMessage that will return just the simple "Hello World" (see Listing 1-3).

Listing 1-3. HelloWorldMessage.java

```
package com.apress.isf.spring;

public class HelloWorldMessage implements MessageService {

        public String getMessage(){
                return "Hello World";
        }
}
```

Listing 1-3 shows the implementation of the interface in Listing 1-2. You can make any implementation you want if you keep following the contract that your interface provides. For example, right now you just return a string, but you can actually call a service or go into a database and pick a random message.

▓ **Note**   All of these examples can be edited using any text editor or any favorite IDE (integrated development environment).

Now you are ready to test your implementation, but you need to add a starting point.

Running the Hello World Application

Listing 1-4 shows the main class where you are going to test your MessageService class implementation (Listing 1-3, the HelloWorldMessage class). Now you need to take a look at Listing 1-4, because I am introducing some annotations (annotations were introduced as a new feature in Java 5). These annotations are markers for the Spring Framework to help understand your classes and they collaborate together. But wait! Spring Framework? Right now you are going to run this example as it is; later in this and the following chapter, you will learn what the Spring Framework is and how it can help you to deliver enterprise-ready applications.

Listing 1-4. Application.java

```
package com.apress.isf.spring;

import org.springframework.context.ApplicationContext;
import org.springframework.context.annotation.Bean;
import org.springframework.context.annotation. AnnotationConfigApplicationContext;
```

```
@Configuration
@ComponentScan
public class Application {

    @Bean          ← Dependency Injection
    MessageService helloWorldMessageService() {
                return new HelloWorldMessage();
    }

    public static void main(String[] args) {   ← Calling the Spring Container
                ApplicationContext context =
                    new AnnotationConfigApplicationContext(Application.class);

                MessageService service =
                                context.getBean(MessageService.class);
                System.out.println(service.getMessage());
    }
}
```

You must have Gradle installed, because this tool will help you to compile, build, and run all your examples. The following command will run the example. Also remember that this command should be executed from the root of the project where the build.gradle file is located.

```
gradle run -DmainClass=com.apress.isf.spring.Application
```

Running the above command should output something similar to the following:

```
isf-book$ gradle run -DmainClass=com.apress.isf.spring.Application
:ch01:compileJava UP-TO-DATE
:ch01:compileGroovy UP-TO-DATE
:ch01:processResources UP-TO-DATE
:ch01:classes UP-TO-DATE
:ch01:run
20:37:08.705 [main] DEBUG o.s.b.f.s.DefaultListableBeanFactory - Returning cached instance of
singleton bean 'helloWorldMessageService'
Hello World
```

■ **Note**   You can also run the gradle command from the project base by just adding the chapter's folder, like so:

```
$ gradle :ch01:run –DmainClass=com.apress.isf.spring.Application.
```

The Spring Framework is based on one simple principle: dependency injection. This is a design pattern that has been around for several years; it works, based on interface design, by injecting through setters or constructors all of the dependencies and implementations that have collaboration and interaction among classes. The Spring Framework creates a container that can handle all of this interaction and collaboration between objects.

This simple example defines an interface. In the main class, you are injecting its implementation by using the @Bean annotation over the helloWorldMessageService method. This will tell the Spring Framework container that the HelloWorldMessage class is the implementation and it will be used at some point.

Then, in your `main` method, you are calling the Spring container by using the `ApplicationContext` class. This class, with help from the other annotations (`@Config`, `@ComponentScan`, and `@Bean`), will create the container and wire everything up for ready to use, so when you call the `context.getBean` method the Spring Container already knows what object to use.

Note that if you change your implementation, it will be the only class to change; the other classes will remain intact. This will create an extensible and robust application, even if it is as simple as the Hello World example.

▮ **Note**   If you need to get more information about dependency injection and how it is used with the Spring Framework, I recommend the Pro Spring series of books from Apress.

In the following chapters, you will get more details on all of the features of the Spring Framework, the Spring Extensions, and subprojects, plus how you can use them.

Spring Boot: Even Easier

With the release of the Spring Framework 4, the Spring team also released a new extension of the Spring technology: Spring Boot. You are going to do a small example (the famous "Hello World") using this new technology and yes, this is also Spring.

Spring Boot makes development even easier. Any Spring application can be reduced to less code with minimum effort, and it will be production-ready. Let's create the folder structure and add the following files:

- `build.gradle`
- ●●● `src`
    - ●●● `main`
        - ●●● `java`
            - ●●● `com`
                - ●●● `apress`
                    - ●●● `isf`
                        - ●●● `spring`
                            - `HelloWorldController.java`

This shows the structure you are going to use and the `HelloWorldController.java` file that it will run. Note that it is necessary to create your `build.gradle` file to run your example (see Listing 1-5).

Listing 1-5. build.gradle

```
apply plugin: 'application'

mainClassName = System.getProperty("mainClass")

dependencies {
    compile("org.springframework.boot:spring-boot-starter-web:1.0.2.RELEASE")
}
repositories {
    mavenCentral()
    maven {
```

```
    url "http://repo.spring.io/libs-snapshot"
    url 'http://repo.spring.io/milestone'
    url 'http://repo.spring.io/libs-release'
    }
}
```

Listing 1-5 shows that instead of adding the Spring Framework dependency, now you are using a spring-boot-starter that will actually help to wire up everything to run this application as a web application.

Listing 1-6 shows your main class, the HelloWorldController; this class introduces new annotations that will help the Spring container know what to do and create the necessary collaboration classes and run it as a web application.

Listing 1-6. HelloWorldController.java

```java
package com.apress.isf.spring;

import org.springframework.boot.SpringApplication;
import org.springframework.boot.autoconfigure.EnableAutoConfiguration;
import org.springframework.stereotype.Controller;
import org.springframework.web.bind.annotation.RequestMapping;
import org.springframework.web.bind.annotation.ResponseBody;

@Controller
@EnableAutoConfiguration
public class HelloWorldController {

    @RequestMapping("/")
    @ResponseBody
    String getMessage() {
        return "<h1>Hello World!</h1>";
    }

    public static void main(String[] args) throws Exception {
        SpringApplication.run(HelloWorldController.class, args);
    }
}
```

The @Controller annotation will mark your class as a web controller that has a @RequestMapping and a @ResponseBody. All this means is that when your web application is running, it will accept requests from the http://localhost:8080/ URL and you should get some response back, such as the famous "Hello World" message.

Running the Spring Boot Application

Run the HelloWorldClass with the following command:

```
gradle - run -DmainClass=com.apress.isf.spring.HelloWorldController
```

You should have the following output after executing the gradle command:

```
isf-book$ gradle run -DmainClass=com.apress.isf.spring.HelloWorldController
:ch01:compileJava UP-TO-DATE
:ch01:compileGroovy UP-TO-DATE
:ch01:processResources UP-TO-DATE
:ch01:classes UP-TO-DATE
:ch01:run
:: Spring Boot ::         (v1.0.2.RELEASE)
INFO 84872 --- [main] .t.TomcatEmbeddedServletContainerFactory : Server initialized with port: 8080
INFO 84872 --- [main] o.apache.catalina.core.StandardService    : Starting service Tomcat
INFO 84872 --- [main] org.apache.catalina.core.StandardEngine   : Starting Servlet Engine: Apache
Tomcat/7.0.52
INFO 84872 --- [ost-startStop-1] o.a.c.c.C.[Tomcat].[localhost].[/]      : Initializing Spring
embedded WebApplicationContext
INFO 84872 --- [ost-startStop-1] o.s.web.context.ContextLoader           : Root
WebApplicationContext: initialization completed in 2030 ms
INFO 84872 --- [main] s.b.c.e.t.TomcatEmbeddedServletContainer : Tomcat started on port(s): 8080/http
INFO 84872 --- [main] c.a.isf.spring.HelloWorldController       : Started HelloWorldController in
7.086 seconds (JVM running for 7.599)
> Building 80% > :ch01:run
```

Now you can go to any browser and type in the URL http://localhost:8080 (see Figure 1-3).

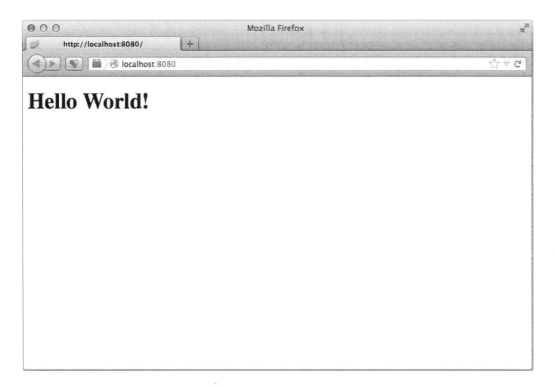

Figure 1-3. *Spring Boot Web Page*

Figure 1-3 shows the result of running the `HelloWorldController.java` file. Spring Boot will know what to do to create a web context and response to any request based on the annotation provided. But why am I showing this? Well if you know how to create a Java web application, you can see that Spring Boot simplifies everything because you're not writing any configuration files for a Java web application; it's configuration free!

Spring Boot, à la Groovy

Spring Boot also provides a powerful interaction with the Groovy programming language, making it even easier to create applications. But wait! Groovy? What is Groovy? The Groovy programming language is based on Java and of course is run on the JVM. If you know Java, you already know Groovy. Groovy is a dynamic programming language that gets rid of all of the boilerplate of any Java class and adds extensible methods to existing Java classes, making it a powerful language.

I am not going into the details of the Groovy language here, but I will say that it is one of the languages in the JVM community that has gathered many followers and developers. So the Spring Team has made the interaction between Groovy and the Spring Framework possible.

Let's continue with the next example. You are going to create only one file; there is no need to create any structure as before. Only one file:

• `app.groovy`

Listing 1-7 shows the `app.groovy` file.

Listing 1-7. app.groovy

```groovy
@Controller
class MyApp {

    @RequestMapping("/")
    @ResponseBody
    String message() {
        return "<h1>Hello World!</h1>"
    }

}
```

But why is Listing 1-7 different from Java? I just said that "if you know Java, you know Groovy." Well, if you add the `public` keywords to the class and the method, and you put a semicolon after every statement, you have a Java class. Note that you are still using some annotations like @controller, @RequestMapping, and @responseBody, similar to Listing 1-6. But now you are not using any imports! That's right! There is no package and there are no imports. Spring Boot will recognize all the annotations used and it will integrate all the libraries in this simple application.

Let's run the code in Listing 1-7, but before you do so, you need to install Spring Boot (see Appendix A for details on how to install Spring Boot on your system). Another difference from the previous example (Listing 1-6) is that you are not using Gradle this time. You are going to use the Spring Boot runtime environment, a command-line tool that will help you to build and run Groovy examples.

Once you have installed Spring Boot, you can execute the following command:

```
spring run app.groovy
```

After executing the above command, you should see something like the following output:

```
spring run app.groovy
Resolving dependencies..
:: Spring Boot ::          (v1.0.2.RELEASE)
INFO 84872 --- [main] .t.TomcatEmbeddedServletContainerFactory : Server initialized with port: 8080
INFO 84872 --- [main] o.apache.catalina.core.StandardService    : Starting service Tomcat
INFO 84872 --- [main] org.apache.catalina.core.StandardEngine   : Starting Servlet Engine: Apache
Tomcat/7.0.52
INFO 84872 --- [ost-startStop-1] o.a.c.c.C.[Tomcat].[localhost].[/]        : Initializing Spring
embedded WebApplicationContext
INFO 84872 --- [ost-startStop-1] o.s.web.context.ContextLoader             : Root
WebApplicationContext: initialization completed in 2030 ms
INFO 84872 --- [main] s.b.c.e.t.TomcatEmbeddedServletContainer : Tomcat started on port(s): 8080/http
INFO 84872 --- [main] c.a.isf.spring.HelloWorldController       : Started HelloWorldController in
7.086 seconds (JVM running for 7.599)
> Building 80% > :ch01:run
```

Now you can go to any web browser and type in the URL http://localhost:8080, and you should see the same as Figure 1-3. The Spring Boot will know what to do when it's running the app.groovy file. It will create a web context and response to any request based on the annotations provided.

Summary

In this chapter, you saw how to create a simple Spring "Hello World" application and run it. You also learned how Spring uses dependency injection to create all the dependencies and collaboration between classes. Thanks to the small example, you saw that it doesn't matter what implementation you create, as long as you follow the interface, Spring will inject its implementation and have it ready when you need it.

You got a small sneak peek of the Spring Boot, a new project by the Spring Team that will be covered in the following chapters. You also saw how Spring plays well with the Groovy programming language.

The following chapters will cover more detail of the Spring Framework, its features, and its Extensions. You'll learn how they work together and how they can be used in your daily development.

CHAPTER 2

Working with Classes and Dependencies

In this chapter, you are going to create an application that will help you understand the features and benefits of using the Spring Framework. In the next sections, I will discuss your application, what it does, and what do you need to do to create it.

You are going to use the book's companion source code, so you need to download it from the `Apress.com` web site. You will use the Gradle build tool to run and test your application.

My Spring Application – My Documents

In this section, I will describe the main application. You are going to name your Spring application "**My Documents**" and the main idea is to have an application where you can add any type of document (Microsoft Office, Apple Office, Open Documents, and PDFs), text notes, and web site links. They can be accessed any time in any device (computer, tablet, smart phone) and they will be organized in a way that makes them easy to find. Figure 2-1 shows a general diagram of the **My Documents** application. This diagram represents how **My Documents** is going to be searchable and the possible types of documents it can contain, such as notes, web links, and any other types (PDFs, for example).

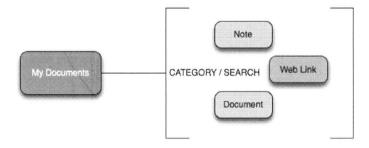

Figure 2-1. *The My Documents Project*

Requirements of **My Documents**

The following list shows the requirements for your **My Documents** application:

- Basic credentials (username, password)
- Ability to add, remove, delete, edit items/documents:
    - Microsoft Office, Apple, Open Documents, and PDF files
- Notes (text notes, limited to 255 characters)
- Web site links (URLs)
- Every item/document can be private or public
    - Private: The owner of the item/documents can see it
    - Public: Everybody can see the document
- Searchable by keyword, name, type, content, tags, category
    - Organizable by category
- Every item/document can be sent by e-mail or external messaging system

These requirements are simple—nothing too complicated. Keep in mind that every application tends to change over time, and this application will be no exception. **My Documents** will be your main Spring application for the entire book!

Defining Classes and Dependencies

The **My Documents** application will use some classes so you can see how dependencies work. You are going to start with something simple (see Figure 2-2).

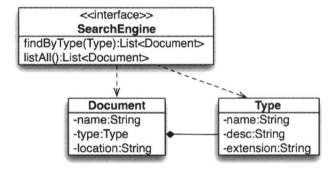

Figure 2-2. *UML Diagram*

Let's start by defining your Document file (see Listing 2-1).

Listing 2-1. Document.java

```
package com.apress.isf.java.model;

import java.util.Date;

public class Document {
        private String name;
        private Type type;
        private String location;
        private Date created;
        private Date modified;

        //Setters/Getters omitted
}
```

Your Document class (Listing 2-1) has a one-to-one relationship with the Type class. The Type class (see Listing 2-2) defines the type of document: a PDF, a note, or a web document.

Listing 2-2. Type.java

```
package com.apress.isf.java.model;
public class Type {
        private String name;
        private String desc;
        private String extension;

        //Setters/Getters omitted
}
```

Listing 2-3 shows your SearchEngine class that will use the Document class and the Type relationship. With this class, you can look for a specific type and retrieve all the relevant documents.

Listing 2-3. SearchEngine.java

```
package com.apress.isf.java.service;
public interface SearchEngine {
        public List<Document> findByType(Type documentType);
        public List<Document> listAll();
}
```

Once you have your base classes, it's time to create the implementation of the SearchEngine class interface, which for now is a simple class that will already have some of the documents listed (see Listing 2-4). You can find all of these files in <isf-book>/ch02/src.

Listing 2-4. MySearchEngine.java

```java
package com.apress.isf.java.service;

import java.util.ArrayList;
import java.util.List;

import com.apress.isf.java.model.Document;
import com.apress.isf.java.model.Type;
import com.apress.isf.java.service.SearchEngine;

public class MySearchEngine implements SearchEngine {

        @Override
        public List<Document> findByType(Type documentType) {
                List<Document> result = new ArrayList<Document>();
                for(Document document : storage()){
                                if(document.getType().getName()
                                        .equals(documentType.getName()))
                                result.add(document);
                }
                return result;
        }

        @Override
        public List<Document> listAll() {
                return storage();
        }

        private List<Document> storage(){
                List<Document> result = new ArrayList<Document>();

                Type type = new Type();
                type.setName("PDF");
                type.setDesc("Portable Document Format");
                type.setExtension(".pdf");

                Document document = new Document();
                document.setName("Book Template");
                document.setType(type);
                document.setLocation("/Documents/Book Template.pdf");

                result.add(document);

                //More Types and Documents omitted

                return result;
        }
}
```

As you can see, you just implemented the findByType and you used a *private storage* method that will retrieve some documents and their types. Also, you implemented the listAll method that directly uses the storage method. Note that this is a naïve example to start showing some of the Spring Framework features. Next, you need to test what you have done. So let's create a unit test using JUnit (see Listing 2-5).

Listing 2-5. MyDocumentsTest.java

```
package com.apress.isf.java.test;

import java.util.List;

import org.junit.Test;
import static org.junit.Assert.*;

import com.apress.isf.java.model.Document;
import com.apress.isf.java.model.Type;
import com.apress.isf.java.service.MySearchEngine;
import com.apress.isf.java.service.SearchEngine;

public class MyDocumentsTest {

        private SearchEngine engine = new MySearchEngine();

        @Test
        public void testFindByType() {
                Type documentType = new Type();
                documentType.setName("WEB");
                documentType.setDesc("Web Link");
                documentType.setExtension(".url");

                List<Document> documents = engine.findByType(documentType);
                assertNotNull(documents);
                assertTrue(documents.size() == 1);
                assertEquals(documentType.getName(),
documents.get(0).getType().getName());
                assertEquals(documentType.getDesc(),
documents.get(0).getType().getDesc());
                assertEquals(documentType.getExtension(),
documents.get(0).getType().getExtension());
        }

        @Test
        public void testListAll() {
                List<Document> documents = engine.listAll();
                assertNotNull(documents);
                assertTrue(documents.size() == 4);
        }

}
```

(handwritten note, pointing to the `private SearchEngine engine = new MySearchEngine();` line) ← this doesn't use Spring Dependency injection see page 20

In Listing 2-5, you are going to test the two methods you implemented. As you can see in the code, you are creating just a simple document and asserting that it belongs to the Documents list that you are getting from calling the findByType method. Now, let's run your test class using Gradle. Listing 2-6 shows the build.gradle file that you are going to use to run your unit test.

Listing 2-6. build.gradle

```
apply plugin: 'java'
apply plugin: 'groovy'
apply plugin: 'eclipse'
apply plugin: 'idea'

group = 'com.apress.isf'
version = '1.0'

repositories {
        mavenCentral()
}

dependencies {
compile 'org.codehaus.groovy:groovy-all:2.2.0'
compile 'org.springframework:spring-context:4.0.5.RELEASE'
        testCompile 'junit:junit:4.11'
}

test {
    testLogging {
        events 'started', 'passed'
    }
}
```

The following command will run the task: test. This will tell the Gradle tool that it needs to look for all the unit tests available in the code and execute them.

```
$ gradle test
```

After executing the above command, you should see something like the following output:

```
:ch02:compileJava
:ch02:compileGroovy
:ch02:processResources UP-TO-DATE
:ch02:classes
:ch02:compileTestJava
:ch02:processTestResources
:ch02:testClasses
:ch02:test

com.apress.isf.java.test.MyDocumentsTest > testFindByType STARTED
com.apress.isf.java.test.MyDocumentsTest > testFindByType PASSED
```

```
com.apress.isf.java.test.MyDocumentsTest > testListAll STARTED
com.apress.isf.java.test.MyDocumentsTest > testListAll PASSED

BUILD SUCCESSFUL

Total time: 12.039 secs
```

■ **Note** The above output shows all the tests in this chapter. You can run from the base project with the following command: `$ gradle :ch02:test`

Using the Spring Framework

As you can see, you started with a simple Java application, and a clean design using interfaces that will promote decoupling and will not depend on a specific implementation because it follows a contract. But there is still some code that you need to refactor in your unit test. Listing 2-5 shows that you need to instantiate a new `MySearchEngine` class, but what happens if you need to add a different implementation? Well, just change the name, and recompile and rerun to test it, right? Or maybe you need to instantiate more of these classes somewhere; it will be some hard work! That's why you need some kind of dependency mechanism tool to avoid this hassle. In other words, you need a way to create this dependency dynamically and avoid instantiating a class every time you add a new implementation.

The Spring Framework's primary goal is to offer a dependency injection container that will facilitate the creation of instances and interaction between objects. But how are you going to use the Spring Framework? And what is the dependency injection thing? Or the Spring container? Well, let's start coding and answer your questions.

You are going to create the file shown in Listing 2-7. If you are using the book's companion source code, you can find it at `<isf-book>/ch02/src/test/resources/META-INF/spring`.

Listing 2-7. mydocuments-context.xml

```xml
<?xml version="1.0" encoding="UTF-8"?>
<beans xmlns="http://www.springframework.org/schema/beans"
       xmlns:xsi="http://www.w3.org/2001/XMLSchema-instance"
       xsi:schemaLocation="http://www.springframework.org/schema/beans
http://www.springframework.org/schema/beans/spring-beans.xsd">

  <bean id="engine" class="com.apress.isf.java.service.MySearchEngine" />

  <bean id="documentType" class="com.apress.isf.java.model.Type">
    <property name="name" value="WEB" />
    <property name="desc" value="Web Link" />
    <property name="extension" value=".url" />
  </bean>

</beans>
```

Listing 2-7 shows an XML file. This file is the configuration that the Spring Framework needs to know in order to inject the dependencies and the interaction between objects. The main tag, `<beans/>`, uses XML namespaces to give your file the correct syntax and usage; and it can contain one or more children. In this case, it uses another tag, `<bean/>`. This is the key to define the dependency; here you are creating an *"engine"* bean that points to an implementation.

In this case, it's the com.apress.isf.java.service.MySearchEngine class and this class will be used by the Spring Framework to create the instance you need. Next, you defined a *"documentType"* bean that will create a new instance of a com.apress.isf.java.model.Type with its values. This will be similar to using the new keyword and the use of setters.

Next, you are going to modify your unit test, and you are going to start using some of the Spring Framework classes that will start up the container. It will instantiate your classes and it will know about the behavior of your application. Listing 2-8 shows your unit test class.

Listing 2-8. MyDocumentsTestWithSpring.java

```java
package com.apress.isf.spring.test;

import static org.junit.Assert.assertEquals;
import static org.junit.Assert.assertNotNull;
import static org.junit.Assert.assertTrue;

import java.util.List;

import org.junit.Before;
import org.junit.Test;
import org.springframework.context.support.ClassPathXmlApplicationContext;

import com.apress.isf.java.model.Document;
import com.apress.isf.java.model.Type;
import com.apress.isf.java.service.SearchEngine;

public class MyDocumentsWithSpringTest {

        private ClassPathXmlApplicationContext context;
        private SearchEngine engine;
        private Type documentType;

        @Before
        public void setup(){
                context = new ClassPathXmlApplicationContext("META-INF/spring/mydocuments-context.xml");
                engine = context.getBean(SearchEngine.class);
                documentType = context.getBean(Type.class);
        }

        @Test
        public void testWithSpringFindByType() {
                List<Document> documents = engine.findByType(documentType);
                assertNotNull(documents);
                assertTrue(documents.size() == 1);
                assertEquals(documentType.getName(),documents.get(0).getType().getName());
                assertEquals(documentType.getDesc(),documents.get(0).getType().getDesc());
                assertEquals(documentType.getExtension(),documents.get(0).getType().getExtension());
        }
}
```

[handwritten note: this uses Spring dependency injection]

```
        @Test
        public void testWithSpringListAll() {
                List<Document> documents = engine.listAll();
                assertNotNull(documents);
                assertTrue(documents.size() == 4);
        }
}
```

As you can see in Listing 2-8, you are using a ClassPathXmlApplicationContext class that will use your configuration file (see Listing 2-7); it will get the instance of the bean when you use the context.getBean method. The Spring Framework will automatically know what bean ID you are referring to because of its type. In this example, it will know that when you call context.getBean(SearchEngine.class) it will get your MySearchEngine implementation and so on for the Type class.

Next, let's run the test using the following command:

```
gradle run –Dtest.single=MyDocumentsWithSpringTest test
```

■ **Note** Remember that you can run the gradle command from the project base directory and execute the command gradle run –Dtest.single=MyDocumentsWithSpringTest :ch02:test.

The following output shows the result of running your unit test:

```
:ch02:compileJava
:ch02:compileGroovy
:ch02:processResources UP-TO-DATE
:ch02:classes
:ch02:compileTestJava
:ch02:compileTestGroovy
:ch02:processTestResources
:ch02:testClasses
:ch02:test

com.apress.isf.spring.test.MyDocumentsWithSpringTest > testWithSpringFindByType STARTED
com.apress.isf.spring.test.MyDocumentsWithSpringTest > testWithSpringFindByType PASSED
com.apress.isf.spring.test.MyDocumentsWithSpringTest > testWithSpringListAll STARTED
com.apress.isf.spring.test.MyDocumentsWithSpringTest > testWithSpringListAll PASSED

BUILD SUCCESSFUL

Total time: 11.33 secs
```

Spring Framework and Dependency Injection

The Spring Framework offers many features, and one of the most used is the dependency injection pattern. The Spring Framework offers this feature as a container that helps to manage your classes though a life cycle that can be used by other objects (also called managed beans) and for other services (see Figure 2-3).

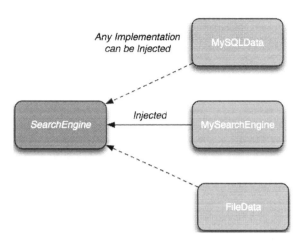

Figure 2-3. *Dependency Injection*

Figure 2-3 shows how any implementation of your SearchEngine interface can be injected. Perhaps you are searching through a database or maybe you're using a file to retrieve some information. The Spring Framework also provides several features such as the following:

- Dependency injection

- Aspect-oriented programming

- Data access

- Transaction management

- Web flow and MVC

- Social frameworks

- Messaging

- Remoting

- Testing

- and more…

Right now you do not need to worry about each of these features. Over the course of the book, you are going to see each one of them in action through your Spring application, **My Documents**.

I was talking about how the Spring Framework creates instances of your declared beans in the XML file (Listing 2-7), and how these are ready when you need them or are injected when required. But how does the Spring Framework know what classes need to be injected? The Spring Framework has several mechanisms to accomplish this: by name or by type. The injection can be either using Setters methods or constructors. But you are going to see this in detail in the following chapters. For now, let's take a look at Figure 2-4 for an overview of the Spring container.

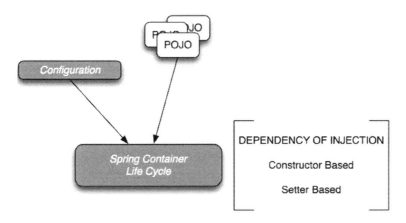

Figure 2-4. *Spring Container/Dependency Injection*

Figure 2-4 shows the Spring dependency injection container and its life cycle, using a configuration based on bean definitions. This configuration can be via XML, as you did, or Java configuration annotations, or programmatically.

In the book's companion source code, you can find the Groovy version of this chapter. You can run it using the following command:

```
gradle run –Dtest.single=MyDocumentsGroovyTest test
```

Summary

In this chapter, you defined your first Spring application, called **My Documents**. This application will evolve over the course of the entire book so you can experiment and add more features using the Spring Framework and its extensions.

You saw the differences using plain Java and you added a Spring flavor to it; the Spring Framework will help you to have a better object-oriented design, applying its dependency injection implementation.

In the next chapters, you will dive deeper into Spring and learn how to enhance your application. You will see how to use collections, how to add some persistence, and how to expose your application on the web, and much more!

CHAPTER 3

Applying Different Configurations

The Spring Framework supports different ways to configure its container and this chapter will cover the XML configuration used previously. Also, you are going to learn how can you accomplish the same configuration using different mechanisms, such as Spring annotations, Java bean configuration class, and the new GroovyBeanDefinitionReader class.

In the previous chapter, you defined your Spring application, **My Documents**, and you saw how to use a XML configuration file to inject your implementation of the SearchEngine interface. In this chapter, you will be using the same XML configuration and you will see what you need to do in order to use all of these new different ways of configuration.

My Documents XML Configuration

Let's start by reviewing your current XML configuration (from the **My Documents** application) context and examine it (see Listing 3-1).

Listing 3-1. mydocuments-context.xml

```xml
<?xml version="1.0" encoding="UTF-8"?>
<beans xmlns="http://www.springframework.org/schema/beans"
       xmlns:xsi="http://www.w3.org/2001/XMLSchema-instance"
       xsi:schemaLocation="http://www.springframework.org/schema/beans
http://www.springframework.org/schema/beans/spring-beans.xsd">

  <bean id="engine" class="com.apress.isf.java.service.MySearchEngine" />

  <bean id="documentType" class="com.apress.isf.java.model.Type">
    <property name="name" value="WEB" />
    <property name="desc" value="Web Link" />
    <property name="extension" value=".url" />
  </bean>

</beans>
```

Listing 3-1 shows how the Spring container needs to know something about the classes and its dependencies. As you saw in the previous chapter, you need to tell it through an XML configuration file. In this XML configuration file, you are telling the Spring container that your implementation of the SearchEngine will be the MySearchEngine bean with an id of "engine". In other words, you are assigning an identifier to your bean definition. Also, you are creating a new instance of the class Type, creating the "documentType" bean.

been

But wait! Bean? What does "bean" mean? In the Java world, this is a concept that has being around since the Java language was created, so the Spring Framework team followed the same naming convention. A Java bean must have some conventions like method naming (set/get/is), construction, and behavior, so it can be reusable and it can interact with other beans and other classes. Later, in the Java community, the Java bean was transformed to the well-known POJO: Plain Old Java Object.

The Spring Framework takes advantage of these conventions to know, create, inject, interact, and even destroy all the declared classes on its container.

A bean is declared as a <bean/> tag in the XML file and can contain the attributes described in Table 3-1.

Table 3-1. *Bean Tag Attributes*

Attribute	Description
id	An identifier for the bean. Only one unique ID can be defined.
class	Points to a concrete class, given the full java package.
scope	Tells the Spring container how it will create the bean; by default if this scope property is not set, the bean will be a singleton instance. Other scopes are prototype (an instance is created every time the bean is required), request (a single instance is created in each HTTP web request), and session (a bean is created and lives during the HTTP session).
init-method	This is the name of the method that will be called after a bean is created. It's useful when you want to set a state after your object is created.
factory-method	This is the name of the method that will be used to create the bean. In other words, you need to provide the method that will create the instance of the object, and this method should have parameters.
destroy-method	This is the name of the method that will be called after you dispose of the bean.
lazy-init	This can be set to true if you want the container to create your bean when it's being called or used by you (when you called the getBean method) or maybe later from another instance class that requires your object.

The Spring Framework has different ways to add information about your classes and their dependencies, and how they interact with each other. All of this will be covered throughout the book by adding some features to your Spring application, **My Documents**.

Listing 3-2 shows your SearchEngine implementation from the previous chapter: MySearchEngine looks like a lot of code, and there is a lot of data hard-coded that has been added to the class. So what happens if you need to add more types or more methods? You need to edit and recompile it again and again with any new changes. Too much work!

Listing 3-2. MySearchEngine.java

```
package com.apress.isf.java.service;

import java.util.ArrayList;
import java.util.List;

import com.apress.isf.java.model.Document;
import com.apress.isf.java.model.Type;
import com.apress.isf.java.service.SearchEngine;
```

```java
public class MySearchEngine implements SearchEngine {

        @Override
        public List<Document> findByType(Type documentType) {
                List<Document> result = new ArrayList<Document>();
                for(Document document : storage()){
                        if(document.getType().getName().equals(documentType.getName()))
                                result.add(document);
                }
                return result;
        }

        @Override
        public List<Document> listAll() {
                return storage();
        }

        private List<Document> storage(){
                List<Document> result = new ArrayList<Document>();

                Type type = new Type();
                type.setName("PDF");
                type.setDesc("Portable Document Format");
                type.setExtension(".pdf");

                Document document = new Document();
                document.setName("Book Template");
                document.setType(type);
                document.setLocation("/Users/felipeg/Documents/Random/Book Template.pdf");

                result.add(document);

                document = new Document();
                document.setName("Sample Contract");
                document.setType(type);
                document.setLocation("/Users/felipeg/Documents/Contracts/Sample Contract.pdf");

                result.add(document);

                type = new Type();
                type.setName("NOTE");
                type.setDesc("Text Notes");
                type.setExtension(".txt");

                document = new Document();
                document.setName("Clustering with RabbitMQ");
                document.setType(type);
                document.setLocation("/Users/felipeg/Documents/Random/Clustering with RabbitMQ.txt");

                result.add(document);
```

```
                type = new Type();
                type.setName("WEB");
                type.setDesc("Web Link");
                type.setExtension(".url");

                document = new Document();
                document.setName("Pro Spring Security Book");
                document.setType(type);
                document.setLocation("http://www.apress.com/9781430248187");

                result.add(document);

                return result;
        }
}
```

So, let's create a new implementation for your SearchEngine interface and use some of the setter-based dependency injections to add some types. Listing 3-3 is an example of your new SearchEngineService class.

Listing 3-3. SearchEngineService.java

```
package com.apress.isf.spring.service;

import java.util.ArrayList;
import java.util.Arrays;
import java.util.List;

import com.apress.isf.java.model.Document;
import com.apress.isf.java.model.Type;
import com.apress.isf.java.service.SearchEngine;
import com.apress.isf.spring.data.DocumentDAO;

public class SearchEngineService implements SearchEngine {

        private DocumentDAO documentDAO;

        public DocumentDAO getDocumentDAO() {
                return documentDAO;
        }

        public void setDocumentDAO(DocumentDAO documentDAO) {
                this.documentDAO = documentDAO;
        }

        public List<Document> findByType(Type documentType) {
                List<Document>  result = new ArrayList<Document>();
                for(Document doc : listAll()){
                        if(doc.getType().getName().equals(documentType.getName()))
                                result.add(doc);
                }
                return result;
        }
}
```

```
        public List<Document> listAll() {
                return Arrays.asList(documentDAO.getAll());
        }
}
```

Let's compare Listing 3-2 and Listing 3-3. In Listing 3-3, you got rid of the hard-coded code, you got rid of the storage method, and you are including a new attribute, documentDAO, which will be injected through its setter method, but you need to help the Spring container to know about this new attribute and the class that will contain the data.

Next, let's create the new classes, DocumentDAO and DocumentRepository. See Listing 3-4 and Listing 3-5. Listing 3-4 shows the DocumentDAO, which is the class that holds all the information about your documents that, for now, will be in memory. Of course, the DocumentRepository (see Listing 3-5) is your implementation of it.

Listing 3-4. DocumentDAO.java

```
package com.apress.isf.spring.data;

import com.apress.isf.java.model.Document;

public interface DocumentDAO {
        public Document[] getAll();
}
```

Listing 3-5 shows your DocumentRepository with four Document properties with their own setters and getters. And yes, you are going to inject four documents through their setters.

Listing 3-5. DocumentRepository.java

```
package com.apress.isf.spring.data;

import com.apress.isf.java.model.Document;

public class DocumentRepository implements DocumentDAO {

        private Document doc1;
        private Document doc2;
        private Document doc3;
        private Document doc4;

        public Document getDoc1() {
                return doc1;
        }

        public void setDoc1(Document doc1) {
                this.doc1 = doc1;
        }

        public Document getDoc2() {
                return doc2;
        }

        public void setDoc2(Document doc2) {
                this.doc2 = doc2;
        }
```

```
        public Document getDoc3() {
                return doc3;
        }

        public void setDoc3(Document doc3) {
                this.doc3 = doc3;
        }

        public Document getDoc4() {
                return doc4;
        }

        public void setDoc4(Document doc4) {
                this.doc4 = doc4;
        }

        public Document[] getAll() {
                return new Document[] { doc1, doc2, doc3, doc4 };
        }

}
```

Well, now this looks a little better. You are separating the way you are extracting the data, but how are you doing this? Well, if you recall, you were using some kind of storage method to retrieve the information, right? (See Listing 3-2.) Then you decided to reimplement your SearchEngine interface by adding a new way to get the data, and the solution was to create an interface that will be injected independent of its implementation, making your class more robust and easy to maintain. But let's see how you are going to modify the XML so the Spring container knows about all of these new modifications. Listing 3-6 is an example of your new modified mydocuments-context.xml configuration file. This configuration holds all the information about your new DocumentDAO class implementation (DocumentRepository) and how it's being injected in your SearchEngine implementation.

Listing 3-6. mydocuments-context.xml

```
<?xml version="1.0" encoding="UTF-8"?>
<beans xmlns="http://www.springframework.org/schema/beans"
        xmlns:xsi="http://www.w3.org/2001/XMLSchema-instance"
        xsi:schemaLocation="http://www.springframework.org/schema/beans
http://www.springframework.org/schema/beans/spring-beans.xsd">

  <bean id="engine" class="com.apress.isf.spring.service.ServiceSearchEngine">
      <property name="documentDAO" ref="documentDAO"/>
  </bean>

  <bean id="documentDAO" class="com.apress.isf.spring.data.DocumentRepository">
      <property name="doc1" ref="doc1"/>
      <property name="doc2" ref="doc2"/>
      <property name="doc3" ref="doc3"/>
      <property name="doc4" ref="doc4"/>
  </bean>
```

```xml
<bean id="doc1" class="com.apress.isf.java.model.Document">
    <property name="name" value="Book Template"/>
    <property name="type" ref="pdfType"/>
    <property name="location" value="/Users/felipeg/Documents/Random/Book Template.pdf"/>
</bean>

 <bean id="doc2" class="com.apress.isf.java.model.Document">
    <property name="name" value="Sample Contract"/>
    <property name="type">
        <bean id="pdfType" class="com.apress.isf.java.model.Type">
                <property name="name" value="PDF" />
                <property name="desc" value="Portable Document Format" />
                <property name="extension" value=".pdf" />
        </bean>
    </property>
    <property name="location" value="/Users/felipeg/Documents/Contracts/Sample Contract.pdf"/>
</bean>

<bean id="doc3" class="com.apress.isf.java.model.Document">
    <property name="name" value="Clustering with RabbitMQ"/>
    <property name="type" ref="noteType"/>
    <property name="location" value="/Users/felipeg/Documents/Random/Clustering with RabbitMQ.txt"/>
</bean>

<bean id="doc4" class="com.apress.isf.java.model.Document">
    <property name="name" value="Pro Spring Security Book"/>
    <property name="type" ref="webType"/>
    <property name="location" value="http://www.apress.com/9781430248187"/>
</bean>

<bean id="webType" class="com.apress.isf.java.model.Type">
  <property name="name" value="WEB" />
  <property name="desc" value="Web Link" />
  <property name="extension" value=".url" />
</bean>

<bean id="pdfType" class="com.apress.isf.java.model.Type">
  <property name="name" value="PDF" />
  <property name="desc" value="Portable Document Format" />
  <property name="extension" value=".pdf" />
</bean>

<bean id="noteType" class="com.apress.isf.java.model.Type">
  <property name="name" value="NOTE" />
  <property name="desc" value="Text Notes" />
  <property name="extension" value=".txt" />
</bean>

</beans>
```

Analyzing Listing 3-6, you can see that you are using some references like the ref attribute to assign a value; there's a new declaration of the ServiceSearchEngine; you are setting a property, documentDAO; and you are referencing the value to another bean with id "documentDAO".

Also, take a look on the bean with id "doc2". You are embedding a new bean as value; this is allowed by the Spring configuration rules.

As you can see, you are putting all your data about the types and documents in your XML file. Maybe there is a better way, but for now let's create your unit test. Listing 3-7 shows your modified unit test.

Listing 3-7. MyDocumentsTest.java

```java
package com.apress.isf.spring.test;

import static org.junit.Assert.*;

import java.util.List;

import org.junit.Before;
import org.junit.Test;
import org.springframework.context.support.ClassPathXmlApplicationContext;

import com.apress.isf.java.model.Document;
import com.apress.isf.java.model.Type;
import com.apress.isf.java.service.SearchEngine;

public class MyDocumentsTest {

        private ClassPathXmlApplicationContext context;
        private SearchEngine engine;
        private Type webType;

        @Before
        public void setup(){
                context = new ClassPathXmlApplicationContext("META-INF/spring/mydocuments-context.xml");
                engine = context.getBean(SearchEngine.class);
                webType = context.getBean("webType",Type.class);
        }

        @Test
        public void testWithSpringFindByType() {
                List<Document> documents = engine.findByType(webType);
                assertNotNull(documents);
                assertTrue(documents.size() == 1);
                assertEquals(webType.getName(),documents.get(0).getType().getName());
                assertEquals(webType.getDesc(),documents.get(0).getType().getDesc());
                assertEquals(webType.getExtension(),documents.get(0).getType().getExtension());
        }

        @Test
        public void testWithSpringListAll() {
                List<Document> documents = engine.listAll();
                assertNotNull(documents);
                assertTrue(documents.size() == 4);
        }

}
```

In Listing 3-7, in your setup() method (this method will run before each method in this class gets executed), you are using the ClassPathXmlApplicationContext class that will run your Spring container by creating and wiring up all the instances and having them ready when you need them.

Now let's run the unit test (see Listing 3-7) with the following command:

```
gradle test
```

Or if you are on the project's base path, you can run it with

```
gradle :ch03:test
```

▓ **Note**   Every chapter will contain several unit test files, so the following command will run a specific test:

```
gradle –Dtest.single=MyDocumentsTest test
```

So far you have seen how to configure the Spring container by adding beans and referencing them so the container knows about the creation and relationship, and gets them ready when you need them. Also, remember that the Spring Framework allows you to have different configurations apart from the XML, so in the next section you are going to see how to use annotations to accomplish the same configuration.

Using Spring Annotations

Java annotations were introduced in Java 5, and they added a great value to the Java language because you can add metadata to a class that can be used at compile time and at runtime, making new ways to develop. The Spring team took advantage of this new feature to provide a Spring annotation-based configuration. This feature was introduced in version 2.5.

But enough talk, let's go to the code and see what you are going to change in order to use the Spring annotation configuration. See Listing 3-8.

Listing 3-8. AnnotatedSearchEngine.java

```
package com.apress.isf.spring.annotated.service;

import java.util.ArrayList;
import java.util.Arrays;
import java.util.List;

import org.springframework.beans.factory.annotation.Autowired;
import org.springframework.stereotype.Service;

import com.apress.isf.java.model.Document;
import com.apress.isf.java.model.Type;
import com.apress.isf.java.service.SearchEngine;
import com.apress.isf.spring.data.DocumentDAO;
                                          ←— create bean with id = 'engine'
@Service("engine")   ←
public class AnnotatedSearchEngine implements SearchEngine {
```

tells Spring to create the instance

```
@Autowired  ⟵
private DocumentDAO documentDAO;

public List<Document> findByType(Type documentType) {
        List<Document>  result = new ArrayList<Document>();
        for(Document doc : listAll()){
                if(doc.getType().getName().equals(documentType.getName()))
                        result.add(doc);
        }
        return result;
}

public List<Document> listAll() {
        return Arrays.asList(documentDAO.getAll());
}
}
```

Listing 3-8 shows your new implementation of the SearchEngine, the AnnotatedSearchEngine class. As you can see, you are using the @Service("engine") and the @Autowired annotations. The Spring Framework supports several annotations (see Table 3-2) that are only markers or stereotypes like the @Service annotation. This annotation can have a value, in this case "engine", meaning that the container will create a bean with id: "engine" and it will point to the AnnotatedSearchEngine class. This is the same as putting the following tag in an XML file:

```
<bean id="engine" class="com.apress.isf.spring.annotated.service AnnotatedSearchEngine" />
```

Table 3-2. *Stereotypes*

Stereotype/Markers	Description
@Component	This is a marker, a generic stereotype that Spring will recognize as a Spring-managed component.
@Repository	This is a specialization of the @Component annotation and it fulfills the idea of the data access object. Classes annotated with this annotation can be processed by other tools or even aspects within the Spring container.
@Service	This is a specialization of the @Component annotation and it fulfills the idea of a service layer.
@Controller	This is also a specialization of the @Component annotation and normally is used on a web context.

Also, you used the @Autowired annotation. This annotation will tell the Spring container to actually create the instance and assign it to the declared variable. This will be the same as the following configuration:

```
<property name="documentDAO" ref="documentDAO" />
```

So, at the end, the AnnotatedSearchEngine class will be like having the following configuration all together:

```
<bean id="engine" class="com.apress.isf.spring.annotated.service AnnotatedSearchEngine">
        <property name="documentDAO" ref="documentDAO" />
</bean>
```

In Listing 3-9, you are going to create the AnnotatedDocumentRepository class. This class will have another marker or stereotype, @Repository, and this class will be injected into your SearchEngine implementation with the @Autowired annotation (see Listing 3-8).

Listing 3-9. AnnotatedDocumentRespository.java

```java
package com.apress.isf.spring.annotated.data;

import java.util.ArrayList;
import java.util.List;

import org.springframework.stereotype.Repository;

import com.apress.isf.java.model.Document;
import com.apress.isf.java.model.Type;
import com.apress.isf.spring.data.DocumentDAO;

@Repository("documentDAO")
public class AnnotatedDocumentRepository implements DocumentDAO {

        public Document[] getAll() {
                return storage();
        }

        private Document[] storage(){
                List<Document> result = new ArrayList<Document>();

                Type type = new Type();
                type.setName("PDF");
                type.setDesc("Portable Document Format");
                type.setExtension(".pdf");

                Document document = new Document();
                document.setName("Book Template");
                document.setType(type);
                document.setLocation("/Users/felipeg/Documents/Random/Book Template.pdf");

                result.add(document);

                document = new Document();
                document.setName("Sample Contract");
                document.setType(type);
                document.setLocation("/Users/felipeg/Documents/Contracts/Sample Contract.pdf");

                result.add(document);

                type = new Type();
                type.setName("NOTE");
                type.setDesc("Text Notes");
                type.setExtension(".txt");
```

```
            document = new Document();
            document.setName("Clustering with RabbitMQ");
            document.setType(type);
            document.setLocation("/Users/felipeg/Documents/Random/Clustering with RabbitMQ.txt");

            result.add(document);

            type = new Type();
            type.setName("WEB");
            type.setDesc("Web Link");
            type.setExtension(".url");

            document = new Document();
            document.setName("Pro Spring Security Book");
            document.setType(type);
            document.setLocation("http://www.apress.com/9781430248187");

            result.add(document);

            return result.toArray(new Document[result.size()]);
        }
}
```

Next, let's take a look at Listing 3-10. It shows your XML configuration file and the necessary tags that will tell the Spring container to look for annotated classes and their annotations. In this file, you are using a special tag: `<context:component-scan-base-package/>`. This tag belongs to an XML namespace that is also declared on your configuration. This new namespace will add more tags that you will see in the following chapters of the book. For now, this tag will instruct the Spring container to start looking for annotated classes from the package specified, in this case `"com.apress.isf.spring.annotated"` and all subpackages.

Listing 3-10. Mydocuments-annotations-context.xml

```
<?xml version="1.0" encoding="UTF-8"?>
<beans xmlns="http://www.springframework.org/schema/beans"
       xmlns:xsi="http://www.w3.org/2001/XMLSchema-instance"
       xmlns:context="http://www.springframework.org/schema/context"
       xsi:schemaLocation="http://www.springframework.org/schema/beans
http://www.springframework.org/schema/beans/spring-beans.xsd
            http://www.springframework.org/schema/context
http://www.springframework.org/schema/context/spring-context-4.0.xsd">

  <context:component-scan base-package="com.apress.isf.spring.annotated"/>

  <bean id="webType" class="com.apress.isf.java.model.Type">
    <property name="name" value="WEB" />
    <property name="desc" value="Web Link" />
    <property name="extension" value=".url" />
  </bean>

</beans>
```

Spring Stereotypes

Spring sterotypes are simply markers that help the Spring container to identify them as Spring-managed components. These markers can be used for external processing tools or can be used as a reference for pointcuts in an aspect-oriented programming context. Nowadays in the Spring community, in many projects, the use of these stereotypes helps not only to understand the code by making it more readable but also by identifying the structure and the architectural layers. The most used stereotypes (by the Spring community and of course in your Spring application **My Documents**) are described in Table 3-2.

Using the Java Bean Configuration

The Spring Framework version 3.0 adopted a new way to configure the Spring container, using a new Java bean configuration class. This began as a separate project, but the Spring Framework team included it in version 3.0 as a part of its core. Nowadays it is one of the most preferable ways to configure the container, because it helps to get a clear picture of the relationship between classes and it shows how it interacts between them. And, in some cases it even helps to avoid all the clutter of using XML files.

Now let's see the following Java configuration class. Listing 3-11 is the equivalent of your XML configuration file (see Listing 3-6). Every bean definition in your XML corresponds to the @Bean annotation placed into the method.

Listing 3-11. MyDocumentsContext.java

```
package com.apress.isf.spring.config;

import java.util.HashMap;
import java.util.Map;

import org.springframework.context.annotation.Bean;
import org.springframework.context.annotation.Configuration;

import com.apress.isf.java.model.Document;
import com.apress.isf.java.model.Type;
import com.apress.isf.java.service.SearchEngine;
import com.apress.isf.spring.data.DocumentDAO;
import com.apress.isf.spring.data.DocumentRepository;
import com.apress.isf.spring.service.ServiceSearchEngine;

@Configuration
public class MyDocumentsContext {

        private Map<String,Document> documents = new HashMap<String,Document>();
        private Map<String,Type> types = new HashMap<String,Type>();

        @Bean
        public Type webType(){
                return getTypeFromMap("web");
        }

        @Bean
        public SearchEngine engine(){
                ServiceSearchEngine engine = new ServiceSearchEngine();
                engine.setDocumentDAO(documentDAO());
                return engine;
        }
```

```java
public MyDocumentsContext(){
        Type type = new Type();
        type.setName("PDF");
        type.setDesc("Portable Document Format");
        type.setExtension(".pdf");

        Document document = new Document();
        document.setName("Book Template");
        document.setType(type);
        document.setLocation("/Users/felipeg/Documents/Random/Book Template.pdf");

        documents.put("doc1", document);
        types.put("pdf",type);

        document = new Document();
        document.setName("Sample Contract");
        document.setType(type);
        document.setLocation("/Users/felipeg/Documents/Contracts/Sample Contract.pdf");

        documents.put("doc2",document);

        type = new Type();
        type.setName("NOTE");
        type.setDesc("Text Notes");
        type.setExtension(".txt");

        document = new Document();
        document.setName("Clustering with RabbitMQ");
        document.setType(type);
        document.setLocation("/Users/felipeg/Documents/Random/Clustering with RabbitMQ.txt");

        documents.put("doc3",document);
        types.put("note",type);

        type = new Type();
        type.setName("WEB");
        type.setDesc("Web Link");
        type.setExtension(".url");

        document = new Document();
        document.setName("Pro Spring Security Book");
        document.setType(type);
        document.setLocation("http://www.apress.com/9781430248187");

        documents.put("doc4",document);
        types.put("web",type);
}
```

```
        private DocumentDAO documentDAO(){
                DocumentRepository documentDAO = new DocumentRepository();
                documentDAO.setDoc1(getDocumentFromMap("doc1"));
                documentDAO.setDoc2(getDocumentFromMap("doc2"));
                documentDAO.setDoc3(getDocumentFromMap("doc3"));
                documentDAO.setDoc4(getDocumentFromMap("doc4"));
                return documentDAO;
        }

        private Document getDocumentFromMap(String documentKey){
                return documents.get(documentKey);
        }

        private Type getTypeFromMap(String typeKey){
                return types.get(typeKey);
        }
}
```

As you can see in Listing 3-10, you are adding @Configuration at the top of the class and in the methods the @Bean annotations. When you use the @Configuration, it is like telling the Spring container, "here are my bean definitions." And when you use the @Bean annotation over a method, it is the same as creating the <bean/> tag and setting its properties. So, this class will tell the Spring container what the beans are and how they will be wired.

Now, let's use this new Java bean configuration feature in your unit test. See Listing 3-12.

Listing 3-12. MyDocumentsBeanConfigurationTest.java

```
package com.apress.isf.spring.test;

import static org.junit.Assert.assertNotNull;
import static org.junit.Assert.assertTrue;
import static org.junit.Assert.assertEquals;

import java.util.List;

import org.junit.Before;
import org.junit.Test;
import org.springframework.context.ApplicationContext;
import org.springframework.context.annotation.AnnotationConfigApplicationContext;

import com.apress.isf.java.model.Document;
import com.apress.isf.java.model.Type;
import com.apress.isf.java.service.SearchEngine;
import com.apress.isf.spring.config.MyDocumentsContext;

public class MyDocumentsBeanConfigurationTest {

        private ApplicationContext context;
        private SearchEngine engine;
        private Type webType;
```

```
        @Before
        public void setup(){
                context = new AnnotationConfigApplicationContext(MyDocumentsContext.class);
                engine = context.getBean(SearchEngine.class);
                webType = context.getBean(Type.class);
        }

        @Test
        public void testWithBeanConfigurationFindByType() {
                List<Document> documents = engine.findByType(webType);
                assertNotNull(documents);
                assertTrue(documents.size() == 1);
                assertEquals(webType.getName(),documents.get(0).getType().getName());
                assertEquals(webType.getDesc(),documents.get(0).getType().getDesc());
                assertEquals(webType.getExtension(),documents.get(0).getType().getExtension());
        }

        @Test
        public void testWithBeanConfigurationListAll() {
                List<Document> documents = engine.listAll();
                assertNotNull(documents);
                assertTrue(documents.size() == 4);
        }
}
```

In Listing 3-12, you are now using the AnnotationConfigApplicationContext class to load your Java configuration class. This will tell the Spring container that the configuration will be based on a class and not on an XML file.

Running your unit test (see Listing 3-12) will be the same as running the gradle command:

```
gradle test
```

Using the GroovyBeanDefinitionReader Class

The new Spring Framework 4 introduces a new way to configure beans using the Groovy programming language. This new feature was based on the Grails Framework, introducing a DSL (domain-specific language) for creating beans.

Let's examine the following example in Listing 3-13.

Listing 3-13. mydocuments.groovy

```
import com.apress.isf.spring.service.ServiceSearchEngine
import com.apress.isf.spring.data.DocumentRepository
import com.apress.isf.java.model.Document

beans {

        engine(ServiceSearchEngine){
                documentDAO = ref("documentDAO")
        }
```

```groovy
    documentDAO(DocumentRepository){
            doc1 = ref("doc1")
            doc2 = ref("doc2")
            doc3 = ref("doc3")
            doc4 = ref("doc4")
    }

    doc1(Document){
            name = "Book Template"
            type = ref("pdfType")
            location = "/Users/felipeg/Documents/Random/Book Template.pdf"
    }

    doc2(Document){
            name = "Sample Contract"
            type = ref("pdfType")
            location = "/Users/felipeg/Documents/Contracts/Sample Contract.pdf"
    }

    doc3(Document){
            name = "Clustering with RabbitMQ"
            type = ref("noteType")
            location = "/Users/felipeg/Documents/Random/Clustering with RabbitMQ.txt"
    }

    doc4(Document){
            name = "Pro Spring Security Book"
            type = ref("webType")
            location = "http://www.apress.com/9781430248187"
    }

    webType(com.apress.isf.java.model.Type){
            name = "WEB"
            desc = "Web Link"
            extension = ".url"
    }

    pdfType(com.apress.isf.java.model.Type){
            name = "PDF"
            desc = "Portable Document Format"
            extension = ".url"
    }

    noteType(com.apress.isf.java.model.Type){
            name = "NOTE"
            desc = "Text Notes"
            extension = ".txt"
    }
}
```

Listing 3-13 shows a new way to represent the XML (see Listing 3-6), the annotated (see Listing 3-9), or the Java configuration class (see Listing 3-10), but now using Groovy as a primary language. Right now you don't need to worry about the syntax because I will be covering it in Chapter 18.

Now, let's create your unit test (see Listing 3-14). In this unit test, you will use a new class to load your bean definitions: the GroovyBeanDefinitionReader. This class will load the mydocuments.groovy Listing 3-13 file.

Listing 3-14. MyDocumentsBeanDefinitionReaderTest.java

```java
package com.apress.isf.spring.test;

import static org.junit.Assert.assertEquals;
import static org.junit.Assert.assertNotNull;
import static org.junit.Assert.assertTrue;

import java.util.List;

import org.junit.Before;
import org.junit.Test;
import org.springframework.context.ApplicationContext;
import org.springframework.context.support.GenericGroovyApplicationContext;

import com.apress.isf.java.model.Document;
import com.apress.isf.java.model.Type;
import com.apress.isf.java.service.SearchEngine;

public class MyDocumentsBeanDefinitionReaderTest {

        private ApplicationContext context;
        private SearchEngine engine;
        private Type webType;

        @Before
        public void setup(){
                context = new GenericGroovyApplicationContext("META-INF/spring/mydocuments.groovy");
                engine = context.getBean(SearchEngine.class);
                webType = context.getBean("webType",Type.class);
        }

        @Test
        public void testWithGroovyFindByType() {
                List<Document> documents = engine.findByType(webType);
                assertNotNull(documents);
                assertTrue(documents.size() == 1);
                assertEquals(webType.getName(),documents.get(0).getType().getName());
                assertEquals(webType.getDesc(),documents.get(0).getType().getDesc());
                assertEquals(webType.getExtension(),documents.get(0).getType().getExtension());
        }

        @Test
        public void testWithGroovyListAll() {
                List<Document> documents = engine.listAll();
                assertNotNull(documents);
                assertTrue(documents.size() == 4);
        }

}
```

In Listing 3-14, you are now using the GenericGroovyApplicationContext class that will load your Groovy script, by passing the groovy file's classpath where it is located (META-INF/spring/mydocuments.groovy); it will start up your Spring Container by creating all the necessary instances, wiring up your classes and having them ready when you need them. Remember that you are now using Groovy! to configure your Spring container.

And now run your unit test with the following command:

```
gradle test
```

Which Configuration to Choose?

Every type of configuration has some differences and some applicable usage (see Table 3-3).

Table 3-3. *Differences and Usage*

Type of Configuration	Usage
XML	This can be used with third party libraries and/or different development environments. It's easy to read and follow but it can grow, and even though it can be split into different files, you need to keep track of them.
Annotations	It is another way to do configurations, but here you are attaching the Spring context to your application. This can be avoided by using your own domain-based annotations and just these can be annotated.
Java Bean Configuration	This is now one of the preferred methods for developers who hate to struggle with the XML, and it can be used for beans or components that don't change too much.
Groovy Bean Configuration	This is a new complete feature that can be used with the power of the Groovy programming language; it's simple and there's less to type.

So it will depend on your needs and how you want to manage your development cycle. Or you may have a team that prefers some configuration because it is easy to manage and doesn't affect your development goals.

Summary

In this chapter, you saw ways to accomplish the same behavior using different styles or conventions to create beans. You saw the different classes that load up your beans, such as ClassPathXmlApplicationContext, AnnotationConfigApplicationContext, and the new GenericGroovyApplicationContext.

You saw how you can annotate classes so the Spring container knows about the beans to use, its dependencies, and relationship with other classes. You saw how the @Repository marks your class as a Spring-managed component that act as a data access object.

Also, you saw how to use the Java configuration class and its @Configuration and @Bean annotations to create the beans and their relationship. And you saw how to use Groovy to expose the beans using the Groovy programming language.

In the next chapter, you are going to start adding more features to your Spring application, **My Documents**. You'll learn how the Spring container initiates your classes and the different approaches you can take in order to get different instances of the same class.

CHAPTER 4

■ ■ ■

Using Beans Scopes

So far you have an application called **My Documents** that for now is exposing a service that returns either all the documents available or it can return a list of documents by specific type. We were talking about the SearchEngine class implementation and the way you had configured it. Based on your XML configuration, you have set its scope to be a Singleton class, meaning that every time you require it by invoking the context.getBean method, you always get the same instance. But what happens if you require different instances, such as another service that is required to handle a fresh instance of your SearchEngine implementation to use its search methods.

In this chapter, I will talk about how the Spring Framework instantiates the classes and its dependencies in the **My Documents** application, by using your existing code and classes such as the SearchEngine implementation. You will see what scopes you can use and the benefits of each one.

Scopes

Right now your existing code doesn't print out any information about what is going on, so let's start by putting some *logs* (recording activity) into your classes so you know what is happening when the Spring container creates and uses them as shown in Listing 4-1.

Listing 4-1. SearchEngineService.java

```java
package com.apress.isf.spring.service;

import java.util.ArrayList;
import java.util.Arrays;
import java.util.List;

import org.slf4j.Logger;
import org.slf4j.LoggerFactory;

import com.apress.isf.java.model.Document;
import com.apress.isf.java.model.Type;
import com.apress.isf.java.service.SearchEngine;
import com.apress.isf.spring.data.DocumentDAO;

public class SearchEngineService implements SearchEngine {
    private static final Logger log =
LoggerFactory.getLogger(ServiceSearchEngine.class);
    private DocumentDAO documentDAO;
```

this doesn't work probably Best to just use

45

[handwritten margin note: Can't Figure out how to make this work to make this visible from commenting out this first line a using log.info]

```java
    public ServiceSearchEngine(){
        if(log.isDebugEnabled())
                log.debug("ServiceSearchEngine created: " + this);
    }

    public DocumentDAO getDocumentDAO() {
        return documentDAO;
    }

    public void setDocumentDAO(DocumentDAO documentDAO) {
        if(log.isDebugEnabled())
                log.debug("Document DAO set: " + documentDAO);

        this.documentDAO = documentDAO;
    }

    public List<Document> findByType(Type documentType) {
        List<Document>  result = new ArrayList<Document>();
        for(Document doc : listAll()){
            if(doc.getType().getName().equals(documentType.getName()))
                    result.add(doc);
        }
        return result;
    }

    public List<Document> listAll() {
        return Arrays.asList(documentDAO.getAll());
    }

}
```

In Listing 4-1 you have just added a Logger into your ServiceSearchEngine class using the SLF4J library. Also, you added a constructor for this class, and you have set the level of debug in the same constructor and in the setter method for your DocumentDAO implementation. With this, every time the container creates an instance, you should see ServiceSearchEngine create: <ID> with some object ID. When the container sets your DocumentDAO implementation, you should see the output Document DAO set: <ID> with some Object ID. For now you haven't changed anything in the code; you only added the Logger just to illustrate what the Spring container is doing when it creates your beans.

Now let's see Listing 4-2, the class MyDocumentTest, because you need to modify it in order to see some of these bean scopes.

Listing 4-2. MyDocumentTest.java

```java
package com.apress.isf.spring.test;

import static org.junit.Assert.*;

import java.util.List;

import org.junit.Before;
import org.junit.Test;
import org.springframework.context.support.ClassPathXmlApplicationContext;
```

```
import com.apress.isf.java.model.Document;
import com.apress.isf.java.model.Type;
import com.apress.isf.java.service.SearchEngine;

public class MyDocumentsTest {

        private ClassPathXmlApplicationContext context;
        private SearchEngine engine;
        private Type webType;

        @Before
        public void setup(){
                context = new ClassPathXmlApplicationContext("META-INF/spring/mydocuments-context.xml");
        }

        @Test
        public void testAll() {
                engine = context.getBean(SearchEngine.class);
                webType = context.getBean("webType",Type.class);

                List<Document> documents = engine.findByType(webType);
                assertNotNull(documents);
                assertTrue(documents.size() == 1);
                assertEquals(webType.getName()
                                ,documents.get(0).getType().getName());
                assertEquals(webType.getDesc()
                                ,documents.get(0).getType().getDesc());
                assertEquals(webType.getExtension()
                                ,documents.get(0).getType().getExtension());

                engine = context.getBean(SearchEngine.class);

                documents = engine.listAll();
                assertNotNull(documents);
                assertTrue(documents.size() == 4);
        }

}
```

In Listing 4-2, you have simply created one test method that contains the call of the getBean method. In this case, you want to know how the Spring container can deal with the creation of the SearchEngine and the injection of your DocumentDAO implementation.

If you run Listing 4-2 without modifying the XML file (mydocuments-context.xml), then you should see the following output:

```
$ gradle  -Dtest.single=MyDocumentsTest test

DEBUG [main] ServiceSearchEngine created: com.apress.isf.spring.service.ServiceSearchEngine@1aee419f
DEBUG [main] Document DAO set: com.apress.isf.spring.data.DocumentRepository@53b97d73
```

this doesn't work

47

The result is *one* SearchEngineService instance and *one* DocumentDAO instance (your concrete class, DocumentRespository). But why? Remember that by default the Spring Framework only creates a Singleton instance of your bean, so even if you call this bean (with the getBean method) several times, you are going to get the same instance.

Now, let's modify the XML and how the Spring container uses the bean scopes. See Listing 4-3 for the XML configuration.

Listing 4-3. mydocuments-context.xml

```
<beans xmlns="http://www.springframework.org/schema/beans"
       xmlns:xsi="http://www.w3.org/2001/XMLSchema-instance"
       xsi:schemaLocation="http://www.springframework.org/schema/beans
http://www.springframework.org/schema/beans/spring-beans.xsd">

  <bean id="engine" class="com.apress.isf.spring.service.ServiceSearchEngine" scope="prototype">
     <property name="documentDAO" ref="documentDAO"/>
  </bean>

  <bean id="documentDAO" class="com.apress.isf.spring.data.DocumentRepository" scope="prototype">
     <property name="doc1" ref="doc1"/>
     <property name="doc2" ref="doc2"/>
     <property name="doc3" ref="doc3"/>
     <property name="doc4" ref="doc4"/>
  </bean>
 <!--Docs and Types omitted -->
</beans>
```

In Listing 4-3, you added the scope prototype attribute to the beans engine and documentDAO. The Spring container will create a new instance of these classes once the getBean method from the application context is called. If you run the test again, you will see the following output:

```
$ gradle –Dtest.simple=MyDocumentTest test

DEBUG [main] ServiceSearchEngine created: com.apress.isf.spring.service.ServiceSearchEngine@2ac1d29e
DEBUG [main] Document DAO set: com.apress.isf.spring.data.DocumentRepository@702557dd
DEBUG [main] ServiceSearchEngine created: com.apress.isf.spring.service.ServiceSearchEngine@23aba7b0
DEBUG [main] Document DAO set: com.apress.isf.spring.data.DocumentRepository@5a8e261b
```

As you can see, now you have different instances because you call the method getBean twice for the engine and every time you get a new instance; the same happens for the documentDAO setter.

Table 4-1 shows how the Bean Scopes are handled by the Spring container. These scopes can be defined as an attribute in the bean tag (XML context) or as a @Scope annotation if you are using annotation or Java configuration classes.

Table 4-1. *Bean Scopes*

Scope	Definition
singleton	The Spring container returns a single instance. This is the default value.
prototype	The Spring container returns a new instance every time it is requested.
request	The Spring container returns a new instance on each HTTP request; this is used in a web context.
session	The Spring container returns a new instance on each HTTP session; this is used in a web context.
globalSession	The Spring container returns a single instance per global HTTP session; this is used in a web context.

In the next sections, you will see different ways to use these bean scopes. You need to be very careful to choose the right scope because that could impact your application.

Using the @Scope Annotation

You need to remember that the Spring Framework has different ways to configure its container: XML, annotations, Java configuration classes, and the new GroovyBeanDefinitionReader. If you are going to use either the annotated beans or the Java bean configuration to get the instance of your beans, then it is necessary to use the @Scope annotation. Listing 4-4 shows the modified code.

Listing 4-4. AnnotatedSearchEngine.java

```
package com.apress.isf.spring.annotated.service;

import java.util.ArrayList;
import java.util.Arrays;
import java.util.List;

import org.slf4j.Logger;
import org.slf4j.LoggerFactory;
import org.springframework.beans.factory.annotation.Autowired;
import org.springframework.context.annotation.Scope;
import org.springframework.stereotype.Service;

import com.apress.isf.java.model.Document;
import com.apress.isf.java.model.Type;
import com.apress.isf.java.service.SearchEngine;
import com.apress.isf.spring.data.DocumentDAO;
import com.apress.isf.spring.service.ServiceSearchEngine;

@Service("engine")
@Scope("prototype")
public class AnnotatedSearchEngine implements SearchEngine {

        private static final Logger log =
LoggerFactory.getLogger(ServiceSearchEngine.class);
```

```
        @Autowired
        private DocumentDAO documentDAO;

        public AnnotatedSearchEngine(){
                if(log.isDebugEnabled())
                        log.debug("AnnotatedSearchEngine created: " + this);
        }

        public List<Document> findByType(Type documentType) {
                List<Document>   result = new ArrayList<Document>();
                for(Document doc : listAll()){
                        if(doc.getType().getName().equals(documentType.getName()))
                                result.add(doc);
                }
                return result;
        }

        public List<Document> listAll() {
                return Arrays.asList(documentDAO.getAll());
        }
}
```

Listing 4-4 shows the @Scope annotation that is placed over your class with a "prototype" value. Also, you can see the use of the Logger.

Listing 4-5 shows a Java configuration class and the use of the @Scope annotation. All these configurations are similar whether you use XML, annotation, or the Java configuration class.

Listing 4-5. MyDocumentsContext.java

```
package com.apress.isf.spring.config;

import java.util.HashMap;
import java.util.Map;

import org.springframework.context.annotation.Bean;
import org.springframework.context.annotation.Configuration;
import org.springframework.context.annotation.Scope;

import com.apress.isf.java.model.Document;
import com.apress.isf.java.model.Type;
import com.apress.isf.java.service.SearchEngine;
import com.apress.isf.spring.data.DocumentDAO;
import com.apress.isf.spring.data.DocumentRepository;
import com.apress.isf.spring.service.ServiceSearchEngine;

@Configuration
public class MyDocumentsContext {
        private static final Logger log =
LoggerFactory.getLogger(MyDocumentsContext.class);

        private Map<String,Document> documents = new HashMap<String,Document>();
        private Map<String,Type> types = new HashMap<String,Type>();
```

```
        @Bean
        public Type webType(){
                return getTypeFromMap("web");
        }

        @Bean
        @Scope("prototype")
        public SearchEngine engine(){
                ServiceSearchEngine engine = new ServiceSearchEngine();
                engine.setDocumentDAO(documentDAO());

if(log.isDebugEnabled())
                        log.debug("SearchEngine created: " + engine);

                return engine;
        }

        public MyDocumentsContext(){


                //...Omitted calls
}

//... Omitted methods
}
```

Running the unit test, you should get the same results. You can find each of these tests in Chapter 4 of the book's companion source code.

Using Bean Scopes in the New GroovyBeanDefinitionReader Context

Using the new Groovy integration will be as easy as setting the word scope in the mydocuments.groovy file (see Listing 4-6).

Listing 4-6. mydocuments.groovy

```
import com.apress.isf.spring.service.ServiceSearchEngine
import com.apress.isf.spring.data.DocumentRepository
import com.apress.isf.java.model.Document

beans {

        engine(SearchEngineService){ bean ->
                bean.scope = "prototype"
                documentDAO = ref("documentDAO")
        }
```

```
documentDAO(DocumentRepository){ bean ->
        bean.scope = "prototype"
        doc1 = ref("doc1")
        doc2 = ref("doc2")
        doc3 = ref("doc3")
        doc4 = ref("doc4")
    }

    //More bean definitions omitted.
}
```

Listing 4-6 shows your Groovy script: mydocuments.groovy. Now you are using a variable to define the scope. You don't need to worry too much about the correct syntax for this Groovy configuration; you are going to see it in detail in Chapter 18.

Running the test, you should get the same results: two different instances of the SearchEngine class implementation (SearchEngineService) and two different instances of the DocumentDAO class implementation (DocumentRepository). But what happens if you combine bean scopes between dependencies? Well, this is an exercise that you can do as homework. You need to put in more logs in order to find out what is happening.

▨ **Note**   In the book's source code, you will find all the tests and classes that have been modified for this chapter. You can use this source code to do your homework, right?

Summary

In this chapter, you added logs to some constructors and methods to discover how the Spring container works. You saw that by default the Spring container will create a single instance because the scope is a singleton, and every time you get that bean you are going to have the same instance. If you change the scope of your beans to prototype, every time you get your bean, the Spring container will create a new fresh instance of your class. In the book's companion source code, you can find the complete examples using the Java bean configuration, XML, annotations, and the GroovyBeanDefinitionReader.

CHAPTER 5

■ ■ ■

Working with Collections and Custom Types

You need to start adding some useful data and some special types to your Spring application. In this chapter, you will learn how to interact with data using collections within the Spring Framework.

So far, you have declared several beans that hold your type of documents, but there should be a better way to do that. I know that you are thinking of some kind of database or some other local storage or even a flat file, but let's see how Spring can help you to define your types in a different way, by using them as a collection.

List, Map, and Properties

First, let's modify the Java classes so you can get an idea of what you will actually need in your final context configuration as shown in Listing 5-1.

Listing 5-1. DocumentRepository.java

```java
package com.apress.isf.spring.data;

import java.util.List;

import org.slf4j.Logger;
import org.slf4j.LoggerFactory;

import com.apress.isf.java.model.Document;

public class DocumentRepository implements DocumentDAO {
        private static final Logger log = LoggerFactory.getLogger(DocumentRepository.class);
        private List<Document> documents = null;

        public List<Document> getDocuments() {
                return documents;
        }

        public void setDocuments(List<Document> documents) {
                this.documents = documents;
        }
```

```
        public Document[] getAll() {
                if(log.isDebugEnabled())
                        log.debug("Start <getAll> Params: ");
                Document[] result = documents.toArray(new Document[documents.size()]);

                if(log.isDebugEnabled())
                        log.debug("End <getAll> Result:" + result);
                return result;
        }

}
```

You need to remember that in your previous DocumentDAO implementation you had several Document objects defined in your implementation. In this new DocumentRepository class (see Listing 5-1) you have removed those documents: doc1, doc2, and so on; you have also added a collection, in this case a List of type Document. Note that you are adding more logs to your class so you know what is going on. Let's review Listing 5-2 and continue with the other classes.

Listing 5-2. TypeDataDAO.java

```
package com.apress.isf.spring.data;

import com.apress.isf.java.model.Type;

public interface TypeDataDAO {
        public Type[] getAll();
        public Type findById(String id);
}
```

In the TypeDataDAO (see Listing 5-2) interface, you have just added a new method, findById. This method will help you just to get the Type based on your id. With this new change, let's modify the classes and implement this method. Now let's take a look at Listing 5-3, your TypeDataDAO implementation.

Listing 5-3. TypeDataRepository.java

```
package com.apress.isf.spring.data;

import java.util.Map;

import org.slf4j.Logger;
import org.slf4j.LoggerFactory;

import com.apress.isf.java.model.Type;

public class TypeDataRepository implements TypeDataDAO{
        private static final Logger log = LoggerFactory.getLogger(TypeDataRepository.class);
        private Map<String,Type> types = null;

        public Map<String, Type> getTypes() {
                return types;
        }
```

```
    public void setTypes(Map<String, Type> types) {
            this.types = types;
    }

    public Type findById(String id){
            if(log.isDebugEnabled())
                    log.debug("Start <findById> Params: " + id);

            Type type = types.get(id);

            if(log.isDebugEnabled())
                    log.debug("End <findById> Params: " + type);
            return type;
    }

    public Type[] getAll() {
            return types.values().toArray(new Type[types.values().size()]);
    }
}
```

In the TypeDataRepository class (see Listing 5-3) you also removed the different fields about the type. You also added a Map that can help you to have in memory at least some of the types you need, like a note, a web URL, a PDF and maybe some Office documents. Furthermore, you implemented the new method findById that the TypeDataDAO (see Listing 5-2) declares; this method will return the type by just giving the Id (using the get method from the Map collection). Then you added some logs to see what method you are calling and what parameters (if any) you are passing. For now it is important to know what is going on; this practice will help to debug your class in case you need to do so. Of course, there are better ways to debug your class, like using an IDE (integrated development environment) such as Eclipse or IntelliJ, but for now, let's do only logs.

Collections in Your XML Configuration

Next, let's see your XML configuration file, as shown in Listing 5-4.

Listing 5-4. mydocuments-context.xml

```xml
<?xml version="1.0" encoding="UTF-8"?>
<beans xmlns="http://www.springframework.org/schema/beans"
       xmlns:xsi="http://www.w3.org/2001/XMLSchema-instance"
       xsi:schemaLocation="http://www.springframework.org/schema/beans
http://www.springframework.org/schema/beans/spring-beans.xsd">

  <bean id="engine" class="com.apress.isf.spring.service.ServiceSearchEngine">
      <property name="documentDAO" ref="documentDAO"/>
  </bean>
```

```xml
<bean id="documentDAO" class="com.apress.isf.spring.data.DocumentRepository">
    <property name="documents">
        <list>
            <ref bean="doc1"/>
            <ref bean="doc2"/>
            <ref bean="doc3"/>
            <ref bean="doc4"/>
        </list>
    </property>
</bean>

<bean id="typeDAO" class="com.apress.isf.spring.data.TypeDataRepository">
    <property name="types">
        <map>
            <entry key="webType" value-ref="webType"/>
            <entry key="pdfType" value-ref="pdfType"/>
            <entry key="noteType" value-ref="noteType"/>
        </map>
    </property>
</bean>

<!-- Docs and Types beans definitions omitted -->
</beans>
```

In the `mydocuments-context.xml` file (see Listing 5-4) you modified the `documentDAO` bean to reflect the new list and also you modified the `typeDAO` bean so now it can accept a Map with some entries, but wait! I think I need to explain how the Spring Framework works with collections, right?

The Spring Framework allows you to use Java Collections right out the box, with the `<list/>` (`java.util.List` type), `<map/>` (`java.util.Map` type), `<props/>` (`java.util.Properties` type) and `<set/>` (`java.util.Set` type) tags shown in Table 5-1.

Table 5-1. *Collections Tags*

Element	Description
`<list />`	This tag allows duplicates. The tags `<value />`, `<ref bean=""/>`, and `<bean />` are the possible children of the `<list />` tag.
`<set />`	This tag doesn't accept duplicates. The tags `<value />`, `<ref bean=""/>`, and `<bean />` are the possible children of the `<set />` tag.
`<props />`	This tag is a name-value pair. Both values are Strings. `<prop key="" value=""/>` and `<prop key=""></prop>` are the children tags. This is a reference to the `java.util.Properties` class.
`<map />`	This tag is a name-value pair; both values can be any type. `<entry key="" value="" />`, `<entry key="" value-ref=""/>`, `<entry key="">`, and `</entry>` are the possible children of the `<map/>` tag. This is a reference of the `java.util.Map` class.

So if you want to apply the `<set/>` to your `documentDAO` bean and `<props/>` to your `typeDAO` bean, first you need to modify your `DocumentRepository` and the `TypeDataRepository` classes to reflect the new type `java.util.Set` and `java.util.Properties`, respectively. Let's review Listing 5-5, your XML configuration.

Listing 5-5. mydocuments-context.xml

```xml
<?xml version="1.0" encoding="UTF-8"?>
<beans xmlns="http://www.springframework.org/schema/beans"
        xmlns:xsi="http://www.w3.org/2001/XMLSchema-instance"
        xsi:schemaLocation="http://www.springframework.org/schema/beans
http://www.springframework.org/schema/beans/spring-beans.xsd">

  <bean id="engine" class="com.apress.isf.spring.service.ServiceSearchEngine">
      <property name="documentDAO" ref="documentDAO"/>
  </bean>

  <bean id="documentDAO" class="com.apress.isf.spring.data.DocumentRepository">
     <property name="documents">
        <set>
            <ref bean="doc1"/>
            <ref bean="doc2"/>
            <ref bean="doc3"/>
            <ref bean="doc4"/>
        </set>
     </set>
  </bean>

  <bean id="typeDAO" class="com.apress.isf.spring.data.TypeDataRepository">
     <property name="types">
        <props>
            <prop key="webType" value-ref="webType"/>
            <prop key="pdfType" value-ref="pdfType"/>
            <prop key="noteType" value-ref="noteType"/>
        </props>
     </property>
  </bean>

  <!-- Docs and Types beans definitions omitted -->
</beans>
```

Merging Collections

The Spring Framework also provides a merge mechanism for the collections. In other words, you can have another bean of the same type with a different set of values and you can actually merge/join collections and avoid duplicates or add more to a set of values. Let's see an example. Imagine you have the typeDAO bean but you want to add more entries that maybe could be in another XML configuration. This approach of merging collections can be beneficial if you are required to have a template or a base where you need to join or inherit some values. See Listing 5-6 for a merge example.

Listing 5-6 Merge Example

```xml
<bean id="typeDAO" abstract="true" class="com.apress.isf.spring.data.TypeDataRepository">
    <property name="types">
        <map>
            <entry key="webType" value-ref="webType"/>
            <entry key="pdfType" value-ref="pdfType"/>
            <entry key="noteType" value-ref="noteType"/>
        </map>
    </property>
</bean>

 <bean id="anotherTypeDAO" parent="typeDAO">
    <property name="types">
        <map merge="true">
            <entry key="pagesType" value-ref="pagesType"/>
            <entry key="numbersType" value-ref="numbersType"/>
            <entry key="keynoteType" value-ref="keynoteType"/>
        </map>
    </property>
</bean>
```

In Listing 5-6, you can get anotherTypeDAO and it will contain the six types. But how does the Spring Framework know about the merging? This is because your typeDAO bean has defined the attribute abstract with a value of true. This means that it cannot be instantiated; it will be seen as a template by the container. All of the children beans that make a reference of this parent bean will inherit all of the properties, such as the case of anotherTypeDAO that inherited all the types properties, in this case the join/merge of the map. Also, you need to see that anotherTypeDAO uses the attribute parent, making the reference to the parent bean the typeDAO.

If you think that Spring has another way to express collections in the XML based configuration, you are right. The Spring Framework also supports, based on a namespace, a "shortcut" for declaring collections. Now you have more options for using collections. See Listing 5-7 for an XML configuration example.

Listing 5-7. mydocuments-util-context.xml

```xml
<?xml version="1.0" encoding="UTF-8"?>
<beans xmlns="http://www.springframework.org/schema/beans"
        xmlns:xsi="http://www.w3.org/2001/XMLSchema-instance"
        xmlns:util="http://www.springframework.org/schema/util"
        xsi:schemaLocation="http://www.springframework.org/schema/beans
http://www.springframework.org/schema/beans/spring-beans.xsd
                http://www.springframework.org/schema/util
http://www.springframework.org/schema/util/spring-util-4.0.xsd">

  <bean id="engine" class="com.apress.isf.spring.service.ServiceSearchEngine">
      <property name="documentDAO" ref="documentDAO"/>
  </bean>

  <bean id="documentDAO" class="com.apress.isf.spring.data.DocumentRepository">
      <property name="documents" ref="docs"/>
  </bean>
```

```xml
<util:list id="docs">
        <ref bean="doc1"/>
        <ref bean="doc2"/>
        <ref bean="doc3"/>
        <ref bean="doc4"/>
</util:list>

<bean id="typeDAO" class="com.apress.isf.spring.data.TypeDataRepository">
    <property name="types" ref="types"/>
</bean>

<util:map id="types">
  <entry key="webType" value-ref="webType"/>
  <entry key="pdfType" value-ref="pdfType"/>
  <entry key="noteType" value-ref="noteType"/>
</util:map>

<!-- Docs and Types beans omitted -->

</beans>
```

In `mydocuments-util-context.xml` (see Listing 5-7) you added the `xmlns:util` namespace that allows you to add the `<util:list/>` and `<util:map/>` tags that accepts the `List` and `Map` types, respectively. Also, the `xmlns:util` namespace has the `<util:set/>`, `<util:properties/>`, and `<util:property-path/>` tags. They are easy to use, so go ahead and do some testing on your own with these collection tags.

After all the modifications you did on the source code, you can run the unit test in the same way you have been running them, by using the gradle tool. If you are in the book's source code base directory, it's

```
gradle :ch05:test
```

Or in the project's directory you can run

```
gradle test
```

You should expect the same result as the following output:

```
com.apress.isf.spring.test.MyDocumentsTest > testAll STARTED

com.apress.isf.spring.service.SearchEngineService@4068f746
Test: test testAll(com.apress.isf.spring.test.MyDocumentsTest) produced standard out/err:
2014-04-22 21:47:27,855 DEBUG [Test worker] Document DAO set: com.apress.isf.spring.data.
DocumentRepository@4ad88414
Test: test testAll(com.apress.isf.spring.test.MyDocumentsTest) produced standard out/err: 2014-04-22
21:47:27,857 DEBUG [Test worker] Start <findByType> Params: Type Definition:
Test: test testAll(com.apress.isf.spring.test.MyDocumentsTest) produced standard out/err: Name: WEB
Test: test testAll(com.apress.isf.spring.test.MyDocumentsTest) produced standard out/err:
Description: Web Link
Test: test testAll(com.apress.isf.spring.test.MyDocumentsTest) produced standard out/err: Extension: .url
```

```
Test: test testAll(com.apress.isf.spring.test.MyDocumentsTest) produced standard out/err: 2014-04-22
21:47:27,857 DEBUG [Test worker] Start <listAll> Params:
Test: test testAll(com.apress.isf.spring.test.MyDocumentsTest) produced standard out/err: 2014-04-22
21:47:27,857 DEBUG [Test worker] Start <getAll> Params:
Test: test testAll(com.apress.isf.spring.test.MyDocumentsTest) produced standard out/err: 2014-04-22
21:47:27,857 DEBUG [Test worker] End <getAll> Result:[Lcom.apress.isf.java.model.Document;@8117683
Test: test testAll(com.apress.isf.spring.test.MyDocumentsTest) produced standard out/err: 2014-04-22
21:47:27,857 DEBUG [Test worker] End <listAll> Result:
[com.apress.isf.java.model.Document@4fdbef0c, com.apress.isf.java.model.Document@20bde8a7,
com.apress.isf.java.model.Document@13f53cbc, com.apress.isf.java.model.Document@496664e0]

Test: test testAll(com.apress.isf.spring.test.MyDocumentsTest) produced standard out/err: 2014-04-22
21:47:27,857 DEBUG [Test worker] End <findByType> Result:
[com.apress.isf.java.model.Document@496664e0] Test:
test testAll(com.apress.isf.spring.test.MyDocumentsTest) produced standard out/err: 2014-04-22
21:47:27,857 DEBUG [Test worker] Start <listAll> Params: Test: test
testAll(com.apress.isf.spring.test.MyDocumentsTest) produced standard out/err: 2014-04-22
21:47:27,857 DEBUG [Test worker] Start <getAll> Params:
Test: test testAll(com.apress.isf.spring.test.MyDocumentsTest) produced standard out/err: 2014-04-22
21:47:27,857 DEBUG [Test worker] End <getAll>
Result:[Lcom.apress.isf.java.model.Document;@5728210a
Test: test testAll(com.apress.isf.spring.test.MyDocumentsTest) produced standard out/err: 2014-04-22
21:47:27,857 DEBUG [Test worker] End <listAll>
Result: [com.apress.isf.java.model.Document@4fdbef0c, com.apress.isf.java.model.Document@20bde8a7,
com.apress.isf.java.model.Document@13f53cbc, com.apress.isf.java.model.Document@496664e0]

com.apress.isf.spring.test.MyDocumentsTest > testAll PASSED
```

Summary

You modified some of your source code, putting in some logs to identify what method you are using, what parameters you are sending, and the result. You also learned how to debug your code in case something happens. You introduced some collections to your code instead of handling each document one at a time. (Imagine if you have thousands of types in your documents. Impractical!!) In a real world scenario, the usage of collections is a nice feature from Spring. Certain values such as user roles or user permissions can be changed easily from an XML configuration file.

You saw how in Spring you can use these collections in a declarative form, by using the list, map, set, and properties tags and the different ways to use collections, like the usage of XML namespaces. Which one should you use? Well, this will be your own preference. This is just a new syntax to accomplish the same, but in a more elegant way.

CHAPTER 6

Using Resource Files

So far, you have been using all your data as bean definitions. Of course, there are better ways to accomplish the same. In this chapter, you are going to employ a useful feature from the Spring Framework, using external files as a data resource for your application.

The resource files will not only help to load the data you are using, but they also can be useful when you want to separate some configuration that may depend on the environment you are working on. They can also be useful if you have an application that you want to be shown in a different language base on the user's browser locale.

Using Resources

You are going to start working on your classes and see how you can use these resource files. These files will just contain some data that will be displayed when you run the application. First, you are going to add a small feature to your application, a simple menu for displaying some options so you can have some interaction with it. The menu will be as simple as showing the following options.

1. Show all documents.

2. Show all document's types.

3. Search by type.

4. Quit.

Let's create a text file under the `src/main/resources/META-INF/data` folder. This will be your menu, as shown in Listing 6-1.

Listing 6-1. src/main/resources/META-INF/data/menu.txt

```
Welcome to My Documents
1. Show all Documents
2. Show all Document's Types
3. Search by Type
4. Quit
```

As you can see, Listing 6-1 is just simple plain text that describes your menu, nothing else. Next, you are going to modify your test so you can see how your menu can be loaded and print it out into the console. See Listing 6-2.

Listing 6-2. MyDocumentsTest.java

```java
package com.apress.isf.spring.test;

import java.io.IOException;
import java.io.InputStream;
import java.util.Scanner;

import org.junit.Before;
import org.junit.Test;
import org.springframework.context.support.ClassPathXmlApplicationContext;
import org.springframework.core.io.Resource;

public class MyDocumentsTest {
        private static final Logger log = LoggerFactory.getLogger(MyDocumentsTest.class);
        private ClassPathXmlApplicationContext context;

        @Before
        public void setup(){
                context = new ClassPathXmlApplicationContext("META-INF/spring/mydocuments-context.xml");
        }

        @Test
        public void testMenu() {
                log.debug("About to read the Resource file: menu.txt ");
                Resource resource = context.getResource("classpath:META-INF/data/menu.txt");
                try{
                        InputStream stream = resource.getInputStream();
                        Scanner scanner = new Scanner(stream);
                        while (scanner.hasNext()) {
                                System.out.println(scanner.nextLine());
                        }
                        scanner.close();
                        stream.close();
                }catch(IOException e){
                        e.printStackTrace();
                }
        }
}
```

The Spring Framework has a utility package, org.springframework.core.io, that contains several helpers for I/O operations, as shown in Listing 6-2. In your test, you are using the org.springframework.core.io.Resource class that will locate your resource file so you can print it out into the console. If you run your unit test using

```
gradle :ch05:test
```

then you should have the following output:

```
2014-02-16 10:12:20,220 DEBUG [main] About to read the Resource file: menu.txt
Welcome to My Documents
1. Show all Documents
2. Show all Document's Types
3. Search by Type
4. Quit
```

▨ **Tip**   The best part of the `Resource` class provided by the Spring Framework is that it can locate the resources in the classpath, an external URL, and on the file system: `classpath: <resourcefile>`, URL: `http://<server>/<resourcefile>`, file: `/unix/path/resourcefile` or file: `c:\\windows\\path\\resourcefile`. Which one to choose? Well, it will depend on your requirements. Perhaps it is necessary to request access through a remote server for special settings on your beans definitions such as passwords or any other credentials, so the `url:http` resource will be the right one.

But wait, loading a resource file in your unit test (see Listing 6-2)? Well, there are different ways that you can accomplish the same, but of course you need to use this in one of your classes, right? So let's use Spring's dependency injection feature, as shown in Listings 6-3, 6-4, and 6-5. Listing 6-3 shows the usage of the `org.springframework.core.io.Resource` class, the `menuFile` as a property with its setters and getters.

Listing 6-3. Menu.java

```java
package com.apress.isf.spring.views;

import java.io.IOException;
import java.io.InputStream;
import java.util.Scanner;
import static java.lang.System.out;

import org.springframework.core.io.Resource;

public class Menu {

        private Resource menuFile = null;

        public Resource getMenuFile() {
                return menuFile;
        }

        public void setMenuFile(Resource menuFile) {
                this.menuFile = menuFile;
        }

        public void printMenu(){
                try{
                                InputStream stream = getMenuFile().getInputStream();
                                Scanner scanner = new Scanner(stream);
```

```
                    while (scanner.hasNext()) {
                            out.println(scanner.nextLine());
                    }
                    scanner.close();
                    stream.close();
              }catch(IOException e){
                    e.printStackTrace();
              }
        }
}
```

Next, Listing 6-4 shows your XML configuration. And the important part to remember is the property of your "menu" bean that points to your menu.txt file, located under src/resources/META-INF/data folder.

Listing 6-4. mydocuments-resource-injection-context.xml

```xml
<?xml version="1.0" encoding="UTF-8"?>
<beans xmlns="http://www.springframework.org/schema/beans"
        xmlns:xsi="http://www.w3.org/2001/XMLSchema-instance"
        xsi:schemaLocation="http://www.springframework.org/schema/beans
http://www.springframework.org/schema/beans/spring-beans.xsd">

  <bean id="menu" class="com.apress.isf.spring.views.Menu">
    <property name="menuFile" value="classpath:META-INF/data/menu.txt"/>
  </bean>

  <!-- Beans definitions omitted -->

</beans>
```

Listing 6-5 shows the unit test that will load the mydocuments-resource-injection-context.xml configuration file (see Listing 6-4).

Listing 6-5. MyDocumentsWithResourceInjectionTest.java

```java
package com.apress.isf.spring.test;

import org.junit.Before;
import org.junit.Test;
import static org.junit.Assert.assertNotNull;
import org.slf4j.Logger;
import org.slf4j.LoggerFactory;
import org.springframework.context.support.ClassPathXmlApplicationContext;
import com.apress.isf.spring.views.Menu;

public class MyDocumentsWithResourceInjectionTest {
        private static final Logger log =
LoggerFactory.getLogger(MyDocumentsWithResourceInjectionTest.class);
        private ClassPathXmlApplicationContext context;

        @Before
        public void setup(){
```

```
            context = new ClassPathXmlApplicationContext("META-INF/spring/
mydocuments-resource-injection-context.xml");
    }

    @Test
    public void testMenu() {
            log.debug("Calling the Menu as Resource Injection:");
            Menu menu = context.getBean(Menu.class);
            assertNotNull(menu);
            menu.printMenu();
    }
}
```

You defined the Menu class and you added the Resource property (see Listing 6-3) that will be injected by the Spring container. One of the important things to mention here is that the Spring Framework will understand that by setting the property menuFile in the XML configuration (see Listing 6-4) it will inject as a Resource class value. In Listing 6-5 you added the testMenu method that will call your bean "menu" and it will print the contents of the menu.txt file.

If you run your unit test with

```
gradle :ch06:test
```

you should have the following result:

```
2014-02-16 11:00:46,377 DEBUG [main] Calling the Menu as Resource Injection:
Welcome to My Documents
1. Show all Documents
2. Show all Document's Types
3. Search by Type
4. Quit
```

Now, what would happen if you want to load the resource dynamically? Maybe you want to change the menu at runtime. Perhaps you have an application that needs to change some values, like some stock market values and definitions. You don't want to stop your application, do the modification, and then redeploy, right? You want to actually make the new changes once you save the resource. The Spring Framework also provides a ResourceLoader class if you want to load some resource and change them based on a business rule. Listing 6-6 shows how to use it.

Listing 6-6. ResourceLoaderMenu.java

```
package com.apress.isf.spring.views;

import static java.lang.System.out;

import java.io.IOException;
import java.io.InputStream;
import java.util.Scanner;

import org.springframework.beans.factory.annotation.Autowired;
import org.springframework.core.io.ResourceLoader;
import org.springframework.stereotype.Component;
```

```
@Component("menu")
public class ResourceLoaderMenu {

        @Autowired
        private ResourceLoader resourceLoader;

        public void printMenu(String menuFile){
                try{
                   InputStream stream = resourceLoader.getResource(menuFile).getInputStream();
                   Scanner scanner = new Scanner(stream);
                   while (scanner.hasNext()) {
                           out.println(scanner.nextLine());
                   }
                   scanner.close();
                   stream.close();
                }catch(IOException e){
                        e.printStackTrace();
                }
        }
}
```

Listing 6-6 shows the usage of the org.springframework.core.io.ResourceLoader class, and also the @Autowired annotation that will be instantiated by the Spring container and get it ready for when it is being used, like in the printMenu method. Next, let's see Listing 6-7, your XML configuration, and Listing 6-8, your unit test.

Listing 6-7. mydocuments-resourceloader-injection=context.xml

```
<?xml version="1.0" encoding="UTF-8"?>
<beans xmlns="http://www.springframework.org/schema/beans"
        xmlns:xsi="http://www.w3.org/2001/XMLSchema-instance"
        xmlns:context="http://www.springframework.org/schema/context"
        xsi:schemaLocation="http://www.springframework.org/schema/beans
http://www.springframework.org/schema/beans/spring-beans.xsd
                http://www.springframework.org/schema/context
http://www.springframework.org/schema/context/spring-context-4.0.xsd">

  <context:component-scan base-package="com.apress.isf.spring.views"/>

  <!-- Beans definitions omitted -->

</beans>
```

Listing 6-7 only shows the <context-component-scan/> tag that will tell the Spring container to look for annotated code and identify all the classes and instances to create.

Listing 6-8 shows your unit test, and how you can load your menu.txt file. As you can see, you have several options for resource files. Running your unit test with

```
gradle :ch06:test
```

Listing 6-8. MyDocumentsWithResourceLoaderInjectionTest.java

```java
package com.apress.isf.spring.test;

import static org.junit.Assert.assertNotNull;

import org.junit.Before;
import org.junit.Test;
import org.slf4j.Logger;
import org.slf4j.LoggerFactory;
import org.springframework.context.support.ClassPathXmlApplicationContext;

import com.apress.isf.spring.views.ResourceLoaderMenu;

public class MyDocumentsWithResourceLoaderInjectionTest {
        private static final Logger log =
                LoggerFactory.getLogger(MyDocumentsWithResourceLoaderInjectionTest.class);
        private ClassPathXmlApplicationContext context;

        @Before
        public void setup(){
                context = new ClassPathXmlApplicationContext("META-INF/spring/
mydocuments-resourceloader-injection-context.xml");
        }

        @Test
        public void testMenu() {
                log.debug("Calling the Menu as Resourceloader Injection:");
                ResourceLoaderMenu menu = context.getBean(ResourceLoaderMenu.class);
                assertNotNull(menu);
                menu.printMenu("classpath:META-INF/data/menu.txt");
        }
}
```

you should have the same result.:

```
2014-04-23 12:20:43,127 DEBUG [main] Calling the Menu as Resource Injection:
Welcome to My Documents
1. Show all Documents
2. Show all Document's Types
3. Search by Type
4. Quit
```

Using Property Files

The Spring Framework can help you read properties files that can contain sensitive data such as username, passwords, URL connections, etc. This feature allows you to separate this sensitive data from your XML configuration files, so it will be easy to deploy applications using the correct properties. A simple use case will have different properties files for different environments such as TEST, QA, and Production.

You are going to add a new interface, a Login class that can help you to authenticate a user providing an e-mail and password and based on the environment you are working on. Let's start by reviewing Listing 6-9 and Listing 6-10. First, you will create your properties files and see how you can use them. Listing 6-9 shows some Development environment values.

Listing 6-9. env_dev.properties

```
user.email=test@mydocuments.com
user.password=test123
```

Listing 6-10 shows some QA environment values.

Listing 6-10. env_qa.properties

```
user.email=qa@mydocuments.com
user.password=3$aqw1
```

Let's continue creating your login interface and its implementation. See Listings 6-11 and 6-12. Listing 6-11 shows a simple interface with only one method that accepts an e-mail and a password. The idea is to authorize a user if these values are correct.

Listing 6-11. Login.java

```java
package com.apress.isf.java.service;

public interface Login {
        public boolean isAuthorized(String email, String pass);
}
```

Listing 6-12. LoginService.java

```java
package com.apress.isf.spring.service;

import com.apress.isf.java.service.Login;

public class LoginService implements Login {

        private String username;
        private String password;

        public String getUsername() {
                return username;
        }

        public void setUsername(String username) {
                this.username = username;
        }

        public String getPassword() {
                return password;
        }
```

```
        public void setPassword(String password) {
                this.password = password;
        }

        public boolean isAuthorized(String email, String pass){
                if(username.equals(email) && password.equals(pass))
                        return true;
                return false;
        }

}
```

As you can see in Listing 6-12, this login and its implementation are trivial for the example you want to do, just do a basic authorization logic by passing an e-mail and password to the isAuthorized method and returning true if the both parameters are equal to the injected properties. For now that's all you need.

Next, let's add your support class and its bean definition to your XML file, the org.springframework.beans. factory.config.PropertyPlaceholderConfigurer class. See Listing 6-13 for your XML configuration file.

Listing 6-13. mydocuments-login-context.xml

```
<?xml version="1.0" encoding="UTF-8"?>
<beans xmlns="http://www.springframework.org/schema/beans"
        xmlns:xsi="http://www.w3.org/2001/XMLSchema-instance"
        xsi:schemaLocation="http://www.springframework.org/schema/beans
http://www.springframework.org/schema/beans/spring-beans.xsd">

  <bean id="environmentProperties"
class="org.springframework.beans.factory.config.PropertyPlaceholderConfigurer">
     <property name="location" value="classpath:META-INF/data/env_dev.properties"/>
  </bean>
  <bean id="login" class="com.apress.isf.spring.service.LoginService">
     <property name="username" value="${user.email}"/>
     <property name="password" value="${user.pass}"/>
  </bean>

  <!-- Beans definitions omitted-->

</beans>
```

In Listing 6-13, you are using the PropertyPlaceholderConfigurer. This class helps to externalize properties values and keep them separate from your XML configuration files. These files follow the Java properties convention and they are useful for customized environment-centric applications by adding values such as password, database URLs, etc. During runtime, the PropertyPlaceholderConfigurer will take the metadata from the properties file and replace it where a placeholder is specified. The placeholders have the form of a ${property} format.

In Listing 6-13, the property username will have the value test@mydocuments.com because it was replaced by using the placeholder ${user.email} matching the property file (see Listing 6-9).

Now, let's create your unit test for this change (see Listing 6-14).

Listing 6-14. MyDocumentsWithLoginTest.java

```java
package com.apress.isf.spring.test;

import org.junit.Before;
import org.junit.Test;
import static org.junit.Assert.assertNotNull;
import static java.lang.System.out;
import org.slf4j.Logger;
import org.slf4j.LoggerFactory;
import org.springframework.context.support.ClassPathXmlApplicationContext;

import com.apress.isf.java.service.Login;

public class MyDocumentsWithLoginTest {
        private static final Logger log = LoggerFactory.getLogger(MyDocumentsWithLoginTest.class);
        private static final String EMAIL = "test@mydocuments.com";
        private static final String PASS = "test123";
        private static final String SUCCESS = "This user is authorized";
        private static final String FAILURE = "WARNING! This user is not authorized!";
        private ClassPathXmlApplicationContext context;

        @Before
        public void setup(){
                context = new ClassPathXmlApplicationContext("META-INF/spring/mydocuments-login-
context.xml");
        }

        @Test
        public void testLogin() {
                log.debug("Login test.");
                Login login = context.getBean(Login.class);
                assertNotNull(login);
                if(login.isAuthorized(EMAIL, PASS))
                        out.println(SUCCESS);
                else
                        out.println(FAILURE);
        }
}
```

Now try to run the test in Listing 6-14 by executing

```
gradle :ch06:test
```

and play with it by changing or augmenting more properties into the configuration file. For example, you can change the password or you can change the name of the property. The following is the result of running the unit test:

```
2014-02-16 13:24:56,897 DEBUG [main] Login test.
This user is authorized
```

Using a Different Language: Do You Speak Spanish?

As a developer, we want everybody to use our application, but what happens when the spoken language is a barrier? You need to start thinking about how to internationalize your application. In other words, your application needs to support different languages. For example, major banks offer their customers the option of changing the language for their entire web site. So what happens if your Spring application, **My Documents**, has a Spanish-speaking user? Is this person able to understand English?

The Spring Framework has some support classes for this purpose. The ResourceBundleMessageSource class allows reading different locales and retrieving the correct message specifying its key based on the properties file.

In order to use this class, it is necessary to have a default properties file with any name, and the locales followed by an underscore and the locale. In your application, you are going to put English as your default language and Spanish as the secondary language. Let's create the files. You need to create three files, two for English and one for Spanish. It's always necessary to have a default dictionary in case of some missing language, and you chose in this case English as a default. Listing 6-15 shows your Default English dictionary file.

Listing 6-15. dictionary.properties. Default English Dictionary

```
main.title=Welcome to My Documents
main.menu.1=Show all My Documents
main.menu.2=Show all Type of Documents
main.menu.3=Search by Type
main.menu.4=Quit

login.success=This user is authorized
login.failure=WARNING! This user is not authorized!
```

Listing 6-16 shows your English dictionary file.

Listing 6-16. dictionary_en.properties. English locale _en

```
main.title=Welcome to My Documents
main.menu.1=Show all My Documents
main.menu.2=Show all Type of Documents
main.menu.3=Search by Type
main.menu.4=Quit

login.success=This user is authorized
login.failure=WARNING! This user is not authorized!
```

Listing 6-17 shows the Spanish Dictionary file.

Listing 6-17. dictionary_es.properties. Spanish local _es

```
main.title=Bienvenido a Mis Documentos
main.menu.1=Mostrar todos Mis Documentos
main.menu.2=Mostrar Tipos de Documentos
main.menu.3=Buscar por Tipo
main.menu.4=Salir

login.success=Usuario Autorizado
login.failure=Alerta! Este usuario no esta autorizado!
```

Next, let's create your XML file configuration and see how you are going to define and use your dictionaries. See Listing 6-18.

Listing 6-18. mydocuments-i18n-context.xml

```xml
<?xml version="1.0" encoding="UTF-8"?>
<beans xmlns="http://www.springframework.org/schema/beans"
       xmlns:xsi="http://www.w3.org/2001/XMLSchema-instance"
       xsi:schemaLocation="http://www.springframework.org/schema/beans
http://www.springframework.org/schema/beans/spring-beans.xsd">

  <bean id="messageSource"
class="org.springframework.context.support.ResourceBundleMessageSource">
    <property name="basename" value="META-INF/data/dictionary"/>
  </bean>

  <!-- Beans definitions omitted -->
</beans>
```

In Listing 6-18, note that the property to use is basename; this will accept a fully qualified name with the extension properties. In this case, it will look up the dictionary files. Remember that you have dictionary.properties, dictionary_en.properties, and dictionary_es.properties. The dictionary without the underscore character is the default dictionary. The _en means the English dictionary and the _es means the Spanish dictionary.

Now let's create your unit test as shown in Listing 6-19.

Listing 6-19. MyDocumentsI18nTest.java

```java
package com.apress.isf.spring.test;

import static java.lang.System.out;

import java.util.Locale;

import org.junit.Before;
import org.junit.Test;
import org.slf4j.Logger;
import org.slf4j.LoggerFactory;
import org.springframework.context.support.ClassPathXmlApplicationContext;

public class MyDocumentsI18nTest {
        private static final Logger log = LoggerFactory.getLogger(MyDocumentsI18nTest.class);
        private ClassPathXmlApplicationContext context;

        @Before
        public void setup(){
                context = new ClassPathXmlApplicationContext
("META-INF/spring/mydocuments-i18n-context.xml");
        }

        @Test
        public void testMenu() {
                log.debug("About to Translate...");
```

```
            String english = context.getMessage("main.title",null, Locale.ENGLISH);
            String spanish = context.getMessage("main.title",null, new Locale("es"));
            out.println("English: " + english);
            out.println("Spanish: " + spanish);
        }
}
```

Listing 6-19 shows your unit test. You are using the context to access the getMessage method that interacts with the ResourceBundleMessageSource class to get the correct language/locale you specified. If you run the Listing 6-19 with

```
gradle :ch06:test
```

this will be the output:

```
2014-02-16 14:15:25,966 DEBUG [main] About to Translate...
English: Welcome to My Documents
Spanish: Bienvenido a Mis Documentos
```

In Listing 6-19, you are using only the main.title property just to make a simple test, but as homework you can modify it and add all the keys to experiment with multiple languages. You can find more about the locales at www.oracle.com/technetwork/java/javase/javase7locales-334809.html.

Summary

In this chapter, you saw how to use resource files. You learned how to use them to get external files and separate them from your XML configuration files, which not only can be text files but also images or any other type of media.

You used the PropertyPlaceholderConfigurer for placeholders for different types of environments such as QA, Development, and Production. You also went international via a simple example using Spanish.

In the next chapter, you will do some unit testing via a Spring test module that will help you to easily configure your Spring container.

CHAPTER 7

■ ■ ■

Testing Your Spring Application

In this chapter, you are going to start using the Spring Framework Features. So far in previous chapters, you have been using the JUnit test framework, which is fine if you want to do simple testing. Previously, every time you needed to declare the application context's implementation like the `ClassPathXmlApplicationContext` class. You did this by calling `context = new ClassPathXmlApplicationContext("META-INF/spring/mydocuments-context.xml")` to load your XML configuration file in order to use the Spring container.

The Spring Framework Test library provides some features like unit testing by using JUnit or TestNG test, and integration testing. You can use mock objects based on environment, JNDI, Servlet, and Portlet APIs. For the integration testing, the Spring Framework provides a caching mechanism between test executions and transaction management, normally the latter regarding JDBC connections.

From now on, your tests for each chapter will be using the integration testing features from the Spring Test library. The primary goals are to support the use of the `ApplicationContext` class so that when your tests start you always have access to the container's beans. Also, this provides the use of dependency injection by using an annotation like `@Autowired`.

Testing with Annotations

You are going to start with annotations, which is one of the common uses of the Spring Test fixtures. So far you have been using the `@Autowired` annotation, but now you use the application context call. So, let's modify your classes to use the testing annotations with no modification of the XML configuration (as shown in Listing 7-1).

Listing 7-1. MyDocumentsTest.java

```
package com.apress.isf.spring.test;

import static org.junit.Assert.assertEquals;
import static org.junit.Assert.assertNotNull;
import static org.junit.Assert.assertTrue;

import java.util.List;

import org.junit.Test;
import org.junit.runner.RunWith;
import org.slf4j.Logger;
import org.slf4j.LoggerFactory;
import org.springframework.beans.factory.annotation.Autowired;
import org.springframework.test.context.ContextConfiguration;
import org.springframework.test.context.junit4.SpringJUnit4ClassRunner;
```

```
import com.apress.isf.java.model.Document;
import com.apress.isf.java.model.Type;
import com.apress.isf.java.service.SearchEngine;

@RunWith(SpringJUnit4ClassRunner.class)
@ContextConfiguration("classpath:META-INF/spring/mydocuments-context.xml")
public class MyDocumentsTest {
        private static final Logger log = LoggerFactory.getLogger(MyDocumentsTest.class);

        @Autowired
        private SearchEngine engine;
        @Autowired
        private Type webType;

        @Test
        public void testUsingSpringTest() {
                log.debug("Using Spring Test fixtures:");

                List<Document> documents = engine.findByType(webType);
                assertNotNull(documents);
                assertTrue(documents.size() == 1);
                assertEquals(webType.getName(),documents.get(0).getType().getName());
                assertEquals(webType.getDesc(),documents.get(0).getType().getDesc());
                assertEquals(webType.getExtension(),documents.get(0).getType().getExtension());

                documents = engine.listAll();
                assertNotNull(documents);
                assertTrue(documents.size() == 4);
        }
}
```

In Listing 7-1, you are using the `@RunWith` annotation. This annotation is just a JUnit annotation that is telling it to use the `SpringJUnit4ClassRunner` class to run the unit tests instead of the JUnit engine. This will allow it to use all the features of the Spring integration testing such as having access to the Spring container. You are also using the `@ContextConfiguration` annotation, which is part of the Spring testing fixtures. This will help to load the beans into the Spring container by passing the location of your XML configuration and have them (the beans) ready and accessible when using the context or, even better, when using the well-known `@Autowired` annotation.

If you run this test (see Listing 7-1) using the gradle tool

```
gradle  :ch07:test
```

then you should have the following output:

```
2014-02-16 17:46:45,744 DEBUG [main] SearchEngineService created: com.apress.isf.spring.service.
SearchEngineService@60d1a23c
2014-02-16 17:46:45,815 DEBUG [main] Document DAO set: com.apress.isf.spring.data.
DocumentRepository@5e2842b6
2014-02-16 17:46:45,839 DEBUG [main] Using Spring Test fixtures:
2014-02-16 17:46:45,839 DEBUG [main] Start <findByType> Params: Type Definition:
Name: WEB
Description: Web Link
```

```
Extension: .url
2014-02-16 17:46:45,839 DEBUG [main] Start <listAll> Params:
2014-02-16 17:46:45,839 DEBUG [main] Start <getAll> Params:
2014-02-16 17:46:45,839 DEBUG [main] End <getAll> Result:[Lcom.apress.isf.java.model.
Document;@bdd6a16
2014-02-16 17:46:45,839 DEBUG [main] End <listAll> Result: [com.apress.isf.java.model.
Document@755fd06f, com.apress.isf.java.model.Document@656d639c, com.apress.isf.java.model.
Document@70a6cac9, com.apress.isf.java.model.Document@564b8be6]
2014-02-16 17:46:45,840 DEBUG [main] End <findByType> Result: [com.apress.isf.java.model.
Document@564b8be6]
2014-02-16 17:46:45,840 DEBUG [main] Start <listAll> Params:
2014-02-16 17:46:45,840 DEBUG [main] Start <getAll> Params:
2014-02-16 17:46:45,840 DEBUG [main] End <getAll> Result:[Lcom.apress.isf.java.model.
Document;@79cdd54c
2014-02-16 17:46:45,840 DEBUG [main] End <listAll> Result: [com.apress.isf.java.model.
Document@755fd06f, com.apress.isf.java.model.Document@656d639c, com.apress.isf.java.model.
Document@70a6cac9, com.apress.isf.java.model.Document@564b8be6]
```

This annotated feature simplifies and reduces the number of lines in your code, which makes it easier to read and understand. It also lets you focus on the real test.

Using Profiles

In Chapter 6, you saw how to use resource files, such as Properties files, that can help you to separate particular properties (for example, username, passwords, database connections, etc.) for different environments, such as Production or QA. Now, this is a nice solution if your project is small and doesn't require too many changes, but what happens when you have a very large project and you have some beans that should be available only in QA or other beans in Production? The Spring Framework team must have had this in mind because with version 3.1 they added the Profiles feature to the Spring container. The Profiles feature can help you to separate environments and gives you an even better and easier way to test them.

Let's start modifying your test and see how the Profiles feature works. Let's look at your XML configuration using Profiles (as shown in Listing 7-2).

Listing 7-2. mydocuments-profiles-context.xml

```xml
<?xml version="1.0" encoding="UTF-8"?>
<beans xmlns="http://www.springframework.org/schema/beans"
       xmlns:xsi="http://www.w3.org/2001/XMLSchema-instance"
       xmlns:context="http://www.springframework.org/schema/context"
       xsi:schemaLocation="http://www.springframework.org/schema/beans http://www.springframework.
       org/schema/beans/spring-beans.xsd
             http://www.springframework.org/schema/context http://www.springframework.org/schema/
             context/spring-context-4.0.xsd">

       <context:component-scan base-package="com.apress.isf.spring.service"/>
       <beans profile="dev">
             <bean id="engine" class="com.apress.isf.spring.service.SearchEngineService">
                    <property name="documentDAO" ref="documentDAO" />
             </bean>
       </beans>
</beans>
```

```xml
    <beans profile="dev,qa">
        <bean id="documentDAO" class="com.apress.isf.spring.data.DocumentRepository">
            <property name="documents">
                <list>
                    <ref bean="doc1" />
                    <ref bean="doc2" />
                    <ref bean="doc3" />
                    <ref bean="doc4" />
                </list>
            </property>
        </bean>

        <!--More Beans definitions omitted -->

    </beans>

</beans>
```

Listing 7-2 shows that the tag `<beans/>` has an attribute of `profile` where you can define any environment or any string as a profile, so in this file you declared two profiles: dev and qa. So you have declared the `profile` dev that has the engine and documentDAO beans, and the `profile` qa that has only the documentDAO bean. But how does the Spring container know what profile to use? You are going to see that with your test class (see Listing 7-3). Also, you added the `<context:component-scan/>` that will search for any annotated class within the `com.apress.isf.spring.service` package. This `<context:component-scan/>` tag will play an important part for your next tests.

Now, let's create your test class, as shown in Listing 7-3. In this test you will use a new annotation: `@ActiveProfiles`. This annotation will tell the Spring container which profile to use and the beans to instantiate for their use.

Listing 7-3. MyDocumentsWithProfilesTest.java

```java
package com.apress.isf.spring.test;

import static org.junit.Assert.assertEquals;
import static org.junit.Assert.assertNotNull;
import static org.junit.Assert.assertTrue;

import java.util.List;

import org.junit.Test;
import org.junit.runner.RunWith;
import org.slf4j.Logger;
import org.slf4j.LoggerFactory;
import org.springframework.beans.factory.annotation.Autowired;
import org.springframework.test.context.ActiveProfiles;
import org.springframework.test.context.ContextConfiguration;
import org.springframework.test.context.junit4.SpringJUnit4ClassRunner;

import com.apress.isf.java.model.Document;
import com.apress.isf.java.model.Type;
import com.apress.isf.java.service.SearchEngine;
```

```java
@RunWith(SpringJUnit4ClassRunner.class)
@ContextConfiguration("classpath:META-INF/spring/mydocuments-profiles-context.xml")
@ActiveProfiles("dev")
public class MyDocumentsWithProfilesTest {
        private static final Logger log = LoggerFactory.getLogger(MyDocumentsWithProfilesTest.class);

        @Autowired
        private SearchEngine engine;
        @Autowired
        private Type webType;

        @Test
        public void testUsingSpringTestWithProfiles() {
                try{
                        log.debug("Using Spring Test fixtures:");

                        List<Document> documents = engine.findByType(webType);
                        assertNotNull(documents);
                        assertTrue(documents.size() == 1);
                        assertEquals(webType.getName(),documents.get(0).getType().getName());
                        assertEquals(webType.getDesc(),documents.get(0).getType().getDesc());
                        assertEquals(webType.getExtension(),documents.get(0).getType().getExtension());

                        documents = engine.listAll();
                        assertNotNull(documents);
                        assertTrue(documents.size() == 4);
                }catch(Exception ex){
                        log.error(ex.getMessage());
                }
        }
}
```

If you run the test in Listing 7-3 with

```
gradle :ch07:test
```

you should get the same result as the previous test (see Listing 7-1). Now, what about the QA environment? Let's create a new class by adding the @Profile annotation, as shown in Listing 7-4. This annotation will mark your FileSearchEngineService class to be instantiated only when the qa profile is activated.

Listing 7-4. FileSearchEngineService.java

```java
package com.apress.isf.spring.service;

import java.util.List;

import org.springframework.context.annotation.Profile;
import org.springframework.stereotype.Component;

import com.apress.isf.java.model.Document;
import com.apress.isf.java.model.Type;
import com.apress.isf.java.service.SearchEngine;
```

```
@Component
@Profile("qa")
public class FileSearchEngineService implements SearchEngine {

        public List<Document> findByType(Type documentType) {
            throw new UnsupportedOperationException("QA Environment. Not yet implemented operation.");
        }

        public List<Document> listAll() {
            throw new UnsupportedOperationException("QA Environment. Not yet implemented operation.");
        }

}
```

Now if you change the @ActiveProfiles to qa, as shown in Listing 7-3, and run it again, then you should get the following output:

```
2014-02-16 18:22:30,110 DEBUG [main] Using Spring Test fixtures:
2014-02-16 18:22:30,113 ERROR [main] QA Environment. Not yet implemented operation.
```

The preceding output is the result of running the Profile as QA, and because you annotated the class FileSearchEngineService with @Profile("qa") the Spring test will use it and you will get that exception.

With profiling, you can get even more detail. You can define a custom Profile by using environment variables; in other words, you can pass a variable name and if it matches with the value given, then the test method will run. For creating a custom Profile you need to implement the ProfileValueSource interface as shown in Listing 7-5.

Listing 7-5. CustomProfile.java

```
package com.apress.isf.spring.test.profile;

import org.springframework.test.annotation.ProfileValueSource;

public class CustomProfile implements ProfileValueSource {

        public String get(String key) {
                if(key.equals("dev"))
                        return "Development";
                else if (key.equals("qa"))
                        return "QA";
                return null;
        }

}
```

In Listing 7-5, you created a CustomProfile class that will help you to reach every method depending on a value passed in a special annotation, and as you can see, you have implemented the get method from the ProfileValueSource interface. Now let's modify your XML and test class as shown in Listing 7-6 and Listing 7-7.

Listing 7-6. mydocuments-custom-profiles-context.xml

```xml
<?xml version="1.0" encoding="UTF-8"?>
<beans xmlns="http://www.springframework.org/schema/beans"
        xmlns:xsi="http://www.w3.org/2001/XMLSchema-instance" xmlns:context=
        "http://www.springframework.org/schema/context"
        xsi:schemaLocation="http://www.springframework.org/schema/beans
        http://www.springframework.org/schema/beans/spring-beans.xsd
                http://www.springframework.org/schema/context
                http://www.springframework.org/schema/context/spring-context-4.0.xsd">

        <bean id="engine" class="com.apress.isf.spring.service.SearchEngineService">
                <property name="documentDAO" ref="documentDAO" />
        </bean>

        <!-- Beans definitions omitted -->

</beans>
```

You just removed the <beans profile=""/>tag from Listing 7-6. Let's look at Listing 7-7 to see what happens to the test.

Listing 7-7. MyDocumentsWithCustomProfilesTest.java

```java
package com.apress.isf.spring.test;

import static org.junit.Assert.assertEquals;
import static org.junit.Assert.assertNotNull;
import static org.junit.Assert.assertTrue;

import java.util.List;

import org.junit.Test;
import org.junit.runner.RunWith;
import org.slf4j.Logger;
import org.slf4j.LoggerFactory;
import org.springframework.beans.factory.annotation.Autowired;
import org.springframework.test.annotation.IfProfileValue;
import org.springframework.test.annotation.ProfileValueSourceConfiguration;
import org.springframework.test.context.ContextConfiguration;
import org.springframework.test.context.junit4.SpringJUnit4ClassRunner;

import com.apress.isf.java.model.Document;
import com.apress.isf.java.model.Type;
import com.apress.isf.java.service.SearchEngine;
import com.apress.isf.spring.test.profile.CustomProfile;

@RunWith(SpringJUnit4ClassRunner.class)
@ContextConfiguration("classpath:META-INF/spring/mydocuments-custom-profiles-context.xml")
@ProfileValueSourceConfiguration(CustomProfile.class)
public class MyDocumentsWithCustomProfilesTest {
        private static final Logger log = LoggerFactory.getLogger(MyDocumentsWithCustomProfilesTest.class);
```

```
        @Autowired
        private SearchEngine engine;
        @Autowired
        private Type webType;

        @IfProfileValue(name = "environment", values = "dev")
        @Test
        public void testUsingSpringTestWithCustomProfilesX() {
                try{
                        log.debug("Using Spring Test fixtures:");

                        List<Document> documents = engine.findByType(webType);
                        assertNotNull(documents);
                        assertTrue(documents.size() == 1);
                        assertEquals(webType.getName(),documents.get(0).getType().getName());
                        assertEquals(webType.getDesc(),documents.get(0).getType().getDesc());
                        assertEquals(webType.getExtension(),documents.get(0).getType().
                        getExtension());

                        documents = engine.listAll();
                        assertNotNull(documents);
                        assertTrue(documents.size() == 4);
                }catch(Exception ex){
                        log.error(ex.getMessage());
                }
        }

        @IfProfileValue(name = "os.name", values = "Unix")
        @Test
        public void testUsingSpringTestWithCustomProfilesY() {
                try{
                        log.debug("Using Spring Test fixtures on Unix:");

                        //More Testing

                }catch(Exception ex){
                        log.error(ex.getMessage());
                }
        }
}
```

Listing 7-7 shows two new annotations: @ProfileValueSourceConfiguration that points to your CustomProfile class and tells the unit test that it will be required in order to perform some business logic, and the @IfProfileValue annotation where you passed a name (key) and the value returned. If you run the test, you are going to see the following output:

```
2014-02-16 19:55:11,903 DEBUG [main] SearchEngineService created: com.apress.isf.spring.service.
SearchEngineService@3b897b54
2014-02-16 19:55:11,993 DEBUG [main] Document DAO set: com.apress.isf.spring.data.
DocumentRepository@2c24be25
2014-02-16 19:55:12,026 DEBUG [main] Using Spring Test fixtures:
2014-02-16 19:55:12,026 DEBUG [main] Start <findByType> Params: Type Definition:
Name: WEB
```

```
Description: Web Link
Extension: .url
2014-02-16 19:55:12,026 DEBUG [main] Start <listAll> Params:
2014-02-16 19:55:12,026 DEBUG [main] Start <getAll> Params:
2014-02-16 19:55:12,026 DEBUG [main] End <getAll> Result:[Lcom.apress.isf.java.model.
Document;@b29b889
2014-02-16 19:55:12,027 DEBUG [main] End <listAll> Result: [com.apress.isf.java.model.
Document@60123018, com.apress.isf.java.model.Document@4a13a8ee, com.apress.isf.java.model.
Document@50b7c740, com.apress.isf.java.model.Document@517a6426]
2014-02-16 19:55:12,027 DEBUG [main] End <findByType> Result: [com.apress.isf.java.model.
Document@517a6426]
2014-02-16 19:55:12,027 DEBUG [main] Start <listAll> Params:
2014-02-16 19:55:12,027 DEBUG [main] Start <getAll> Params:
2014-02-16 19:55:12,027 DEBUG [main] End <getAll> Result:[Lcom.apress.isf.java.model.
Document;@3a452494
2014-02-16 19:55:12,027 DEBUG [main] End <listAll> Result: [com.apress.isf.java.model.
Document@60123018, com.apress.isf.java.model.Document@4a13a8ee, com.apress.isf.java.model.
Document@50b7c740, com.apress.isf.java.model.Document@517a6426]
2014-02-16 19:55:12,029 DEBUG [main] Using Spring Test fixtures on Unix:
```

The two tests run because the correct value is returned in each.

■ **Note** If you removed the @ProfileValueSourceConfiguration, then the unit test will be based on the System.getProperty(propertyKey). This means that if you add the Environment variable os.name with value Unix, then the test method testUsingSpringTestWithCustomProfilesY will be executed.

More Test Annotations

The Spring Framework provides even more annotations to test with. Let's see some examples. Listing 7-8 shows the @Timed and @Repeat annotations that can be used only when using the SpringJUnit4ClassRunner or JUnit support classes.

Listing 7-8. MyDocumentsMoreAnnotationsTest.java (@Timed, @Repeat)

```java
package com.apress.isf.spring.test;

import static org.junit.Assert.assertEquals;
import static org.junit.Assert.assertNotNull;
import static org.junit.Assert.assertTrue;

import java.util.List;

import org.junit.Test;
import org.junit.runner.RunWith;
import org.slf4j.Logger;
import org.slf4j.LoggerFactory;
import org.springframework.beans.factory.annotation.Autowired;
```

```java
import org.springframework.test.annotation.Repeat;
import org.springframework.test.annotation.Timed;
import org.springframework.test.context.ContextConfiguration;
import org.springframework.test.context.junit4.SpringJUnit4ClassRunner;

import com.apress.isf.java.model.Document;
import com.apress.isf.java.model.Type;
import com.apress.isf.java.service.SearchEngine;

@RunWith(SpringJUnit4ClassRunner.class)
@ContextConfiguration("classpath:META-INF/spring/mydocuments-context.xml")
public class MyDocumentsMoreAnnotationsTest {
        private static final Logger log = LoggerFactory.getLogger(MyDocumentsMoreAnnotationsTest.class);

        @Autowired
        private SearchEngine engine;
        @Autowired
        private Type webType;

        @Timed(millis=2000)
        @Test
        public void testUsingSpringTimedAnnotationTest() throws InterruptedException {
                log.debug("Using Spring Test fixtures:");

                List<Document> documents = engine.findByType(webType);
                assertNotNull(documents);
                assertTrue(documents.size() == 1);
                assertEquals(webType.getName(),documents.get(0).getType().getName());
                assertEquals(webType.getDesc(),documents.get(0).getType().getDesc());
                assertEquals(webType.getExtension(),documents.get(0).getType().getExtension());

                Thread.sleep(500);

                documents = engine.listAll();
                assertNotNull(documents);
                assertTrue(documents.size() == 4);
        }

        @Repeat(10)
        @Test
        public void testUsingSpringRepeatedAnnotationTest() {
                log.debug("This message should be printed 10 times..");
        }
}
```

If you run the test (see Listing 7-8) with

```
gradle :ch07:test
```

you should get the following output:

```
2014-02-16 20:08:53,797 DEBUG [main] SearchEngineService created: com.apress.isf.spring.service.
SearchEngineService@3553d71d
2014-02-16 20:08:53,843 DEBUG [main] Document DAO set: com.apress.isf.spring.data.
DocumentRepository@31da28a
2014-02-16 20:08:53,860 DEBUG [main] Using Spring Test fixtures:
2014-02-16 20:08:53,861 DEBUG [main] Start <findByType> Params: Type Definition:
Name: WEB
Description: Web Link
Extension: .url
2014-02-16 20:08:53,861 DEBUG [main] Start <listAll> Params:
2014-02-16 20:08:53,861 DEBUG [main] Start <getAll> Params:
2014-02-16 20:08:53,861 DEBUG [main] End <getAll> Result:[Lcom.apress.isf.java.model.
Document;@42704d54
2014-02-16 20:08:53,861 DEBUG [main] End <listAll> Result: [com.apress.isf.java.model.
Document@5ae4e7df, com.apress.isf.java.model.Document@6a331017, com.apress.isf.java.model.
Document@3e658c79, com.apress.isf.java.model.Document@7ce97bef]
2014-02-16 20:08:53,861 DEBUG [main] End <findByType> Result: [com.apress.isf.java.model.
Document@7ce97bef]
2014-02-16 20:08:54,361 DEBUG [main] Start <listAll> Params:
2014-02-16 20:08:54,362 DEBUG [main] Start <getAll> Params:
2014-02-16 20:08:54,362 DEBUG [main] End <getAll> Result:[Lcom.apress.isf.java.model.
Document;@44c7c7fa
2014-02-16 20:08:54,362 DEBUG [main] End <listAll> Result: [com.apress.isf.java.model.
Document@5ae4e7df, com.apress.isf.java.model.Document@6a331017, com.apress.isf.java.model.
Document@3e658c79, com.apress.isf.java.model.Document@7ce97bef]
2014-02-16 20:08:54,366 DEBUG [main] This message should be printed 10 times..
2014-02-16 20:08:54,367 DEBUG [main] This message should be printed 10 times..
2014-02-16 20:08:54,367 DEBUG [main] This message should be printed 10 times..
2014-02-16 20:08:54,368 DEBUG [main] This message should be printed 10 times..
2014-02-16 20:08:54,368 DEBUG [main] This message should be printed 10 times..
2014-02-16 20:08:54,369 DEBUG [main] This message should be printed 10 times..
2014-02-16 20:08:54,369 DEBUG [main] This message should be printed 10 times..
2014-02-16 20:08:54,370 DEBUG [main] This message should be printed 10 times..
2014-02-16 20:08:54,370 DEBUG [main] This message should be printed 10 times..
2014-02-16 20:08:54,370 DEBUG [main] This message should be printed 10 times..
```

So the @Timed annotation will fail if the test takes more than the milliseconds parameter provided. Maybe you want to test some process time that should not take too long or maybe you need to test the response of the external call to another system that should not exceed the time you specified. And the @Repeat annotation will repeat the test as many times as the number provided. You can use the @Repeat in a test when you need to measure the average of process executing by repeating the same test several times.

Summary

In this chapter, I covered the Spring Framework Testing extension. You discovered how easy it is to use it. In previous chapters, you instantiated the ApplicationContext with the ClassPathXMLApplicationContext class and every time you needed a bean you had to call the getBean method. But thanks to the annotations provided by the Spring Framework Test extension, you can have better readable code and faster development because you can focus on the test cases. If you download the companion source code, you can find other versions of the classes, which convert to the Spring Test extension, even the Groovy classes.

PART II

Spring Framework

In Part II, you will continue to learn more about the Spring Framework and some of its extensions like AOP, JDBC, Email, Scheduling, JMS, AMQP, and Web.

You will start by using AOP (aspect-oriented programming) to separate concerns by focusing on your business logic. You'll work with JDBC to save information into an in-memory database. Then you will show your Spring application on the Web by creating a small web application.

Later, you will integrate your Spring application with external systems by using JMS and AMQP and you will expose a RESTful API so external clients can post information to your Spring application.

And finally, you will learn how to send e-mail and schedule tasks that will perform validation of your data within your Spring application.

CHAPTER 8

Give Advice to Your Spring Application

In this chapter, you will review part of your logic and refactor some of the classes to make the application more functional. In the previous chapters, I introduced some Spring concepts for your application, like dependency injection, how to use collections, how to load external resources, and how to use Profiles and testing. You did a little testing with them, but you need to actually see something real, right? So in this chapter you are going to give **advice** to your **My Documents** app.

Advice to My Documents

So what is this "advice" thingy anyway? Remember your SearchEngineService.java class from previous chapters? You just added logs everywhere in order to find out what was going on in every method (if you were passing the correct parameter or not, and if the result was what you expected). Now imagine for a moment that this class needs some new logic added to it, something like a security checkpoint for every method written where only users with a username and password are allowed to execute certain logic, or maybe audit checks for some methods, or some particular business logic you have, like having a counter to see how many times a user uses a particular method call. This new logic would become a nightmare—too much code to add for something that should be simple! You would end up having too many calls to do security or audit checks, and the same code would be all over the place. Let's look at Listing 8-1, which is your SearchEngineService class.

Listing 8-1. SearchEngineService.java

```
package com.apress.isf.spring.service;

import java.util.ArrayList;
import java.util.Arrays;
import java.util.List;

import org.slf4j.Logger;
import org.slf4j.LoggerFactory;

import com.apress.isf.java.model.Document;
import com.apress.isf.java.model.Type;
import com.apress.isf.java.service.SearchEngine;
import com.apress.isf.spring.data.DocumentDAO;
```

```java
public class SearchEngineService implements SearchEngine {
        private static final Logger log = LoggerFactory.getLogger(SearchEngineService.class);
        private DocumentDAO documentDAO;

        public SearchEngineService(){
                if(log.isDebugEnabled())
                        log.debug("SearchEngineService created: " + this);
        }

        public DocumentDAO getDocumentDAO() {
                return documentDAO;
        }

        public void setDocumentDAO(DocumentDAO documentDAO) {
                if(log.isDebugEnabled())
                        log.debug("Document DAO set: " + documentDAO);

                this.documentDAO = documentDAO;
        }

        public List<Document> findByType(Type documentType) {
                if(log.isDebugEnabled())
                        log.debug("Start <findByType> Params: " + documentType);

                List<Document>  result = new ArrayList<Document>();
                for(Document doc : listAll()){
                        if(doc.getType().getName().equals(documentType.getName()))
                                result.add(doc);
                }

                if(log.isDebugEnabled())
                        log.debug("End <findByType> Result: " + result);
                return result;
        }

        public List<Document> listAll() {
                if(log.isDebugEnabled())
                        log.debug("Start <listAll> Params: ");
                List<Document> result = Arrays.asList(documentDAO.getAll());
                if(log.isDebugEnabled())
                        log.debug("End <listAll> Result: " + result);
                return result;
        }

}
```

In Listing 8-1 you are using the "if" statement because debugging is enabled and it is calling the log.debug method. But take a closer look; those "if" statements are in every method: in the constructor, in the findByType, listAll, and in the setter of the DocumentDAO. Also these statements are in different classes as well. This is called tangling and scattering code, as shown in Figure 8-1.

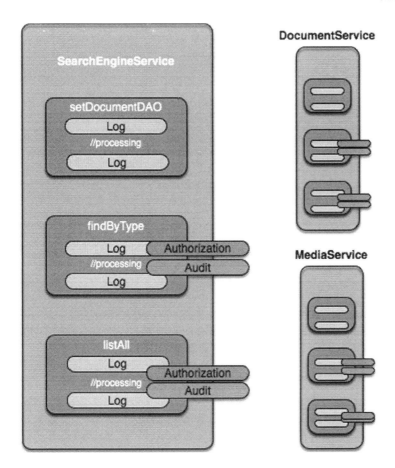

Figure 8-1. *Tangling and Scattering Code*

Figure 8-1 shows how your logging mechanism is in every method of your SearchEngine implementation, and that it could be in other classes like the DocumentService or MediaService classes. The code is all over the place! This is called scattering and its implementation is not modular. But that's not all. As I mentioned before, you can have the same code, such as authorization or audit, in places where there is a particular business logic happening, making it not cohesive. This is called tangling. There should be a better way to solve these issues.

AOP to the Rescue

You need to start thinking about how to modularize your code into independent modules. But how can you accomplish that? Aspect-oriented programming (AOP) was created to accomplish this hard task by modularizing this cross-cutting functionality into better manageable modules. In other words, AOP is going to take care of your concerns (such as logging, authorization, and audit, in your case), so you can focus only on the business logic without having to worry about checkpoints or logging.

AOP Concepts

Let's quickly review some of the AOP concepts over your SearchEngineService.java class (as shown in Listing 8-1). Let's also start thinking about the logging concerns (see Figure 8-2 and Table 8-1). Start by writing your concerns.

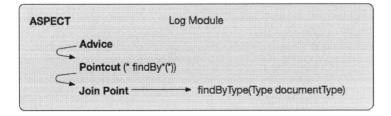

Figure 8-2. *AOP Definitions*

Table 8-1. *AOP Concepts*

ASPECT	A set of pointcuts and related advices.
ADVICE	An action that will be executed at the join points in a particular pointcut.
POINTCUT	A pattern (expression language) that bounds an advice with a single or many joint points.
JOIN POINT	A method exception where the advice will be executed.

Figure 8-2 explains the Table 8-1 concepts that you will find within your Log module. But I'll explain them more in detail here. In your case, you need to create a Log module that will log every method call you have. Figure 8-2 shows the Log module that will define an **advice**.

Figure 8-2 shows how the **aspect** will be applied. So in this case, the Log module defines an **advice**, this **advice** will be executed based on the defined **pointcut**. Figure 8-2 shows the (* findBy*(*)) **pointcut** expression. This expression means the following:

- Select a method that has any return type (***** findBy*(*)), that is what the first asterisk means.

- Select a method that contains a prefix findBy. (* **findBy***(*)).

- With any number of parameters (* findBy*(*****)), that is what the last asterisk means.

So based on the preceding explanation, then **joint point** will be the findByType(Type Document) method that will execute the **advice**. In other words, the method findByType will be intercepted and the Log module logic will be executed. All of this working together is an **aspect**.

The Spring Framework provides an AOP extension and supports four types of advices:

- **Before advice**: Runs before every method call.

- **After returning advice**: Runs after a method call and returns a result.

- **Around advice**: Runs before and after a method call, and combines advices.

- **After throwing advice**: Runs after throwing an exception.

Let's start modifying your code and getting rid of the logs from your classes. Remember that you need to take care of the logging concern by separating it from the classes to avoid scattering and tangling. You are going to start with the SearchEngine.java class, adding a new method just for testing one of your advice types (see Listing 8-2), then your SearchEngineService.java class (see Listing 8-3).

Listing 8-2. SearchEngine.java

```
package com.apress.isf.java.service;

import java.util.List;

import com.apress.isf.java.model.Document;
import com.apress.isf.java.model.Type;

public interface SearchEngine {

        public List<Document> findByType(Type documentType);

        public List<Document> listAll();

        public List<Document> findByLocation(String location);
}
```

Listing 8-3. SearchEngineService.java

```
package com.apress.isf.spring.service;

import java.util.ArrayList;
import java.util.Arrays;
import java.util.List;

import com.apress.isf.java.model.Document;
import com.apress.isf.java.model.Type;
import com.apress.isf.java.service.SearchEngine;
import com.apress.isf.spring.data.DocumentDAO;

public class SearchEngineService implements SearchEngine {
        private DocumentDAO documentDAO;

        public SearchEngineService(){
        }

        public DocumentDAO getDocumentDAO() {
                return documentDAO;
        }

        public void setDocumentDAO(DocumentDAO documentDAO) {
                this.documentDAO = documentDAO;
        }
```

```
        public List<Document> findByType(Type documentType) {
                List<Document>  result = new ArrayList<Document>();
                for(Document doc : listAll()){
                        if(doc.getType().getName().equals(documentType.getName()))
                                result.add(doc);
                }
                return result;
        }

        public List<Document> listAll() {
                List<Document> result = Arrays.asList(documentDAO.getAll());
                return result;
        }

        public List<Document> findByLocation(String location) {
                throw new UnsupportedOperationException("findByLocation not yet implemented.");
        }
}
```

You have just added the findByLocation method on the SearchEngine.java class, as shown in Listing 8-2. Then you removed all the log details from your SearchEngineService.java implementation class. You need to remove every logging concern. Now, remember your XML file? Let's review your mydocuments-aop-context.xml file, as shown in Listing 8-4.

Listing 8-4. mydocuments-aop-context.xml

```
<?xml version="1.0" encoding="UTF-8"?>
<beans xmlns="http://www.springframework.org/schema/beans"
        xmlns:xsi="http://www.w3.org/2001/XMLSchema-instance"
        xsi:schemaLocation="http://www.springframework.org/schema/beans
http://www.springframework.org/schema/beans/spring-beans.xsd">

  <bean id="engine" class="com.apress.isf.spring.service.SearchEngineService">
      <property name="documentDAO" ref="documentDAO"/>
  </bean>

  <bean id="documentDAO" class="com.apress.isf.spring.data.DocumentRepository">
     <property name="documents">
        <list>
            <ref bean="doc1"/>
            <ref bean="doc2"/>
            <ref bean="doc3"/>
            <ref bean="doc4"/>
        </list>
     </property>
  </bean>

  <!-- Bean definitions omitted -->
</beans>
```

As you can see in Listing 8-4, the file is nothing out of the ordinary; in fact, it's the same file as in previous chapters. The file contains your SearchEngineService and your DocumentRepository classes defined with a list of references of documents. But you will be modifying the file in the following sections. First, let's review your unit test (see Listing 8-5).

Listing 8-5. MyDocumentsAOPTest.java

```java
package com.apress.isf.spring.test;

import static org.junit.Assert.assertEquals;
import static org.junit.Assert.assertNotNull;
import static org.junit.Assert.assertTrue;

import java.util.List;

import org.junit.Test;
import org.junit.runner.RunWith;
import org.slf4j.Logger;
import org.slf4j.LoggerFactory;
import org.springframework.beans.factory.annotation.Autowired;
import org.springframework.test.context.ContextConfiguration;
import org.springframework.test.context.junit4.SpringJUnit4ClassRunner;

import com.apress.isf.java.model.Document;
import com.apress.isf.java.model.Type;
import com.apress.isf.java.service.SearchEngine;

@RunWith(SpringJUnit4ClassRunner.class)
@ContextConfiguration("classpath:META-INF/spring/mydocuments-aop-context.xml")
public class MyDocumentsAOPTest {
        private static final Logger log = LoggerFactory.getLogger(MyDocumentsAOPTest.class);

        @Autowired
        private SearchEngine engineProxy;
        @Autowired
        private Type webType;

        @Test
        public void testUsingSpringAOP() {
                log.debug("Using Spring AOP:");

                List<Document> documents = engineProxy.findByType(webType);
                assertNotNull(documents);
                assertTrue(documents.size() == 1);
                assertEquals(webType.getName(),documents.get(0).getType().getName());
                assertEquals(webType.getDesc(),documents.get(0).getType().getDesc());
                assertEquals(webType.getExtension(),documents.get(0).getType().getExtension());

                documents = engineProxy.listAll();
                assertNotNull(documents);
                assertTrue(documents.size() == 4);
```

```
        try{
                engineProxy.findByLocation("/some/path/");
        }catch(Exception ex){
                log.error(ex.getMessage());
        }
    }
}
```

If you run this test with

`gradle :ch08:test`

you will have the following output:

```
2014-02-23 20:04:06,217 DEBUG [main] Using Spring AOP:
2014-02-23 20:04:06,404 ERROR [main] findByLocation not yet implemented.
```

Where are the logs? Well, you removed them from your implementation (see SearchEngineService.java, which is shown in Listing 8-3). You also added a new method in your interface (see Listing 8-2). And in your implementation you just throw an UnsupportedOperationException exception, that's why you are seeing the error log.

Next, let's learn more about each advice type: before, after, around, and after throw.

Before Advice

You are going to create your first advice type. Spring AOP provides a MethodBeforeAdvice interface, and it provides a before method for its implementation. This method will be called before the object's method execution (see Listing 8-6). In other words, you are intercepting a method call before its execution.

Listing 8-6. BeforeLoggingModule.java

```
package com.apress.isf.spring.aop;

import java.lang.reflect.Method;

import org.slf4j.Logger;
import org.slf4j.LoggerFactory;
import org.springframework.aop.MethodBeforeAdvice;

public class BeforeLoggingModule implements MethodBeforeAdvice {
        private static final Logger log = LoggerFactory.getLogger(BeforeLoggingModule.class);

        public void before(Method method, Object[] args, Object target)
                        throws Throwable {
                if(log.isDebugEnabled()){
                        log.debug("@@@@(BEFORE) Method called: " + method.getName());
                        if(args.length ==0 )
                                log.debug("@@@@(BEFORE) No arguments passed.");
                        for(Object arg:args)
                                log.debug("@@@@(BEFORE) Argument passed:" + arg);
                }
        }

}
```

How will this code interact with your SearchEngine implementation? Well, you only need to declare the BeforeLoggingModule class (see Listing 8-6) in your XML file, as well as declare a Proxy class (I am going to discuss this in the next section). Spring will take care of the rest. Next, you will add the beans you need, as shown in Listing 8-7.

Listing 8-7. mydocuments-aop-context.xml

```xml
<?xml version="1.0" encoding="UTF-8"?>
<beans xmlns="http://www.springframework.org/schema/beans"
        xmlns:xsi="http://www.w3.org/2001/XMLSchema-instance"
        xsi:schemaLocation="http://www.springframework.org/schema/beans
http://www.springframework.org/schema/beans/spring-beans.xsd">

  <!-- AOP -->
  <bean id="beforeLogging" class="com.apress.isf.spring.aop.BeforeLoggingModule" />

  <!-- AOP Proxy -->
  <bean id="engineProxy" class="org.springframework.aop.framework.ProxyFactoryBean">
    <property name="proxyTargetClass" value="true"/>
    <property name="target" ref="engine" />
    <property name="interceptorNames">
      <list>
        <value>beforeLogging</value>
      </list>
    </property>
  </bean>

  <bean id="engine" class="com.apress.isf.spring.service.SearchEngineService">
      <property name="documentDAO" ref="documentDAO"/>
  </bean>

  <!-- Bean definitions omitted -->

</beans>
```

You added your beforeLogging bean that points to your class where your interface MethodBeforeAdvice is implemented. Then there is a new bean, engineProxy, that points to the org.springframework.aop.framework. ProxyFactoryBean class. This class will create a proxy using the JDK reflection. Or you can choose to use a CGLib (Code Generation Library) that will help to create the necessary code to be in place when the methods are called. Because here you are using the CGLib, you set the property proxyTargetClass to true. You also defined two more properties, the target that refers to your SearchEngineService class and the property interceptorNames that has the value beforeLogging which matches with your bean definition or your advice. This will help the Spring container to advise all the methods in your SearchEngineService.

If you run the same unit test (see Listing 8-5) using

```
gradle :ch08:test
```

you should have the following output:

```
2014-02-23 20:29:30,119 DEBUG [main] Using Spring AOP:
2014-02-23 20:29:30,152 DEBUG [main] @@@@(BEFORE) Method called: findByType
2014-02-23 20:29:30,152 DEBUG [main] @@@@(BEFORE) Argument passed:Type(name: WEB, description:
Web Link, extension: .url)
```

```
2014-02-23 20:29:30,241 DEBUG [main] @@@@(BEFORE) Method called: listAll
2014-02-23 20:29:30,241 DEBUG [main] @@@@(BEFORE) No arguments passed.
2014-02-23 20:29:30,241 DEBUG [main] @@@@(BEFORE) Method called: findByLocation
2014-02-23 20:29:30,241 DEBUG [main] @@@@(BEFORE) Argument passed:/some/path/
2014-02-23 20:29:30,241 ERROR [main] findByLocation not yet implemented.
```

It's magic! Yes! You are now advising your code, removing the entire scattering and tangling of the logs. Your SearchEngine implementation is now clean and you can just focus on your business logic.

After Advice

The after advice will be after the method call, and you can get a hold of the return value. This advice is done by implementing the AfterReturningAdvice interface class. See Listing 8-8 for an example.

Listing 8-8. AfterLoggingModule.java

```java
package com.apress.isf.spring.aop;

import java.lang.reflect.Method;

import org.slf4j.Logger;
import org.slf4j.LoggerFactory;
import org.springframework.aop.AfterReturningAdvice;

public class AfterLoggingModule implements AfterReturningAdvice {
        private static final Logger log = LoggerFactory.getLogger(AfterLoggingModule.class);

        public void afterReturning(Object returnValue, Method method,
                        Object[] args, Object target) throws Throwable {
                if(log.isDebugEnabled()){
                        log.debug("@@@@(AFTER) Method called: " + method.getName());
                        if(args.length ==0 )
                                log.debug("@@@@(AFTER) No arguments passed.");
                        for(Object arg:args)
                                log.debug("@@@@(AFTER) Argument passed:" + arg);
                        log.debug("@@@(AFTER) Result: " + returnValue);
                }
        }

}
```

Listing 8-8 implements the method afterReturning that will have the returned value, the method that was intercepted, the arguments of the method, and the object where the method was intercepted.

Now let's modify your XML. Remember it will almost be the same as Listing 8-7, but now you are going to change some ids, as shown in Listing 8-9.

Listing 8-9. mydocuments-aop-context.xml

```xml
<?xml version="1.0" encoding="UTF-8"?>
<beans xmlns="http://www.springframework.org/schema/beans"
        xmlns:xsi="http://www.w3.org/2001/XMLSchema-instance"
        xsi:schemaLocation="http://www.springframework.org/schema/beans
http://www.springframework.org/schema/beans/spring-beans.xsd">

  <!-- AOP -->
  <bean id="afterLogging" class="com.apress.isf.spring.aop.AfterLoggingModule" />

  <!-- AOP Proxy -->
  <bean id="engineProxy" class="org.springframework.aop.framework.ProxyFactoryBean">
    <property name="proxyTargetClass" value="true"/>
    <property name="target" ref="engine" />
    <property name="interceptorNames">
      <list>
        <value>afterLogging</value>
      </list>
    </property>
  </bean>

  <bean id="engine" class="com.apress.isf.spring.service.SearchEngineService">
      <property name="documentDAO" ref="documentDAO"/>
  </bean>

  <!-- Bean definitions omitted -->

</beans>
```

Running the unit test (see Listing 8-5) with

```
gradle :ch08:test
```

will have the following output:

```
2014-02-23 20:39:40,683 DEBUG [main] Using Spring AOP:
2014-02-23 20:39:40,747 DEBUG [main] @@@@(AFTER) Method called: findByType
2014-02-23 20:39:40,748 DEBUG [main] @@@@(AFTER) Argument passed:Type(name: WEB, description: Web
Link, extension: .url)
2014-02-23 20:39:40,748 DEBUG [main] @@@(AFTER) Result: [Documents(name: Pro Spring Security Book,
type: Type(name: WEB, description: Web Link, extension: .url), location:
http://www.apress.com/9781430248187)]
2014-02-23 20:39:40,748 DEBUG [main] @@@@(AFTER) Method called: listAll
2014-02-23 20:39:40,748 DEBUG [main] @@@@(AFTER) No arguments passed.
2014-02-23 20:39:40,748 DEBUG [main] @@@(AFTER) Result: [Documents(name: Book Template, type:
Type(name: PDF, description: Portable Document Format, extension: .pdf), location: /Users/
felipeg/Documents/Random/Book Template.pdf), Documents(name: Sample Contract, type: Type(name:
PDF, description: Portable Document Format, extension: .pdf), location: /Users/felipeg/Documents/
Contracts/Sample Contract.pdf), Documents(name: Clustering with RabbitMQ, type: Type(name: NOTE,
```

description: Text Notes, extension: .txt), location: /Users/felipeg/Documents/Random/Clustering with RabbitMQ.txt), Documents(name: Pro Spring Security Book, type: Type(name: WEB, description: Web Link, extension: .url), location: http://www.apress.com/9781430248187)]
2014-02-23 20:39:40,749 ERROR [main] findByLocation not yet implemented.

The output shows how this advice intercepts the method after it is called, so you can get a hold of the return value. A different scenario would be to have an audit advice that will trigger an alarm after a special value is returned by the method intercepted, such as an audit of a bank account that returns a big amount.

Around Advice

This advice, as you may have guessed already, is the combination of the before and after advices, but you can have more control over it because it will intercept the method call, then you can execute that call and get back a result. You are executing the after and before advices in one advice. In order to implement this advice, you need to use the MethodInterceptor interface class (see Listing 8-10).

Listing 8-10. AroundLoggingModule.java

```java
package com.apress.isf.spring.aop;

import org.aopalliance.intercept.MethodInterceptor;
import org.aopalliance.intercept.MethodInvocation;
import org.slf4j.Logger;
import org.slf4j.LoggerFactory;

public class AroundLoggingModule implements MethodInterceptor {
        private static final Logger log = LoggerFactory.getLogger(AroundLoggingModule.class);

        public Object invoke(MethodInvocation invocation) throws Throwable {
                Object result = null;
                if(log.isDebugEnabled()){
                        log.debug("@@@@(AROUND-BEFORE) Method called: " +
                                invocation.getMethod().getName());
                        if(invocation.getArguments().length ==0 )
                                log.debug("@@@@(AROUND-BEFORE) No arguments passed.");
                        for(Object arg:invocation.getArguments())
                                log.debug("@@@@(AROUND-BEFORE) Argument passed:" + arg);
                }

                try{
                        if(log.isDebugEnabled())
                                log.debug("@@@(AROUND) Processing...");

                        result = invocation.proceed();

                        if(log.isDebugEnabled())
                                log.debug("@@@(AROUND-AFTER) Result: " + result);

                        return result;
                }catch(IllegalArgumentException ex){
```

```
            log.error("@@@(AROUND) Throws an exception: " + ex.getMessage());
            throw ex;
        }
    }
}
```

Listing 8-10 shows the implementation of the invoke method that has the MethodInvocation class as a parameter, which is in fact the object that it is advising. With the MethodInvocation class you can get the method that was intercepted and its arguments. You can execute the method by calling proceed() to get the result of the execution.

Next, let's modify your XML to point to your new advice, the AroundLoggingModule class as shown in Listing 8-11.

Listing 8-11. mydocuments-aop-context.xml

```xml
<?xml version="1.0" encoding="UTF-8"?>
<beans xmlns="http://www.springframework.org/schema/beans"
       xmlns:xsi="http://www.w3.org/2001/XMLSchema-instance"
       xsi:schemaLocation="http://www.springframework.org/schema/beans
http://www.springframework.org/schema/beans/spring-beans.xsd">

  <!-- AOP -->
  <bean id="aroundLogging" class="com.apress.isf.spring.aop.AroundLoggingModule" />

  <!-- AOP Proxy -->
  <bean id="engineProxy" class="org.springframework.aop.framework.ProxyFactoryBean">
    <property name="proxyTargetClass" value="true"/>
    <property name="target" ref="engine" />
    <property name="interceptorNames">
      <list>
        <value>aroundLogging</value>
      </list>
    </property>
  </bean>

  <bean id="engine" class="com.apress.isf.spring.service.SearchEngineService">
      <property name="documentDAO" ref="documentDAO"/>
  </bean>

  <!-- Bean definitions omitted -->

</beans>
```

Running the unit test (see Listing 8-5) with

```
gradle :ch08:test
```

you will get the following output:

```
2014-02-23 20:46:25,679 DEBUG [main] Using Spring AOP:
2014-02-23 20:46:25,689 DEBUG [main] @@@@(AROUND-BEFORE) Method called: findByType
2014-02-23 20:46:25,689 DEBUG [main] @@@@(AROUND-BEFORE) Argument passed:Type(name: WEB,
description: Web Link, extension: .url)
```

101

```
2014-02-23 20:46:25,689 DEBUG [main] @@@(AROUND) Processing...
2014-02-23 20:46:25,732 DEBUG [main] @@@(AROUND-AFTER) Result: [Documents(name: Pro Spring
Security Book, type: Type(name: WEB, description: Web Link, extension: .url), location:
http://www.apress.com/9781430248187)]
2014-02-23 20:46:25,732 DEBUG [main] @@@@(AROUND-BEFORE) Method called: listAll
2014-02-23 20:46:25,732 DEBUG [main] @@@@(AROUND-BEFORE) No arguments passed.
2014-02-23 20:46:25,732 DEBUG [main] @@@(AROUND) Processing...
2014-02-23 20:46:25,732 DEBUG [main] @@@(AROUND-AFTER) Result: [Documents(name: Book Template,
type: Type(name: PDF, description: Portable Document Format, extension: .pdf), location: /Users/
felipeg/Documents/Random/Book Template.pdf), Documents(name: Sample Contract, type: Type(name:
PDF, description: Portable Document Format, extension: .pdf), location: /Users/felipeg/Documents/
Contracts/Sample Contract.pdf), Documents(name: Clustering with RabbitMQ, type: Type(name: NOTE,
description: Text Notes, extension: .txt), location: /Users/felipeg/Documents/Random/Clustering with
RabbitMQ.txt), Documents(name: Pro Spring Security Book, type: Type(name: WEB, description: Web
Link, extension: .url), location: http://www.apress.com/9781430248187)]
2014-02-23 20:46:25,733 DEBUG [main] @@@@(AROUND-BEFORE) Method called: findByLocation
2014-02-23 20:46:25,733 DEBUG [main] @@@@(AROUND-BEFORE) Argument passed:/some/path/
2014-02-23 20:46:25,733 DEBUG [main] @@@(AROUND) Processing...
2014-02-23 20:46:25,733 ERROR [main] findByLocation not yet implemented.
```

As you can see in the output, you are intercepting a method before it's actually called. You are logging its name and its parameters (if any), and then you are executing the object's method and logging the result. Another way to use the around advice is to use a cache mechanism to a database or a remote site. So if there are several calls to the same method, you can cache some data in memory instead of going to a database or going to the remote site. You will see more examples in the following sections.

After Throwing Advice

In order to use this advice, your class needs to implement the ThrowsAdvice interface class. This will be after any exception occurs in your code. Now, remember that you added a new method in your SearchEngine interface (as shown in Listing 8-2). And in your implementation (as shown in Listing 8-3) you throw the UnsupportedOperationException. Let's see how this will work (see Listing 8-12).

Listing 8-12. ThrowsLoggingModule.java

```java
package com.apress.isf.spring.aop;

import java.lang.reflect.Method;

import org.slf4j.Logger;
import org.slf4j.LoggerFactory;
import org.springframework.aop.ThrowsAdvice;

public class ThrowsLoggingModule implements ThrowsAdvice {
        private static final Logger log = LoggerFactory.getLogger(ThrowsLoggingModule.class);

        public void afterThrowing(Method m, Object[] args, Object target, Exception ex) {
                if(log.isDebugEnabled()){
                        log.debug("@@@(THROWS) Method called: " + m.getName());
                        if(args.length ==0 )
                                log.debug("@@@@(THROWS) No arguments passed.");
```

```
                      for(Object arg:args)
                            log.debug("@@@@(THROWS) Argument passed:" + arg);
                      log.debug("@@@(THORWS) Error: " + ex.getMessage());
               }
        }
}
```

Listing 8-12 shows the implementation of the afterThrowing method that has the method, the arguments of the method, the object that is being adviced, and the exception that occurred as parameters.

Next, let's modify your XML configuration file (see Listing 8-13) by adding the ThrowsLoggingModule class and making a reference to the bean on the interceptorNames within the engineProxy bean.

Listing 8-13. mydocuments-aop-context.xml

```xml
<?xml version="1.0" encoding="UTF-8"?>
<beans xmlns="http://www.springframework.org/schema/beans"
        xmlns:xsi="http://www.w3.org/2001/XMLSchema-instance"
        xsi:schemaLocation="http://www.springframework.org/schema/beans
http://www.springframework.org/schema/beans/spring-beans.xsd">

  <!-- AOP -->
  <bean id="throwsLogging" class="com.apress.isf.spring.aop.ThrowsLoggingModule" />

  <!-- AOP Proxy -->
  <bean id="engineProxy" class="org.springframework.aop.framework.ProxyFactoryBean">
    <property name="proxyTargetClass" value="true"/>
    <property name="target" ref="engine" />
    <property name="interceptorNames">
      <list>
        <value>throwsLogging</value>
      </list>
    </property>
  </bean>

  <bean id="engine" class="com.apress.isf.spring.service.SearchEngineService">
      <property name="documentDAO" ref="documentDAO"/>
  </bean>

  <!-- Bean definitions omitted -->

</beans>
```

And again if you run the unit test (see Listing 8-5) with

```
gradle :ch08:test
```

you will get following output:

```
2014-02-23 21:01:01,860 DEBUG [main] Using Spring AOP:
2014-02-23 21:01:01,924 DEBUG [main] @@@(THROWS) Method called: findByLocation
2014-02-23 21:01:01,924 DEBUG [main] @@@@(THROWS) Argument passed:/some/path/
2014-02-23 21:01:01,924 DEBUG [main] @@@(THORWS) Error: findByLocation not yet implemented.
2014-02-23 21:01:01,924 ERROR [main] findByLocation not yet implemented.
```

As you can see, aspect-oriented programming can help you modularize your concerns by using logging or maybe caching to separate them from your business logic and thereby avoiding scattering and tangling.

But wait, how will caching use these advices? Well, let's find out by reviewing Listing 8-14. You are going to use the around advice type to achieve caching.

Listing 8-14. CachingModule.java

```java
package com.apress.isf.spring.aop;

import java.util.HashMap;
import java.util.Map;

import org.aopalliance.intercept.MethodInterceptor;
import org.aopalliance.intercept.MethodInvocation;
import org.slf4j.Logger;
import org.slf4j.LoggerFactory;

import com.apress.isf.java.model.Type;

public class CachingModule implements MethodInterceptor {
        private static final Logger log = LoggerFactory.getLogger(CachingModule.class);
        private static final Map<String, Object> cache = new HashMap<String,Object>();

        public Object invoke(MethodInvocation invocation) throws Throwable {
                Object result = null;
                Type documentType = null;

                log.debug("@@@(Caching) review if this call is cachable...");

                if("findByType".equals(invocation.getMethod().getName()) &&
                                invocation.getArguments().length == 1 &&
                                        invocation.getArguments()[0] instanceof Type){
                        documentType = (Type)invocation.getArguments()[0];
                        log.debug("@@@(Caching) Is cachable!!");
                        if(cache.containsKey(documentType.getName())){
                                log.debug("@@@(Caching) Found in Cache!");
                                return cache.get(documentType.getName());
                        }
                        log.debug("@@@(Caching) Not Found! but is cachable!");
                        result = invocation.proceed();
                        cache.put(documentType.getName(), result);
                        return result;
                }

                return invocation.proceed();
        }

}
```

Listing 8-14 shows the implementation of the invoke method; here you are going to specialize your logic. You are going to declare a Map class that will hold the values from different keys; these keys will be the document's type. You are going to cache only the findByType method, so if it is called you can see if the document's type exists in the Map. If not, you add it into the Map and return it; if it exists in the Map, then just return it.

Now, let's do your XML. This should be very easy (see Listing 8-15) because you only need to declare your CachingModule class and make a reference into the engineProxy bean.

Listing 8-15. mydocuments-aop-context.xml

```xml
<?xml version="1.0" encoding="UTF-8"?>
<beans xmlns="http://www.springframework.org/schema/beans"
        xmlns:xsi="http://www.w3.org/2001/XMLSchema-instance"
        xsi:schemaLocation="http://www.springframework.org/schema/beans
http://www.springframework.org/schema/beans/spring-beans.xsd">

  <!-- AOP -->
  <bean id="caching" class="com.apress.isf.spring.aop.CachingModule" />

  <!-- AOP Proxy -->
  <bean id="engineProxy" class="org.springframework.aop.framework.ProxyFactoryBean">
    <property name="proxyTargetClass" value="true"/>
    <property name="target" ref="engine" />
    <property name="interceptorNames">
      <list>
        <value>caching</value>
      </list>
    </property>
  </bean>

  <bean id="engine" class="com.apress.isf.spring.service.SearchEngineService">
      <property name="documentDAO" ref="documentDAO"/>
  </bean>

  <!-- Bean definitions omitted -->

</beans>
```

Next, you are going to add an extra method call of findByType in your test so you can see that the caching is really working (see Listing 8-16).

Listing 8-16. MyDocumentAOPTest.java

```java
package com.apress.isf.spring.test;

import static org.junit.Assert.assertEquals;
import static org.junit.Assert.assertNotNull;
import static org.junit.Assert.assertTrue;

import java.util.List;

import org.junit.Test;
import org.junit.runner.RunWith;
import org.slf4j.Logger;
import org.slf4j.LoggerFactory;
import org.springframework.beans.factory.annotation.Autowired;
```

```java
import org.springframework.test.context.ContextConfiguration;
import org.springframework.test.context.junit4.SpringJUnit4ClassRunner;

import com.apress.isf.java.model.Document;
import com.apress.isf.java.model.Type;
import com.apress.isf.java.service.SearchEngine;

@RunWith(SpringJUnit4ClassRunner.class)
@ContextConfiguration("classpath:META-INF/spring/mydocuments-aop-context.xml")
public class MyDocumentsAOPTest {
        private static final Logger log = LoggerFactory.getLogger(MyDocumentsAOPTest.class);

        @Autowired
        private SearchEngine engineProxy;
        @Autowired
        private Type webType;

        // The Previous test goes here

        @Test
        public void testUsingSpringAOPCaching() {
                log.debug("Testing Caching Module...");

                List<Document> documents = engineProxy.findByType(webType);
                assertNotNull(documents);
                int count = documents.size();

                log.debug("It should be now cached!");
                documents = engineProxy.findByType(webType);
                assertNotNull(documents);
                assertEquals(count, documents.size());

                log.debug("It should be now cached!");
                documents = engineProxy.findByType(webType);
                assertNotNull(documents);
                assertEquals(count, documents.size());
        }
}
```

If you run Listing 8-16 with the new method for testing the cache with

```
gradle :ch08:test
```

you should have the following output:

```
2014-02-23 21:07:04,630 DEBUG [main] Testing Caching Module...
2014-02-23 21:07:04,639 DEBUG [main] @@@(Caching) review if this call is cachable...
2014-02-23 21:07:04,639 DEBUG [main] @@@(Caching) Is cachable!!
2014-02-23 21:07:04,640 DEBUG [main] @@@(Caching) Not Found! but is cachable!
2014-02-23 21:07:04,680 DEBUG [main] It should be now cached!
2014-02-23 21:07:04,680 DEBUG [main] @@@(Caching) review if this call is cachable...
```

```
2014-02-23 21:07:04,680 DEBUG [main] @@@(Caching) Is cachable!!
2014-02-23 21:07:04,680 DEBUG [main] @@@(Caching) Found in Cache!
2014-02-23 21:07:04,680 DEBUG [main] It should be now cached!
2014-02-23 21:07:04,680 DEBUG [main] @@@(Caching) review if this call is cachable...
2014-02-23 21:07:04,680 DEBUG [main] @@@(Caching) Is cachable!!
2014-02-23 21:07:04,680 DEBUG [main] @@@(Caching) Found in Cache!
```

AOP with Annotations

The Spring Framework also supports and plays nice with AspectJ. AspectJ is the library that initially started providing AOP support for Java by providing a compiler and a new aspect programming language; later it provided some Java 5 annotation features. So the Spring Framework AOP extension provides support for @Aspect, @Before, @After, @AfterReturning, @Around, and @AfterThrowing annotations. Listing 8-17 is an example of your caching solution using AspectJ and Spring.

Listing 8-17. Caching.java

```
package com.apress.isf.spring.annotated.aop;

import java.util.HashMap;
import java.util.Map;

import org.aspectj.lang.ProceedingJoinPoint;
import org.aspectj.lang.annotation.Around;
import org.aspectj.lang.annotation.Aspect;
import org.slf4j.Logger;
import org.slf4j.LoggerFactory;
import org.springframework.stereotype.Component;

import com.apress.isf.java.model.Type;
import com.apress.isf.spring.aop.CachingModule;

@Component
@Aspect
public class Caching {
        private static final Logger log = LoggerFactory.getLogger(CachingModule.class);
        private static final Map<String, Object> cache = new HashMap<String,Object>();

        @Around("execution(* com.apress.isf.java.service.SearchEngine.*(..))")
        public Object caching(ProceedingJoinPoint pjp) throws Throwable {
                Object result = null;
                Type documentType = null;

                log.debug("@@@(Caching) review if this call is cachable...");

                if("findByType".equals(pjp.getSignature().getName()) &&
                            pjp.getArgs().length == 1 && pjp.getArgs()[0] instanceof Type){
                        documentType = (Type)pjp.getArgs()[0];
                        log.debug("@@@(Caching) Is cachable!!");
```

```
                       if(cache.containsKey(documentType.getName())){
                               log.debug("@@@(Caching) Found in Cache!");
                               return cache.get(documentType.getName());
                       }
                       log.debug("@@@(Caching) Not Found! but is cachable!");
                       result = pjp.proceed();
                       cache.put(documentType.getName(), result);
                       return result;
               }

               return pjp.proceed();
        }
}
```

In Listing 8-17 you added the @Aspect annotation to define your class as an aspect. You used the @Around annotation advice that accepts the pointcut as an expression; in this case, this will be read as "every method that is on SearchEngine with any return type and any arguments." Listing 8-18 shows your XML; remember you are using annotations and you need to scan your packages so the Spring container knows about them.

Listing 8-18. mydocuments-aop-annotated-context.xml

```
<?xml version="1.0" encoding="UTF-8"?>
<beans xmlns="http://www.springframework.org/schema/beans"
        xmlns:xsi="http://www.w3.org/2001/XMLSchema-instance"
        xmlns:aop="http://www.springframework.org/schema/aop"
        xmlns:context="http://www.springframework.org/schema/context"
        xsi:schemaLocation="http://www.springframework.org/schema/beans
http://www.springframework.org/schema/beans/spring-beans.xsd
                http://www.springframework.org/schema/context
http://www.springframework.org/schema/context/spring-context-4.0.xsd
                http://www.springframework.org/schema/aop
http://www.springframework.org/schema/aop/spring-aop-4.0.xsd">

  <context:component-scan base-package="com.apress.isf.spring.annotated.aop"/>

  <!-- AOP -->
  <aop:aspectj-autoproxy/>

  <bean id="engine" class="com.apress.isf.spring.service.SearchEngineService">
      <property name="documentDAO" ref="documentDAO"/>
  </bean>

  <!-- Bean definitions omitted -->

</beans>
```

In Listing 8-18, you added the <xmlns:aop /> and <xmlns:context /> namespaces to your XML, and you added the <context:component-scan /> tag to scan your packages. Then you added the <aop:aspect-autoproxy/> tag; this tag will be doing the magic for the AOP to work. For this to run, you need some jar dependencies in your build.gradle file. See this book's companion source code and the integration of these libraries (aspectjrt and aspectjweaver) for more information.

You can run your unit test (Listing 8-16) with

`gradle :ch08:test`

and you should see the same output as the previous run.

▧ **Note**   The book's companion source code shows the other methods Spring supports, such as Java configuration style, annotations and Groovy style. Check it out!

Summary

In this chapter, you saw how AOP (aspect-oriented programming) can help you separate and modularize your application concerns and get rid of scattering and tangling code. You don't want to have code all over the place or some of your concerns mixed with different business logic that it doesn't need to know about. If you need more information about the AspectJ and Spring Framework AOP extension, take a look at the Pro Spring and Spring Recipes series from Apress.

You also saw all the advice types that Spring supports, as well as how to use them. You will continue to use AOP for the rest of the book. In later chapters, you will learn what to do when you need some caching, security, or transaction management.

CHAPTER 9

■ ■ ■

Adding Persistence to Your Spring Application

In this chapter, you are going to add some persistence to your **My Documents** application. So far you have been using bean definitions and some hard-coded logic to retrieve information about the documents and types of documents. For testing purposes, hard-coded data is fine, but in a real-world application like the **My Documents** Spring application, you need some other mechanisms to retrieve all the information because the data can grow and it will be a hard to keep putting the data in like that.

The Spring Framework supports a persistence mechanisms using JDBC (Java Database Connectivity) to query, update, insert, and delete data from databases.

In the **My Documents** Spring application you are going to use a small footprint database engine called the HSQLDB engine. This engine allows you to run the database in memory. The idea behind using this HSQLDB database engine is to avoid spending time setting up a database server and trying to configure it, but later in this chapter you will see how to use different engines such as MySQL (which is one of the most commonly used databases engines by the open source community).

But enough talk! Let's see how to add some persistence to your **My Documents** Spring application.

Adding Persistence

First, you are going to modify the Model classes and establish the relationship that you have been adding since the beginning. Figure 9-1 shows this relationship.

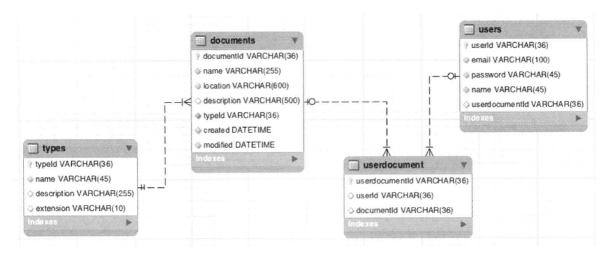

Figure 9-1. *My Documents Relationships*

Figure 9-1 shows how the Model classes are related to each other. The Documents table has a one-to-one relationship with its document type (Types table), and the Users table has a many-to-many relationship with the Documents table. In other words, a document can have only one type and a user can have many documents.

Now let's take a look at these classes and the code behind to see the relationship. Let's start with the Document class as shown in Listing 9-1.

Listing 9-1. Document.java

```java
package com.apress.isf.java.model;

import java.util.Date;

public class Document {
        private String documentId;
        private String name;
        private Type type;
        private String location;
        private String description;
        private Date created;
        private Date modified;

        public String getDocumentId() {
                return documentId;
        }

        public void setDocumentId(String documentId) {
                this.documentId = documentId;
        }

        public String getName() {
                return name;
        }
```

```java
public void setName(String name) {
        this.name = name;
}

public Type getType() {
        return type;
}

public void setType(Type type) {
        this.type = type;
}

public String getLocation() {
        return location;
}

public void setLocation(String location) {
        this.location = location;
}

public String getDescription() {
        return description;
}

public void setDescription(String description) {
        this.description = description;
}

public Date getCreated() {
        return created;
}

public void setCreated(Date created) {
        this.created = created;
}

public Date getModified() {
        return modified;
}

public void setModified(Date modified) {
        this.modified = modified;
}

public String toString(){
        StringBuilder builder = new StringBuilder("Documents(");
        builder.append("id: ");
        builder.append(documentId);
        builder.append("name: ");
        builder.append(name);
        builder.append(", type: ");
        builder.append(type);
```

```
                builder.append(", location: ");
                builder.append(location);
                builder.append(")");
                return builder.toString();
        }
}
```

Listing 9-1 shows the Document class; here you added the **Type** class that will hold the relationship shown in Figure 9-1. You also added new properties like the created and modified dates, and a documentId. Now let's take a look at Listing 9-2, which shows the Type class.

Listing 9-2. Type.java

```
package com.apress.isf.java.model;

public class Type {

        private String typeId;
        private String name;
        private String desc;
        private String extension;

        public Type(){

        }

        public Type(String name,String extension){
                this.name = name;
                this.extension = extension;
        }

        public String getTypeId() {
                return typeId;
        }

        public void setTypeId(String typeId) {
                this.typeId = typeId;
        }

        public String getName() {
                return name;
        }

        public void setName(String name) {
                this.name = name;
        }

        public String getDesc() {
                return desc;
        }
```

```java
        public void setDesc(String desc) {
                this.desc = desc;
        }

        public String getExtension() {
                return extension;
        }

        public void setExtension(String extension) {
                this.extension = extension;
        }

        public String toString(){
                StringBuilder builder = new StringBuilder("Type(");
                builder.append("id: ");
                builder.append(typeId);
                builder.append("name: ");
                builder.append(name);
                builder.append(", description: ");
                builder.append(desc);
                builder.append(", extension: ");
                builder.append(extension);
                builder.append(")");
                return builder.toString();
        }
}
```

Listing 9-2 shows the Type class. This class has some properties like the typeId that will be the reference for the relationship in the Document class. Also, you added the name, description, and extension properties. Let's review Listing 9-3, which shows the User class in action.

Listing 9-3. User.java

```java
package com.apress.isf.java.model;

import java.util.ArrayList;
import java.util.List;

public class User {
        private String userId;
        private String email;
        private String password;
        private String name;
        List<Document> documents = new ArrayList<Document>();

        public String getUserId() {
                return userId;
        }

        public void setUserId(String userId) {
                this.userId = userId;
        }
```

```java
        public String getEmail() {
                return email;
        }

        public void setEmail(String email) {
                this.email = email;
        }

        public String getPassword() {
                return password;
        }

        public void setPassword(String password) {
                this.password = password;
        }

        public String getName() {
                return name;
        }

        public void setName(String name) {
                this.name = name;
        }

        public List<Document> getDocuments() {
                return documents;
        }

        public void setDocuments(List<Document> documents) {
                this.documents = documents;
        }

}
```

Listing 9-3 shows the User class, which has several properties, such as the userId that will be part of the relationship of the document. You also added a list of documents.

For purposes of the application and just for this chapter, these relationships will be enough to show how to use persistence in **My Documents**. In later chapters, you are going to use a different mechanism of persistence.

Remember the DocumentDAO interface and its implementation? It contained some examples of only the implementation of the interface methods, and in another example it had a storage method that provided all the data. Now you are going to modify it in order to use JDBC; see Listing 9-4.

Listing 9-4. DocumentRepository.java

```java
package com.apress.isf.spring.data;

import java.sql.Connection;
import java.sql.ResultSet;
import java.sql.SQLException;
import java.sql.Statement;
import java.util.ArrayList;
import java.util.List;
```

```java
import javax.sql.DataSource;

import com.apress.isf.java.model.Document;
import com.apress.isf.java.model.Type;

public class DocumentRepository implements DocumentDAO {

        private DataSource dataSource;

        public void setDataSource(DataSource dataSource) {
                this.dataSource = dataSource;
        }

        public List<Document> getAll() {
                List<Document> result = new ArrayList<Document>();
                Connection connection = null;
                Statement statement = null;
                ResultSet resultSet = null;
                Document document = null;
                Type type=null;
                try {
                        connection = dataSource.getConnection();
                        statement = connection.createStatement();
                        resultSet = statement.executeQuery("select * from documents");
                        while (resultSet.next()) {
                                document = new Document();
                                document.setDocumentId(resultSet.getString("documentId"));
                                document.setName(resultSet.getString("name"));
                                document.setLocation(resultSet.getString("location"));
                                document.setCreated(resultSet.getDate("created"));
                                document.setModified(resultSet.getDate("modified"));
                                document.setDescription("doc_desc");
                                result.add(document);
                        }
                } catch (SQLException ex) {
                        throw new RuntimeException(ex);
                } finally {
                        if (null != connection) {
                                try {
                                        connection.close();
                                } catch (SQLException ex) {
                                }
                        }
                }
                return result;
        }

}
```

Listing 9-4 shows new elements used in JDBC, so let's talk about them.

- You added a DataSource class. It provides all the necessary information to connect to a database engine like username, password, driver, and URL.

- You added a Connection class. It establishes a connection to the database, in this case to the HSQLDB engine.

- You added a Statement class. With this class you can create all SQL related calls (INSERT, DELETE, UPDATE, SELECT).

- You added a ResultSet class. It will return the result of the executed query.

You can see that the DataSource is being injected, so you need to provide all the information about the database you are going to use. Listing 9-5 shows the XML configuration that holds your bean definitions.

Listing 9-5. mydocuments-jdbc-context.xml

```xml
<?xml version="1.0" encoding="UTF-8"?>
<beans xmlns="http://www.springframework.org/schema/beans"
       xmlns:xsi="http://www.w3.org/2001/XMLSchema-instance"
       xmlns:context="http://www.springframework.org/schema/context"
       xsi:schemaLocation="http://www.springframework.org/schema/beans
http://www.springframework.org/schema/beans/spring-beans.xsd
                http://www.springframework.org/schema/context
http://www.springframework.org/schema/context/spring-context-4.0.xsd">

  <context:property-placeholder location="jdbc.properties"/>

  <bean id="dataSource" class="org.springframework.jdbc.datasource.DriverManagerDataSource">
          <property name="driverClassName" value="${jdbc.driverClassName}"/>
          <property name="url" value="${jdbc.url}"/>
          <property name="username" value="${jdbc.username}"/>
          <property name="password" value="${jdbc.password}"/>
  </bean>

  <bean id="engine" class="com.apress.isf.spring.service.SearchEngineService">
             <property name="documentDAO" ref="documentDAO"/>
  </bean>

  <bean id="documentDAO" class="com.apress.isf.spring.data.DocumentRepository"
init-method="initialize">
             <property name="dataSource" ref="dataSource"/>
  </bean>

</beans>
```

In Listing 9-5, you got rid of the whole bean definitions. Finally! The Spring Framework provides a manager (DriverManagerDataSource class) for the DataSource that will be injected in the DocumentDAO implementation. Also, you can see that you are using the <xmlns:context/> namespace (as a property holder) to use a jdbc.properties file (see Listing 9-6).

Listing 9-6. jdbc.properties

```
jdbc.driverClassName=org.hsqldb.jdbcDriver
jdbc.url=jdbc:hsqldb:mem:mydocuments;shutdown=false
jdbc.username=SA
jdbc.password=
```

Listing 9-6 shows the JDBC parameters that are used to connect to the database engine, and you can see that in the jdbc.url (format: jdbc:<engine>:<server>:<port>[:|/]<database>;<parameters>) property you are using an in-memory database. Next, you need to create the unit test class to test the persistence (see Listing 9-7).

Listing 9-7. Unit Test Class

```
package com.apress.isf.spring.test;

import static org.junit.Assert.assertEquals;
import static org.junit.Assert.assertNotNull;
import static org.junit.Assert.assertTrue;

import java.util.List;

import org.junit.Test;
import org.junit.runner.RunWith;
import org.slf4j.Logger;
import org.slf4j.LoggerFactory;
import org.springframework.beans.factory.annotation.Autowired;
import org.springframework.test.context.ContextConfiguration;
import org.springframework.test.context.junit4.SpringJUnit4ClassRunner;

import com.apress.isf.java.model.Document;
import com.apress.isf.java.model.Type;
import com.apress.isf.java.service.SearchEngine;

@RunWith(SpringJUnit4ClassRunner.class)
@ContextConfiguration("classpath:META-INF/spring/mydocuments-jdbc-context.xml")
public class MyDocumentsJDBCTest {
        private static final Logger log = LoggerFactory.getLogger(MyDocumentsJDBCTest.class);

        @Autowired
        private SearchEngine engine;

        private Type webType = new Type("WEB",".url");

        @Test
        public void testUsingSpringJDBC() {
                log.debug("Using Spring JDBC...");

                List<Document> documents = engine.listAll();
                assertNotNull(documents);
                assertTrue(documents.size() == 4);

                documents = engine.findByType(webType);
                assertNotNull(documents);
                assertTrue(documents.size() == 1);
```

```
                    assertEquals(webType.getName(),documents.get(0).getType().getName());
                    assertEquals(webType.getExtension(),documents.get(0).getType().getExtension());
                    log.debug("Found WEB Document: " + documents.get(0));
            }
    }
```

Before you run your test, you need to add the HSDQLDB jar file in the class path or even better, use the gradle tool, the build.gradle file, to include it. So, in the build.gradle file let's add in the libraries you need in the dependencies section (you can find the complete source in the book's companion source code):

```
dependencies {
        //other libraries here
        runtime 'hsqldb:hsqldb:1.8.0.10'
}
```

If you run Listing 9-7 with

```
gradle :ch09:test
```

it will fail, but why? Well, you need to add some data first, right? Yes, you don't have any data to use for this test; you need to add some documents and their types. So let's create the database schema (see Listing 9-8) and add some data (see Listing 9-9) as separate files, and then you can read them to initialize your database.

Listing 9-8. schema.sql

```
CREATE TABLE types (
  typeId varchar(36) NOT NULL,
  name varchar(45) NOT NULL,
  description varchar(255) DEFAULT NULL,
  extension varchar(10) DEFAULT NULL,
  PRIMARY KEY (typeId)
);

CREATE TABLE documents (
  documentId varchar(36) NOT NULL,
  name varchar(255) NOT NULL,
  location varchar(600) NOT NULL,
  description varchar(600),
  typeId varchar(36) NOT NULL,
  created datetime NOT NULL,
  modified datetime NOT NULL,
  PRIMARY KEY (documentId),
  CONSTRAINT documentType FOREIGN KEY (typeId) REFERENCES types (typeId)
);

CREATE TABLE users (
  userId varchar(36) NOT NULL,
  email varchar(100) NOT NULL,
  password varchar(45) NOT NULL,
  name varchar(45) NOT NULL,
  userdocumentId varchar(36) DEFAULT NULL,
  PRIMARY KEY (userId)
);
```

```
CREATE TABLE userdocument (
  userdocumentId varchar(36) NOT NULL,
  userId varchar(36) DEFAULT NULL,
  documentId varchar(36) DEFAULT NULL,
  PRIMARY KEY (userdocumentId),
  CONSTRAINT users FOREIGN KEY (userId) REFERENCES users (userId) ON DELETE NO ACTION
ON UPDATE NO ACTION,
  CONSTRAINT documents FOREIGN KEY (documentId) REFERENCES documents (documentId) ON DELETE NO
ACTION ON UPDATE NO ACTION
);
```

Listing 9-8 shows the database schema where you specified the tables that will hold all the information about the documents, types, and users. If you need more information about database concepts, you can take a look at some of the SQL books from Apress. Next, you need to have some data (see Listing 9-9).

Listing 9-9. data.sql

```
INSERT INTO types (typeId, name, description, extension) VALUES
('41e2d211-6396-4f23-9690-77bc2820d84b', 'PDF', 'Portable Document Format', '.pdf');
INSERT INTO types (typeId, name, description, extension) VALUES
('e8e5310b-6345-4d08-86b6-d5c3c299aa7f', 'NOTE', 'Text Notes', '.txt');
INSERT INTO types (typeId, name, description, extension) VALUES
('4980d2e4-a424-4ff4-a0b2-476039682f43', 'WEB', 'Web Link', '.url');
INSERT INTO types (typeId, name, description, extension) VALUES
('c9f1a16d-852d-4132-b4b8-ead20aafc6ef', 'WORD', 'Microsoft Word', '.doc?');

INSERT INTO documents (documentId, name, location, description, typeId, created, modified) VALUES
('1acbb68a-a859-49c9-ac88-d9e9322bac55', 'Book Template', '/docs/isfbook/Documents/Random/Book
Template.pdf', 'A book template for creating new books', '41e2d211-6396-4f23-9690-77bc2820d84b',
'2014-02-24 11:52', '2014-02-26 13:45');
INSERT INTO documents (documentId, name, location, description, typeId, created, modified) VALUES
('cf7fec3e-55bf-426d-8a6f-2ca752ae34ac', 'Sample Contract', '/docs/isfbook/Documents/Contracts/
Sample Contract.pdf', 'Just a Contract', '41e2d211-6396-4f23-9690-77bc2820d84b', '2014-02-24 15:23',
'2014-02-28 10:20');
INSERT INTO documents (documentId, name, location, description, typeId, created, modified) VALUES
('3580f482-7f12-4787-bb60-c98023d47b6c', 'Clustering with RabbitMQ', '/Users/isfbook/Documents/
Random/Clustering with RabbitMQ.txt', 'Simple notes ', 'e8e5310b-6345-4d08-86b6-d5c3c299aa7f',
'2014-02-18', '2014-02-20 14:50');
INSERT INTO documents (documentId, name, location, description, typeId, created, modified)
VALUES ('431cddbf-f3c0-4076-8c1c-564e7dce16c9', 'Pro Spring Security Book',
'http://www.apress.com/9781430248187', 'Excellent Book', '4980d2e4-a424-4ff4-a0b2-476039682f43',
'2014-02-14', '2014-02-20');
```

Listing 9-9 shows the SQL statements you need, which in your case are the INSERT statements.

▓ **Note** You can find the files used in Listing 9-8 and Listing 9-9 in the book's companion source code at the `src/main/resources/META-INF/data` path.

Now that you have your Schema and Data files, let's access them, read them, and, of course, initialize the database. Let's look at Listing 9-10 to see how you are going to modify the DocumentDAO implementation.

Listing 9-10. DocumentRepository.java

```java
package com.apress.isf.spring.data;

import java.io.IOException;
import java.io.InputStream;
import java.sql.Connection;
import java.sql.ResultSet;
import java.sql.SQLException;
import java.sql.Statement;
import java.util.ArrayList;
import java.util.List;
import java.util.Scanner;

import javax.sql.DataSource;

import org.springframework.core.io.Resource;

import com.apress.isf.java.model.Document;
import com.apress.isf.java.model.Type;

public class DocumentRepository implements DocumentDAO {
        private String queryAll;
        private DataSource dataSource;
        private Resource schema;
        private Resource data;

        public void setQueryAll(String queryAll) {
                this.queryAll = queryAll;
        }

        public void setDataSource(DataSource dataSource) {
                this.dataSource = dataSource;
        }

        public void setSchema(Resource schema) {
                this.schema = schema;
        }

        public void setData(Resource data) {
                this.data = data;
        }

        public void initialize() {
                try {
                        InputStream stream = schema.getInputStream();
                        Scanner scanner = new Scanner(stream);
                        StringBuilder sql = new StringBuilder();
```

```java
while (scanner.hasNext()) {
        sql.append(scanner.nextLine());
        sql.append("\n");
}
scanner.close();
stream.close();
Connection connection = null;
Statement statement = null;
try {
        connection = dataSource.getConnection();
        statement = connection.createStatement();
        statement.execute(sql.toString());
} catch (SQLException ex) {
        ex.printStackTrace();
        throw new RuntimeException(ex);
} finally {
        if (null != connection) {
                try {
                        connection.close();
                } catch (SQLException ex) {
                }
        }
}

stream = data.getInputStream();
scanner = new Scanner(stream);
sql = new StringBuilder();
while (scanner.hasNext()) {
        sql.append(scanner.nextLine());
        sql.append("\n");
}
scanner.close();
stream.close();
connection = null;
statement = null;
try {
        connection = dataSource.getConnection();
        statement = connection.createStatement();
        statement.executeUpdate(sql.toString());
} catch (SQLException ex) {
        ex.printStackTrace();
        throw new RuntimeException(ex);
} finally {
        if (null != connection) {
                try {
                        connection.close();
                } catch (SQLException ex) {
                }
        }
}
```

```
                    } catch (IOException e) {
                            e.printStackTrace();
                    }
        }

        public List<Document> getAll() {
                List<Document> result = new ArrayList<Document>();
                Connection connection = null;
                Statement statement = null;
                ResultSet resultSet = null;
                Document document = null;
                Type type=null;
                try {
                        connection = dataSource.getConnection();
                        statement = connection.createStatement();
                        resultSet = statement.executeQuery(queryAll);
                        while (resultSet.next()) {
                                document = new Document();
                                document.setDocumentId(resultSet.getString("documentId"));
                                document.setName(resultSet.getString("name"));
                                document.setLocation(resultSet.getString("location"));
                                document.setCreated(resultSet.getDate("created"));
                                document.setModified(resultSet.getDate("modified"));
                                document.setDescription("doc_desc");
                                type = new Type();
                                type.setTypeId(resultSet.getString("typeId"));
                                type.setName(resultSet.getString("type_name"));
                                type.setDesc(resultSet.getString("type_desc"));
                                type.setExtension(resultSet.getString("extension"));
                                document.setType(type);

                                result.add(document);
                        }
                } catch (SQLException ex) {
                        throw new RuntimeException(ex);
                } finally {
                        if (null != connection) {
                                try {
                                        connection.close();
                                } catch (SQLException ex) {
                                }
                        }
                }
                return result;
        }

}
```

Listing 9-10 shows a new method called `initialize`, where you read the resource files, the `schema.sql` and `data.sql` files, and you inject the query through the `queryAll` property. Also, you are exposing a better way to build the `Document` object because you are adding the type; just remember that the `Document` contains this relationship. Look at Figure 9-1 and Listing 9-8 where you have this relationship between the documents and types, and the users and documents.

But wait! How do you tell Spring to call the `initialize` method? Let's see how by reviewing the XML file in Listing 9-11.

Listing 9-11. mydocuments-jdbc-context.xml

```xml
<?xml version="1.0" encoding="UTF-8"?>
<beans xmlns="http://www.springframework.org/schema/beans"
        xmlns:xsi="http://www.w3.org/2001/XMLSchema-instance"
        xmlns:context="http://www.springframework.org/schema/context"
        xsi:schemaLocation="http://www.springframework.org/schema/beans
http://www.springframework.org/schema/beans/spring-beans.xsd
                http://www.springframework.org/schema/context
http://www.springframework.org/schema/context/spring-context-4.0.xsd">

  <context:property-placeholder location="jdbc.properties"/>

  <bean id="dataSource" class="org.springframework.jdbc.datasource.DriverManagerDataSource">
     <property name="driverClassName" value="${jdbc.driverClassName}"/>
     <property name="url" value="${jdbc.url}"/>
     <property name="username" value="${jdbc.username}"/>
     <property name="password" value="${jdbc.password}"/>
  </bean>

  <bean id="engine" class="com.apress.isf.spring.service.SearchEngineService">
      <property name="documentDAO" ref="documentDAO"/>
  </bean>

  <bean id="documentDAO" class="com.apress.isf.spring.data.DocumentRepository"
init-method="initialize">
      <property name="dataSource" ref="dataSource"/>
      <property name="schema" value="classpath:META-INF/data/schema.sql"/>
      <property name="data" value="classpath:META-INF/data/data.sql"/>
      <property name="queryAll">
        <value>
          select d.documentId, d.name, d.location, d.description as doc_desc, d.typeId,
          d.created, d.modified,
              t.name as type_name, t.description as type_desc, t.extension from documents d
              join types t
              on d.typeId = t.typeId
        </value>
      </property>
  </bean>

</beans>
```

If you run Listing 9-7 with

```
gradle :ch09:test
```

then the test will pass, because you have added the `initialize` method and you can count on the data being there.

Embedding a Database

In the XML configuration (see Listing 9-11) you can see the `DocumentRepository` class and the `initialize` method; there should be a better way to initialize your database, right? Well, the Spring Framework offers different ways to use the JDBC; for test purposes it provides a way to use the HSQLDB in an embedded way through an `xmlns:jdbc` namespace. Let's modify the XML configuration to use these new features from the xmlns:jdbc namespace (see Listing 9-12).

Listing 9-12. mydocuments-jdbc-embedded-context.xml

```
<?xml version="1.0" encoding="UTF-8"?>
<beans xmlns="http://www.springframework.org/schema/beans"
        xmlns:xsi="http://www.w3.org/2001/XMLSchema-instance"
        xmlns:context="http://www.springframework.org/schema/context"
        xmlns:jdbc="http://www.springframework.org/schema/jdbc"
        xsi:schemaLocation="http://www.springframework.org/schema/jdbc
http://www.springframework.org/schema/jdbc/spring-jdbc-4.0.xsd
                http://www.springframework.org/schema/beans
http://www.springframework.org/schema/beans/spring-beans.xsd
                http://www.springframework.org/schema/context
http://www.springframework.org/schema/context/spring-context-4.0.xsd">

    <context:component-scan base-package="com.apress.isf.spring.annotated"/>
    <jdbc:embedded-database id="dataSource">
        <jdbc:script location="classpath:META-INF/data/schema.sql"/>
        <jdbc:script location="classpath:META-INF/data/data.sql"/>
    </jdbc:embedded-database>

</beans>
```

Listing 9-12 shows the `<jdbc:embedded-database/>` tag where you can pass the location of the schema and data. The Spring Framework can use this tag to create and populate your database using the schema and data files. Also, you are using annotations with the `<context:component-scan/>` tag because the Spring Framework use a `@Repository` as a marker for any data access. Listing 9-13 shows the `DocumentDAO` implementation using the embedded database feature.

Listing 9-13. AnnotatedDocumentRepository.java

```
package com.apress.isf.spring.annotated.data;

import java.sql.Connection;
import java.sql.ResultSet;
import java.sql.SQLException;
import java.sql.Statement;
import java.util.ArrayList;
import java.util.List;
```

```java
import javax.sql.DataSource;

import org.springframework.beans.factory.annotation.Autowired;
import org.springframework.stereotype.Repository;

import com.apress.isf.java.model.Document;
import com.apress.isf.java.model.Type;
import com.apress.isf.spring.data.DocumentDAO;

@Repository("documentDAO")
public class AnnotatedDocumentRepository implements DocumentDAO {
        private static final String queryAll = " select d.documentId, d.name, d.location,
d.description as doc_desc," +
                                                "d.typeId, d.created, d.modified, "+
                                                "t.name as type_name, t.description as type_desc," +
                                "t.extension from documents d join types t on d.typeId = t.typeId";

        @Autowired
        private DataSource dataSource;

        public List<Document> getAll() {
                List<Document> result = new ArrayList<Document>();
                Connection connection = null;
                Statement statement = null;
                ResultSet resultSet = null;
                Document document = null;
                Type type=null;
                try {
                        connection = dataSource.getConnection();
                        statement = connection.createStatement();
                        resultSet = statement.executeQuery(queryAll);
                        while (resultSet.next()) {
                                document = new Document();
                                document.setDocumentId(resultSet.getString("documentId"));
                                document.setName(resultSet.getString("name"));
                                document.setLocation(resultSet.getString("location"));
                                document.setCreated(resultSet.getDate("created"));
                                document.setModified(resultSet.getDate("modified"));
                                document.setDescription("doc_desc");
                                type = new Type();
                                type.setTypeId(resultSet.getString("typeId"));
                                type.setName(resultSet.getString("type_name"));
                                type.setDesc(resultSet.getString("type_desc"));
                                type.setExtension(resultSet.getString("extension"));
                                document.setType(type);

                                result.add(document);
                        }
                } catch (SQLException ex) {
                        throw new RuntimeException(ex);
                } finally {
```

```
                              if (null != connection) {
                                   try {
                                         connection.close();
                                   } catch (SQLException ex) {
                                   }
                              }
                         }
                         return result;
            }

}
```

Listing 9-13 shows how you can avoid writing too much code to initialize the database. You removed the initialize code that had a lot of lines to read two files in order to create and populate the database with the information you needed.

Now, let's see the unit test (see Listing 9-14).

Listing 9-14. MyDocumentsJDBCEmbeddedAnnotatedTest.java

```java
package com.apress.isf.spring.test;

import static org.junit.Assert.assertEquals;
import static org.junit.Assert.assertNotNull;
import static org.junit.Assert.assertTrue;

import java.util.List;

import org.junit.Test;
import org.junit.runner.RunWith;
import org.springframework.beans.factory.annotation.Autowired;
import org.springframework.test.context.ContextConfiguration;
import org.springframework.test.context.junit4.SpringJUnit4ClassRunner;

import com.apress.isf.java.model.Document;
import com.apress.isf.java.model.Type;
import com.apress.isf.java.service.SearchEngine;

@RunWith(SpringJUnit4ClassRunner.class)
@ContextConfiguration("classpath:META-INF/spring/mydocuments-jdbc-embedded-context.xml")
public class MyDocumentsJDBCEmbeddedAnnotatedTest {

        @Autowired
        private SearchEngine engine;
        private Type webType = new Type("WEB",".url");

        @Test
        public void testJDBCEmbedded() {

                List<Document> documents = engine.findByType(webType);
                assertNotNull(documents);
                assertTrue(documents.size() == 1);
                assertEquals(webType.getName(),documents.get(0).getType().getName());
                assertEquals(webType.getExtension(),documents.get(0).getType().getExtension());
```

```
                documents = engine.listAll();
                assertNotNull(documents);
                assertTrue(documents.size() == 4);
        }
}
```

That's it! As you can see, the unit test (see Listing 9-14) didn't change at all, and if you run it, the test should pass without any problems.

A New Way to Collect Data: JdbcTemplate and RowMapper

Reviewing your DocumentDAO implementation (see Listing 9-13), you have a lot of code still. The good news is that Spring Framework provides a JdbcTemplate that can help you to execute any query and map the document class by implementing a RowMapper class, but how you can accomplish this? How can you reduce all this code? Well, let's look at Listing 9-15; it shows you how to use the JdbcTemplate.

Listing 9-15. DocumentJdbcTemplateRepository.java

```
package com.apress.isf.spring.jdbc;

import java.util.List;

import javax.sql.DataSource;

import org.springframework.jdbc.core.JdbcTemplate;

import com.apress.isf.java.model.Document;
import com.apress.isf.spring.data.DocumentDAO;

public class DocumentJdbcTemplateRepository implements DocumentDAO {

        private JdbcTemplate jdbcTemplate;
        private DataSource dataSource;
        private String query;

        public void setDataSource(DataSource dataSource) {
                this.dataSource = dataSource;
                this.jdbcTemplate = new JdbcTemplate(this.dataSource);
        }

        public void setQuery(String query){
                this.query = query;
        }

        public List<Document> getAll() {
                return jdbcTemplate.query(query, new DocumentRowMapper());
        }

}
```

Listing 9-15 shows how you can reduce the amount of code by using the JdbcTemplate class, where you can pass the query and the row mapper. The JdbcTemplate implements a Template Design pattern that does the heavy work of calling the JDBC directly, and therefore provides easy methods for executing SQL statements.

Next, let's create the DocumentRowMapper class as shown in Listing 9-16.

Listing 9-16. DocumentRowMapper

```
package com.apress.isf.spring.jdbc;

import java.sql.ResultSet;
import java.sql.SQLException;

import org.springframework.jdbc.core.RowMapper;

import com.apress.isf.java.model.Document;
import com.apress.isf.java.model.Type;

public class DocumentRowMapper implements RowMapper<Document> {

    public Document mapRow(ResultSet rs, int rowNum) throws SQLException {
        Document document = new Document();
        document.setDocumentId(rs.getString("documentId"));
        document.setName(rs.getString("name"));
        document.setLocation(rs.getString("location"));
        document.setCreated(rs.getDate("created"));
        document.setModified(rs.getDate("modified"));
        document.setDescription("doc_desc");
        Type type = new Type();
        type.setTypeId(rs.getString("typeId"));
        type.setName(rs.getString("type_name"));
        type.setDesc(rs.getString("type_desc"));
        type.setExtension(rs.getString("extension"));
        document.setType(type);
        return document;
    }

}
```

Listing 9-16 shows how to implement the RowMapper interface. You can see that the Spring Framework will iterate every row and create the result list you need: the Document model. If you take this approach, you will have more readable code.

Next, let's create the XML configuration that will contain the new reference to the DocumentJdbcTemplateRepository class as shown in Listing 9-17.

Listing 9-17. mydocuments-jdb-template-context.xml

```
<?xml version="1.0" encoding="UTF-8"?>
<beans xmlns="http://www.springframework.org/schema/beans"
       xmlns:xsi="http://www.w3.org/2001/XMLSchema-instance"
       xmlns:context="http://www.springframework.org/schema/context"
       xmlns:jdbc="http://www.springframework.org/schema/jdbc"
```

```xml
        xsi:schemaLocation="http://www.springframework.org/schema/jdbc
http://www.springframework.org/schema/jdbc/spring-jdbc-4.0.xsd
                http://www.springframework.org/schema/beans
http://www.springframework.org/schema/beans/spring-beans.xsd
                http://www.springframework.org/schema/context
http://www.springframework.org/schema/context/spring-context-4.0.xsd">

  <jdbc:embedded-database id="dataSource">
      <jdbc:script location="classpath:META-INF/data/schema.sql"/>
      <jdbc:script location="classpath:META-INF/data/data.sql"/>
  </jdbc:embedded-database>

   <bean id="engine" class="com.apress.isf.spring.service.SearchEngineService">
      <property name="documentDAO" ref="documentDAO"/>
   </bean>

   <bean id="documentDAO" class="com.apress.isf.spring.jdbc.DocumentJdbcTemplateRepository">
      <property name="dataSource" ref="dataSource"/>
       <property name="query">
        <value>
          select d.documentId, d.name, d.location, d.description as doc_desc, d.typeId,
d.created, d.modified,
               t.name as type_name, t.description as type_desc, t.extension from documents d
               join types t
               on d.typeId = t.typeId
        </value>
      </property>
   </bean>

</beans>
```

In Listing 9-17, you set the DocumentDAO bean reference to the DocumentJdbcTemplateRepository class; practically nothing changes except this reference to the class. Next, let's create the unit test class (see Listing 9-18).

Listing 9-18. MyDocumentsJDBCTemplateTest.java

```java
package com.apress.isf.spring.test;

import static org.junit.Assert.assertEquals;
import static org.junit.Assert.assertNotNull;
import static org.junit.Assert.assertTrue;

import java.util.List;

import org.junit.Test;
import org.junit.runner.RunWith;
import org.springframework.beans.factory.annotation.Autowired;
import org.springframework.test.context.ContextConfiguration;
import org.springframework.test.context.junit4.SpringJUnit4ClassRunner;
```

```
import com.apress.isf.java.model.Document;
import com.apress.isf.java.model.Type;
import com.apress.isf.java.service.SearchEngine;

@RunWith(SpringJUnit4ClassRunner.class)
@ContextConfiguration("classpath:META-INF/spring/mydocuments-jdbc-template-context.xml")
public class MyDocumentsJDBCTemplateTest {

        @Autowired
        private SearchEngine engine;
        private Type webType = new Type("WEB",".url");

        @Test
        public void testJDBCTemplate() {

                List<Document> documents = engine.findByType(webType);
                assertNotNull(documents);
                assertTrue(documents.size() == 1);
                assertEquals(webType.getName(),documents.get(0).getType().getName());
                assertEquals(webType.getExtension(),documents.get(0).getType().getExtension());

                documents = engine.listAll();
                assertNotNull(documents);
                assertTrue(documents.size() == 4);
        }
}
```

Now when you run Listing 9-18 with

```
gradle :ch09:test
```

your test will pass without any errors.

Summary

In this chapter, you saw how to read from the database engine and how to combine profiles in order to access different environments, such as development. You also saw where you can embed a database in memory.

You also looked at how to use a JDBC configuration in different ways, such as pure JDBC with connections and prepared statements. You also saw how to use the JDBCTemplate to query, insert, and update data. In addition, we covered how to use the JDBCTemplate to row map the data with the domain classes.

There are even more ways to persist data, which I will cover in the following chapters.

CHAPTER 10

Showing Your Spring Application on the Web

In this chapter, you are going to show your Spring application called **My Documents** on the Web. You are going to use Spring annotations so the code is clean and easy to read. Also, you are going to continue to use the embedded database and the RowMapper from Chapter 9 so you can see something real in action.

To put your Spring application on the Web, you need to know about the MVC design pattern. The MVC design pattern is the most used pattern for web applications. Let's start coding, and as we go along I will talk more about this famous pattern.

Persistence Layer

First, let's start with the Persistence layer. Listing 10-1 shows your modified DocumentDAO implementation (this class is from Chapter 9).

Listing 10-1. DocumentRepository.java.

```
package com.apress.isf.spring.data;

import java.util.List;

import javax.sql.DataSource;

import org.springframework.beans.factory.annotation.Autowired;
import org.springframework.jdbc.core.JdbcTemplate;
import org.springframework.stereotype.Repository;

import com.apress.isf.java.model.Document;

@Repository("documentDAO")
public class DocumentRepository implements DocumentDAO {

        @Autowired
        private DataSource dataSource;
        @Autowired
        private String query;
```

```java
    public List<Document> getAll() {
            return new JdbcTemplate(this.dataSource).query(query, new DocumentRowMapper());
    }

}
```

As you can see, Listing 10-1 has been reduced to its minimal size in lines compared with other chapters. This is awesome! Next is Listing 10-2, the Mapper, but this class doesn't have any new changes.

Listing 10-2. DocumentRowMapper.java

```java
package com.apress.isf.spring.data;

import java.sql.ResultSet;
import java.sql.SQLException;

import org.springframework.jdbc.core.RowMapper;

import com.apress.isf.java.model.Document;
import com.apress.isf.java.model.Type;

public class DocumentRowMapper implements RowMapper<Document> {

        public Document mapRow(ResultSet rs, int rowNum) throws SQLException {
                Document document = new Document();
                document.setDocumentId(rs.getString("documentId"));
                document.setName(rs.getString("name"));
                document.setLocation(rs.getString("location"));
                document.setCreated(rs.getDate("created"));
                document.setModified(rs.getDate("modified"));
                document.setDescription("doc_desc");
                Type type = new Type();
                type.setTypeId(rs.getString("typeId"));
                type.setName(rs.getString("type_name"));
                type.setDesc(rs.getString("type_desc"));
                type.setExtension(rs.getString("extension"));
                document.setType(type);
                return document;
        }

}
```

Before you continue, you need to prepare your project, **My Documents**, with the necessary structure, creating folders and files essential for your web application. In the Java world, there is a standard way to develop web applications and you will be following it. Every web application must have the structure shown:

```
└── src
     └── main
          └── java
          └── resources
          └── webapp
                   └── WEB-INF
```

After creating the web application structure (this is the standard structure for a web application) and before you continue with the code, let's talk about the MVC design pattern and how the Spring MVC extension helps you to use this pattern effectively.

Spring MVC

The Spring Framework provides the Spring MVC extension that supports the MVC pattern and features such as i18n, support for different view engines, theming, and others. Figure 10-1 shows the Spring MVC at a high level.

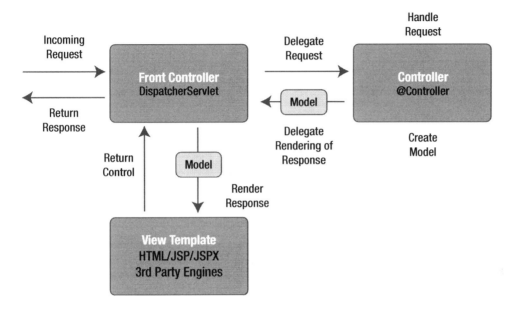

Figure 10-1. *Spring MVC*

Figure 10-1 shows how the MVC design pattern works; first there is a request from the user to the front controller (the Spring's DispatcherServlet); then it delegates its request to a controller (your own implementation) that will create a model; then it will delegate the response to the view, in this case the view template (a JSP/JSPX) that will return the control to the front controller and return the response to the user.

But let's start coding, so we can see your Spring application on the Web. First, you are going to start creating a controller that will create the model, and then this controller will delegate the rendering response (with the name of the view) through the DispatcherServlet. Listing 10-3 shows the delegate.

Listing 10-3. SearchController.java

```
package com.apress.isf.spring.web;

import org.springframework.beans.factory.annotation.Autowired;
import org.springframework.stereotype.Controller;
import org.springframework.ui.Model;
import org.springframework.web.bind.annotation.RequestMapping;
import org.springframework.web.bind.annotation.RequestMethod;

import com.apress.isf.spring.data.DocumentDAO;
```

```
@Controller
@RequestMapping("/search")
public class SearchController {

        @Autowired
        DocumentDAO documentDAO;

        @RequestMapping(value="/all",method=RequestMethod.GET)
        public String searchAll(Model model){
                model.addAttribute("docs", documentDAO.getAll());
                return "search/all";
        }
}
```

As you can see in Listing 10-3, the controller is very simple and it uses different annotations, but let's see each one and its meaning.

- **@Controller:** This will mark your class as the controller so the DispatcherServlet know where to delegate the request.

- **@RequestMapping:** This annotation tells how to access this controller, in this case through the path/search. Later on in the method you will have the same annotation that is telling you that it will only execute with the path /all and will only accept GET requests. At the end, the path will be http://<server>/<context>/<servletname>/search/all.

- **@Autowired:** This will inject the DocumentDAO implementation.

Next, you need to add the web.xml that will define how the web application should start up. In any Java web application, the web.xml file is necessary for most application servers so they know what to do to start the web application; this is a standard way to deploy web apps. Nowadays this has been simplified by removing the web.xml file (like in Java 6 EE, and of course when using Spring), but in this case you are going to follow the same standard. Later (in Chapter 19) you will see that no web.xml or any other configuration file is required for web applications.

Listing 10-4 shows the web.xml file; this file should be put in the src/main/webapp/WEB-INF/ folder.

Listing 10-4. web.xml

```
<?xml version="1.0" encoding="UTF-8"?>
<web-app version="3.0" xmlns="http://java.sun.com/xml/ns/javaee"
xmlns:xsi="http://www.w3.org/2001/XMLSchema-instance" xsi:schemaLocation="http://java.sun.com/xml/
ns/javaee
http://java.sun.com/xml/ns/javaee/web-app_3_0.xsd">
  <servlet>
        <servlet-name>mydocuments</servlet-name>
        <servlet-class>org.springframework.web.servlet.DispatcherServlet</servlet-class>
        <load-on-startup>1</load-on-startup>
    </servlet>
    <servlet-mapping>
        <servlet-name>mydocuments</servlet-name>
        <url-pattern>/mydocuments/*</url-pattern>
    </servlet-mapping>
</web-app>
```

The DispatcherServlet defined in your web.xml, as shown in Listing 10-4, will be the front controller that is taking care of sending requests to the controller (see Listing 10-3) and the response back with the correct view. Now you need to tell the Spring MVC where your views will be. Listing 10-5 contains the Spring XML configuration needed for the Spring container to instantiate the necessary beans.

Listing 10-5. mydocuments-servlet.xml

```xml
<?xml version="1.0" encoding="UTF-8"?>
<beans xmlns="http://www.springframework.org/schema/beans"
        xmlns:xsi="http://www.w3.org/2001/XMLSchema-instance"
        xmlns:context="http://www.springframework.org/schema/context"
        xmlns:jdbc="http://www.springframework.org/schema/jdbc"
        xmlns:mvc="http://www.springframework.org/schema/mvc"
        xsi:schemaLocation="http://www.springframework.org/schema/jdbc http://www.springframework.
        org/schema/jdbc/spring-jdbc-4.0.xsd
                http://www.springframework.org/schema/mvc http://www.springframework.org/schema/mvc/
                spring-mvc-4.0.xsd
                http://www.springframework.org/schema/beans http://www.springframework.org/schema/
                beans/spring-beans.xsd
                http://www.springframework.org/schema/context http://www.springframework.org/schema/
                context/spring-context-4.0.xsd">

    <context:component-scan base-package="com.apress.isf.spring"/>
    <mvc:annotation-driven />

    <bean class="org.springframework.web.servlet.view.InternalResourceViewResolver">
      <property name="prefix" value="/WEB-INF/views/"/>
        <property name="suffix" value=".jspx"/>
    </bean>

    <jdbc:embedded-database id="dataSource">
      <jdbc:script location="classpath:/META-INF/data/schema.sql" />
      <jdbc:script location="classpath:/META-INF/data/data.sql" />
    </jdbc:embedded-database>

    <bean id="query" class="java.lang.String">
                <constructor-arg>
                        <value>
                                select d.documentId, d.name, d.location, d.description as doc_desc,
                                d.typeId, d.created, d.modified,
                                t.name as type_name, t.description as type_desc, t.extension from
                                documents d
                                join types t
                                on d.typeId = t.typeId
                        </value>
                </constructor-arg>
        </bean>

</beans>
```

Do you see anything new in Listing 10-5? Yes, that's right, the `<xmlns:mvc />` namespace. This namespace will help you to set up everything and get it ready for your MVC. Also, you need to add the `<mvc:annotation-driven />` tag. This tag will tell the Spring container to look for any annotated class with the `@Controller` annotation, so it knows the controller will be the delegate from the front controller (`DispatcherServlet`). Next, you need to specify what view engine you are going to use; in this case it will be the `InternalResourceViewResolver` with two properties. The first property will be the prefix where your web pages will live and the second property will be the suffix where it tells the Spring MVC that your views will be JSPX pages.

▧ **Note** Your Spring context XML file needs to be named after the name of the servlet definition, followed by `-servlet.xml`, so the format will be `<name of the servlet>-servlet.xml`. In your case, you define your servlets as `mydocuments`, so the name of the XML file will be `mydocuments-servlet.xml`. This is one of the many standards we will use.

Next, you need to add your JSPX file. JSPX is an XML variation of a JSP which is used to create dynamic web pages but using an XML syntax. This file will live in the `WEB-INF/views/search/` folder and it will be named `all.jspx`. Listing 10-6 shows your view.

Listing 10-6. all.jspx

```
<html
  xmlns:jsp="http://java.sun.com/JSP/Page"
  xmlns:c="http://java.sun.com/jsp/jstl/core"
  xmlns:spring="http://www.springframework.org/tags"
  version="2.0">
<jsp:directive.page contentType="text/html;charset=UTF-8" />
<jsp:output omit-xml-declaration="yes" />
<head>
<title>My Documents</title>
</head>
<body style="font-family: verdana;">
  <h2>My Documents - Search</h2>
  <c:if test="${not empty docs}">
    <table>
      <tbody>
        <c:forEach items="${docs}" var="doc" varStatus="status">
          <tr>
            <td>
              <table>
                <tbody>
                  <tr>
                    <td align="right">Name:</td>
                    <td>${doc.name}</td>
                  </tr>
                  <tr>
                    <td align="right">Type:</td>
                    <td>${doc.type.name}</td>
                  </tr>
```

```
            <tr>
              <td align="right">Location</td>
              <td>${doc.location}:</td>
            </tr>
          </tbody>
        </table>
      </td>
    </tr>
  </c:forEach>
    </tbody>
  </table>
</c:if>
</body>
</html>
```

The idea of this view is to iterate over all the documents saved in the database (In-memory HSQL), and display them one by one. But how are you going to accomplish this? Well, first you need to add some dependencies to the build.gradle file. Listing 10-7 shows you how to do that.

Listing 10-7. build.gradle

```
apply plugin: 'jetty'

//... more configuration options

dependencies {
        //... more dependencies

        compile 'org.springframework:spring-webmvc:4.0.5.RELEASE'
        runtime 'jstl:jstl:1.2'

        //... more dependencies
}
```

Running this application as a web application will require a web container. In your case, you will use Jetty, a light container. The definition is in Listing 10-7: apply plugin: 'jetty'. Also, you are going to require a JSTL (Java Standard Tag Library) runtime that will help you to add logic embedded in your page and in this case to iterate through the list returned by the controller. Of course, you need to have the Spring Web MVC extension dependency at compile time.

Now if you run as gradle :ch10:jettyRun, you should get the following output:

```
.....
10:35:26.324 [main] DEBUG o.s.web.servlet.DispatcherServlet - Published WebApplicationContext of
servlet 'mydocuments' as ServletContext attribute with name [org.springframework.web.servlet.
FrameworkServlet.CONTEXT.mydocuments]
10:35:26.325 [main] INFO  o.s.web.servlet.DispatcherServlet - FrameworkServlet 'mydocuments':
initialization completed in 3881 ms
10:35:26.325 [main] DEBUG o.s.web.servlet.DispatcherServlet - Servlet 'mydocuments' configured
successfully
> Building 80% > :ch10:jettyRun > Running at http://localhost:8080/ch10
```

> ■ **Note** Remember if you are using the book's companion source code, at the root of the project you can run `gradle :ch10:jettyRun`; if you are in the ch10 folder, just run `gradle jettyRun`.

Now you can go to the following URL: `http://localhost:8080/ch10/mydocuments/search/all`. Figure 10-2 shows the result.

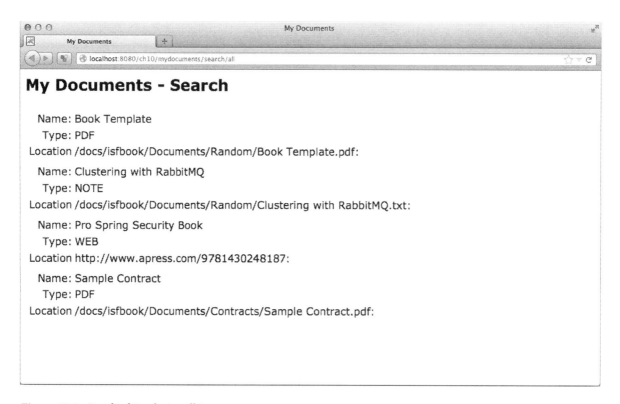

Figure 10-2. *Result of Rendering all.jspx*

The following segment shows the output of the logs used by the Jetty container when I accessed the web page. You can see the JDBC calls in action and how they are being rendered.

```
10:38:27.615 [1141619556@qtp-568919009-0] DEBUG o.s.web.servlet.DispatcherServlet -
DispatcherServlet with name 'mydocuments' processing GET request for [/ch10/mydocuments/search/all]
10:38:27.616 [1141619556@qtp-568919009-0] DEBUG o.s.w.s.m.m.a.RequestMappingHandlerMapping - Looking
up handler method for path /search/all
10:38:27.618 [1141619556@qtp-568919009-0] DEBUG o.s.w.s.m.m.a.RequestMappingHandlerMapping -
Returning handler method [public java.lang.String com.apress.isf.spring.web.SearchController.
searchAll(org.springframework.ui.Model)]
10:38:27.618 [1141619556@qtp-568919009-0] DEBUG o.s.b.f.s.DefaultListableBeanFactory - Returning
cached instance of singleton bean 'searchController'
```

```
10:38:27.619 [1141619556@qtp-568919009-0] DEBUG o.s.web.servlet.DispatcherServlet - Last-Modified
value for [/ch10/mydocuments/search/all] is: -1
10:38:27.634 [1141619556@qtp-568919009-0] DEBUG o.s.jdbc.core.JdbcTemplate - Executing SQL query [
      select d.documentId, d.name, d.location, d.description as doc_desc,
      d.typeId, d.created, d.modified,
      t.name as type_name, t.description as type_desc, t.extension from
      documents d
      join types t
      on d.typeId = t.typeId
   ]
10:38:27.635 [1141619556@qtp-568919009-0] DEBUG o.s.jdbc.datasource.DataSourceUtils - Fetching JDBC
Connection from DataSource
10:38:27.635 [1141619556@qtp-568919009-0] DEBUG o.s.j.d.SimpleDriverDataSource - Creating new JDBC
Driver Connection to [jdbc:hsqldb:mem:dataSource]
```

Internationalization: i18n

I said that the Spring MVC has other features like i18n (Internationalization). Chapter 6 talked about the message bundles; the Spring MVC has that capability too. Let's see how to do it.

First, you need to add some extra bean definitions to the XML configuration file in order for it to be ready for this particular feature. Listing 10-8 shows you how it's done.

Listing 10-8. mydocuments-servlet.xml

```xml
<?xml version="1.0" encoding="UTF-8"?>
<beans xmlns="http://www.springframework.org/schema/beans"
  xmlns:xsi="http://www.w3.org/2001/XMLSchema-instance"
  xmlns:context="http://www.springframework.org/schema/context"
  xmlns:jdbc="http://www.springframework.org/schema/jdbc"
  xmlns:mvc="http://www.springframework.org/schema/mvc"
  xmlns:p="http://www.springframework.org/schema/p"
  xsi:schemaLocation="http://www.springframework.org/schema/jdbc http://www.springframework.org/
  schema/jdbc/spring-jdbc-4.0.xsd
    http://www.springframework.org/schema/mvc http://www.springframework.org/schema/mvc/spring-mvc-4.0.xsd
    http://www.springframework.org/schema/beans http://www.springframework.org/schema/beans/spring-
    beans.xsd
    http://www.springframework.org/schema/context http://www.springframework.org/schema/context/
    spring-context-4.0.xsd">

<context:component-scan base-package="com.apress.isf.spring"/>
<mvc:annotation-driven />

<mvc:interceptors>
   <bean class="org.springframework.web.servlet.i18n.LocaleChangeInterceptor" p:paramName="lang" />
</mvc:interceptors>

<bean id="messageSource" class="org.springframework.context.support.
ReloadableResourceBundleMessageSource"
   p:basenames="WEB-INF/i18n/messages" p:fallbackToSystemLocale="false"/>
<bean id="localeResolver" class="org.springframework.web.servlet.i18n.CookieLocaleResolver"
   p:cookieName="locale"/>
```

```xml
<bean class="org.springframework.web.servlet.view.InternalResourceViewResolver">
  <property name="prefix" value="/WEB-INF/views/"/>
  <property name="suffix" value=".jspx"/>
</bean>

<jdbc:embedded-database id="dataSource">
  <jdbc:script location="classpath:/META-INF/data/schema.sql" />
  <jdbc:script location="classpath:/META-INF/data/data.sql" />
</jdbc:embedded-database>

<bean id="query" class="java.lang.String">
  <constructor-arg>
    <value>
      select d.documentId, d.name, d.location, d.description as doc_desc,
      d.typeId, d.created, d.modified,
      t.name as type_name, t.description as type_desc, t.extension from
      documents d
      join types t
      on d.typeId = t.typeId
    </value>
  </constructor-arg>
</bean>

</beans>
```

In Listing 10-8, you add an interceptor the `LocaleChangeInterceptor`. It will help you with a parameter named `lang` to change the locale. (If omitted, the default parameter will be `locale`.) Next, you have the `ReloadableResourceBundleMessageSource` class, which helps you find the path where your bundle message will be. In your case, `WEB-INF/i18n/` is the path and `messages` is the name of the bundle. Also, you are defining a `CookieLocaleResolver` that will help you to save the state of your locale selected during your session.

After modifying the XML file, you need to add the `messages.properties` file with its translations. In Chapter 6, I talked about using resource files. In this example, you will be using Spanish. You are going to create three files, one of which will be the default: `messages.properties`, `messages_en.properties` (for English), and `messages_es.properties` (for Spanish). Listing 10-9, 10-10, and 10-11 contain the messages bundles.

Listing 10-9. WEB-INF/i18n/messages.properties

```
main.title=Welcome to My Documents
search.subtitle=.:: My Documents - Search ::.
search.name=Name:
search.type=Type:
search.location=Location:
```

Listing 10-9 shows the default `message.properties` file. Now let's take a look at the English properties. See Listing 10-10.

Listing 10-10. WEB-INF/i18n/messages_en.properties

```
main.title=Welcome to My Documents
search.subtitle=.:: My Documents - Search ::.
search.name=Name:
search.type=Type:
search.location=Location:
```

Listing 10-10 shows the English message_en.properties file. Next, let's look at Listing 10-11, which is the Spanish version.

Listing 10-11. WEB-INF/i18n/message_es.properties

```
main.title=Bienvenido a Mis Documentos
search.subtitle=.:: Mis Documentos - Busqueda ::.
search.name=Nombre:
search.type=Tipo:
search.location=Localidad:
```

Listing 10-11 shows the Spanish message_es.properties file. As you can see, the only thing that changed in all these files is the value of every property. Now let's run the application using gradle :ch10:jettyRun. If you add the parameter ?lang=es your page will be in Spanish! Figure 10-3 shows the results in Spanish and then Figure 10-4 shows it set back to English.

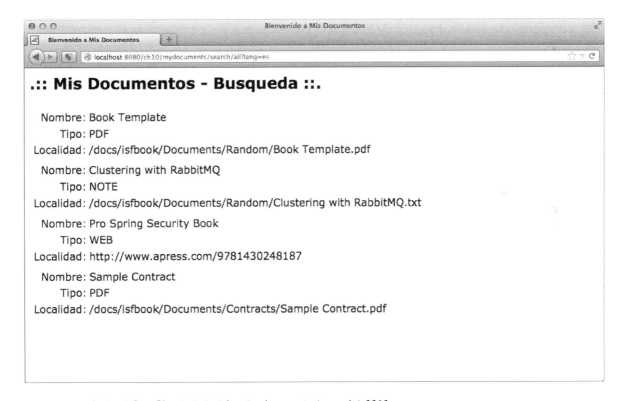

Figure 10-3. *http://localhost:8080/ch10/mydocuments/search/all?lang=es*

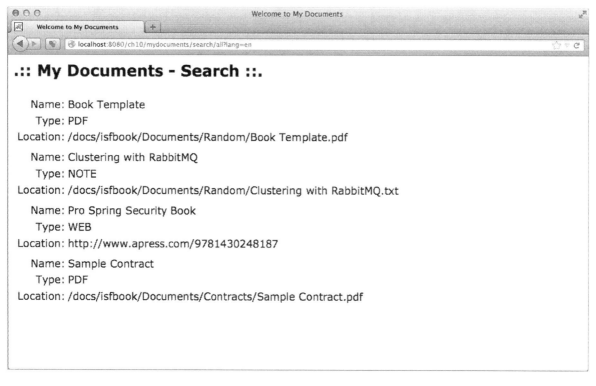

Figure 10-4. *http://localhost:8080/ch10/mydocuments/search/all?lang=en*

And what happens if you are not passing any parameter? Well, the container will take the default messages.properties file and you will get the English version.

But wait! I have been saying that Spring simplifies everything, right? Of course it does. What about getting rid of all the XML files, even the web.xml (the standard Java way)? Yes, you can! You can use Java configuration. Take a look at the book's companion source code for more information about how to do this.

Summary

In this chapter, you used Java's standard way of deploying web applications using a web structure and a web.xml configuration file to show your Spring application, **My Document**, in a web page. You also saw how to internationalize your application by using Message bundles for multiple languages.

In the next chapters, you will still use the Spring MVC, but this time you will see how it interacts with other services besides the Web, such as JMS or AMQP.

CHAPTER 11

■ ■ ■

Integrating Your Spring Application with External Systems

In this chapter, you are going to learn how to integrate your Spring application, **My Documents**, with external or existing systems. Let's imagine for a moment that you have two friends. The first friend wants to send you some document information: the same Document class model that you have in XML format. But this friend only knows JMS (Java Message Service). The second friend wants to only receive document information in XML format as well, but this friend only knows AMQP (Advance Message Queue Protocol).

Figure 11-1 shows how you should communicate between these systems. At the end of this chapter you will know how to integrate your **My Documents** Spring application with external systems, either JMS or AMQP technologies.

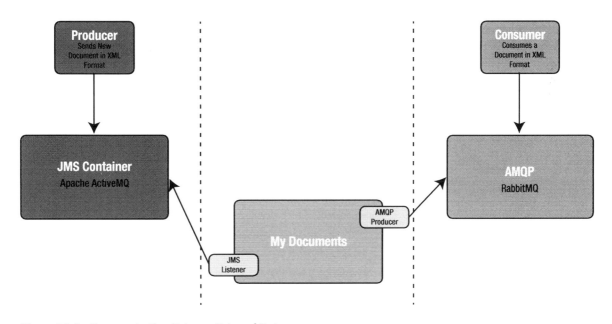

Figure 11-1. *Communication Between External Systems*

Figure 11-1 shows how the **My Documents** application will interact with JMS. There will be a producer that only talks JMS, and it will send messages to a JMS container, in this case Apache ActiveMQ. Then **My Documents**, after receiving the message in a String XML format, will save it into the database; after that it will send the same message but using AMPQ to the RabbitMQ broker. You are going to create both the producer and consumer for the JMS and a producer and consumer for the AMQP.

Java Message Service

Let's start by setting **My Documents** up to receive XML messages from a JMS service. But wait, what is this JMS thing? The Java Message Service API was developed by the Java community (JSR 914) as an effort to connect different and distributed clients (MOM—message-oriented middleware) in an asynchronous way and loosely couple. The clients can send and receive messages in a point-to-point (queues) or a publish-subscribe (topics) way.

To emulate your friend that only talks to JMS, you are going to install Apache ActiveMQ. This is a JMS container. You can download it from http://activemq.apache.org/. (For more information about how to install ApacheMQ, see Appendix A.)

Listing 11-1 shows the XML that you are going to use to send document information to your Spring application. The XML contains some documentIds, a name, location, description, the date created and modified, and the type with its attributes.

Listing 11-1. XML Document Info (META-INF/data/jms.txt)

```
<document>
  <documentId>df569fa4-a513-4252-9810-818cade184ca</documentId>
  <name>Apress Books</name>
  <type>
    <typeId>4980d2e4-a424-4ff4-a0b2-476039682f43</typeId>
    <name>WEB</name>
    <desc>Web Link</desc>
    <extension>.url</extension>
  </type>
  <location>http://www.apress.com</location>
  <description>Apress Books</description>
  <created>2014-03-11 03:02:18.490 UTC</created>
  <modified>2014-03-11 03:02:18.490 UTC</modified>
</document>
```

Next, start the Apache ActiveMQ, go to the main page (http://localhost:8161/hawtio), and create a queue (destination) with the name of mydocumentsQueue. On the Hawtio web page, go to the left side and select the localhost node. Some tabs will appear; select the + Create tab. It will display a Create Queue dialog. Set the name and choose the Queue option, then click the Create Queue button. See Figure 11-2.

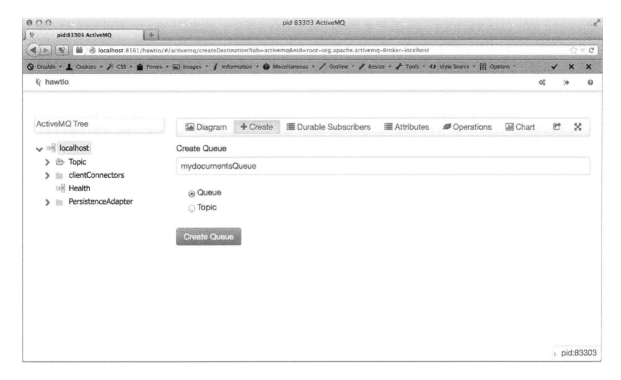

Figure 11-2. *Creating a Queue Named mydocumentsQueue*

After creating the queue, you are going to actually send a message. Remember that you are going to simulate your friend sending a message with new document information, so you can pick up that message and save it into the database.

To send a message on the web page (hawtio), you need to select the localhost node from the left side, then select Queue, and then choose the created queue (mydocumentsQueue). You will see several options; select Send, and it will show a dialog where you need to copy and paste the XML contents (from Listing 11-1). Figure 11-3 and 11-4 show how it's done.

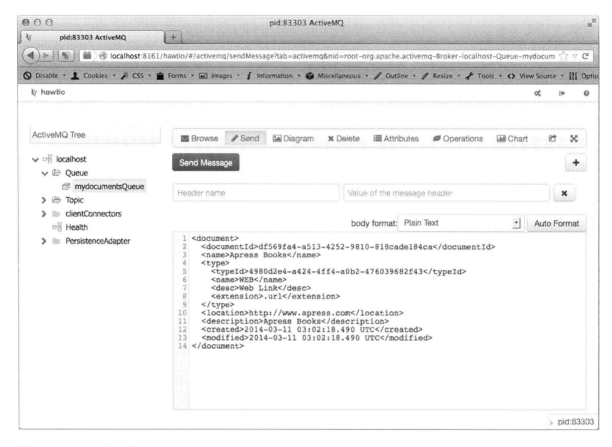

Figure 11-3. *Pasting the XML Message*

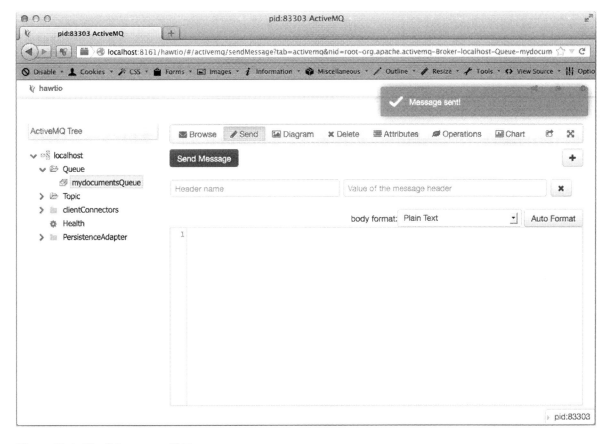

Figure 11-4. *The "Message sent!" Message*

After pasting the XML contents (from Listing 11-1), see Figure 11-3. Click the Send Message button. This will send the XML message to the mydocumentsQueue; take a look at Figure 11-4.

Figure 11-4 displays a "Message sent!" message in green. This means that your message is now waiting in the queue. And if you click the Browse button (next to the Send button) you can see the message listed and ready to be consumed by any client, as shown in Figure 11-5.

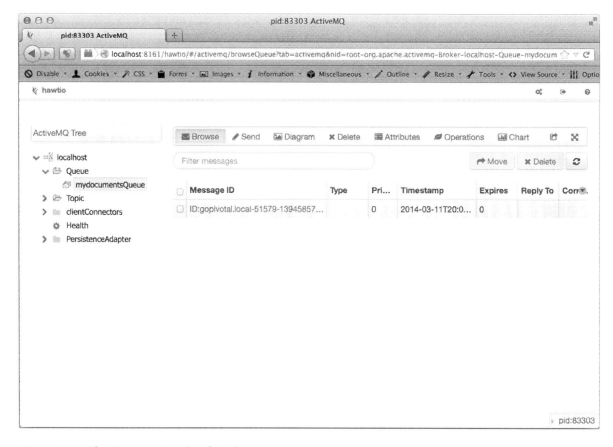

Figure 11-5. *The Message Is Listed and Ready*

Figure 11-5 shows the message that you sent to the queue.

Spring JMS

Next, you are going to create a consumer that will consume that message. The Spring Framework already has a template (for sending JMS messages to any JMS broker) and a Simple Listener container (that connects to a JMS broker and listens for any new messages incoming from a queue or topic). Listing 11-2 shows the consumer you are going to use to consume the XML message from the Apache ActiveMQ container.

Listing 11-2. JMSConsumer.java

```java
package com.apress.isf.spring.jms;

import javax.jms.JMSException;
import javax.jms.Message;
import javax.jms.MessageListener;
import javax.jms.TextMessage;

import org.springframework.beans.factory.annotation.Autowired;
import org.springframework.stereotype.Component;
```

```java
import com.apress.isf.java.model.Document;
import com.apress.isf.java.utils.XmlUtils;
import com.apress.isf.spring.data.DocumentDAO;

@Component
public class JMSConsumer implements MessageListener{

        @Autowired
        DocumentDAO documentDAO;

        @Override
        public void onMessage(Message message) {
                TextMessage textMessage = (TextMessage)message;
                try{
                        Document document = XmlUtils.fromXML(textMessage.getText(), Document.class);
                        documentDAO.save(document);
                }catch(JMSException ex){
                        ex.printStackTrace();
                }
        }

}
```

Let's analyze what you are doing in Listing 11-2. First, you are implementing the javax.jms.MessageListener. The JMS API exposes this interface where you need to implement the onMessage method; this method accepts a javax.jms.Message that will contain the message. Also, you are using a small Utility class, which will help to convert the XML into a document object and be saved into the database using the DocumentDAO implementation. Next, take a look at Listing 11-3, which shows the Utility class that is used in the consumer.

Listing 11-3. XmlUtils.java

```java
package com.apress.isf.java.utils;

import com.thoughtworks.xstream.XStream;

public class XmlUtils {

        public static <T> String toXML(T object){
                XStream xstream = new XStream();
                xstream.alias(object.getClass().getSimpleName().toLowerCase(), object.getClass());
                return xstream.toXML(object);
        }

        @SuppressWarnings({ "unchecked"})
        public static <T> T fromXML(String xml, Class<T> _class){
                XStream xstream = new XStream();
                xstream.alias(_class.getSimpleName().toLowerCase(), _class);
                return (T)xstream.fromXML(xml);
        }
}
```

Listing 11-3 uses XStream, a library that serializes/deserializes objects into an XML String back and forth. Because you need to save an actual document object, it is necessary to add this helper to the application. Note in Listing 11-2 that there is a documentDAO.save(document)call. This is a new method that you will add to the DocumentDAO implementation that will save a Document object. See Listing 11-4, the DocumentRepository class.

Listing 11-4. DocumentRepository.java

```java
package com.apress.isf.spring.data;

import java.util.Date;
import java.util.List;

import javax.sql.DataSource;

import org.springframework.beans.factory.annotation.Autowired;
import org.springframework.dao.EmptyResultDataAccessException;
import org.springframework.jdbc.core.JdbcTemplate;
import org.springframework.stereotype.Repository;

import com.apress.isf.java.model.Document;

@Repository("documentDAO")
public class DocumentRepository implements DocumentDAO {

        @Autowired
        private DataSource dataSource;

        @Autowired
        private String query;
        @Autowired
        private String insert;
        @Autowired
        private String find;
        @Autowired
        private String update;

        public List<Document> getAll() {
                return new JdbcTemplate(dataSource).query(query,
                                new DocumentRowMapper());
        }

        public Document findById(String id) {
                Document updateDocument = null;
                JdbcTemplate template = new JdbcTemplate(dataSource);

                try {
                        updateDocument = template.queryForObject(find,
                                        new Object[] { id },
                                        new DocumentRowMapper());
                } catch (EmptyResultDataAccessException ex) {}
                return updateDocument;
        }
}
```

```
        public void save(Document document) {
                try {
                        JdbcTemplate template = new JdbcTemplate(dataSource);
                        if (null == findById(document.getDocumentId()))
                                template.update(
                                insert,
                                new Object[] { document.getDocumentId(),
                                        document.getName(), document.getLocation(),
                                        document.getDescription(),
                                        document.getType().getTypeId(),
                                        document.getCreated(), document.getModified() });
                        else
                                template.update(
                                        update,
                                        new Object[] { document.getName(),
                                                document.getLocation(),
                                                document.getDescription(),
                                                document.getType().getTypeId(), new Date(),
                                                document.getDocumentId() });
                } catch (Exception ex) {
                        ex.printStackTrace();
                }
        }

}
```

You have a more complete DocumentDAO implementation, right? See Listing 11-4, where you are saving, updating, and finding documents by id. Also notice that the save method will be used to save a new document or update an existing one; this is because you are checking to see if that document exists first by calling the findById method.

So how will the JMSConsumer class (see Listing 11-2) be called or used to consume the message from the Apache ActiveMQ? Well, the Spring Framework will take care of this, but you need to help it a little bit. See Listing 11-5, the XML configuration.

Listing 11-5. mydocuments-context.xml

```
<?xml version="1.0" encoding="UTF-8"?>
<beans xmlns="http://www.springframework.org/schema/beans"
        xmlns:xsi="http://www.w3.org/2001/XMLSchema-instance"
        xmlns:jms="http://www.springframework.org/schema/jms"
        xmlns:context="http://www.springframework.org/schema/context"
        xmlns:jdbc="http://www.springframework.org/schema/jdbc"
        xsi:schemaLocation="
http://www.springframework.org/schema/jdbc http://www.springframework.org/schema/jdbc/spring-jdbc-4.0.xsd
    http://www.springframework.org/schema/jms http://www.springframework.org/schema/jms/spring-jms-4.0.xsd
    http://www.springframework.org/schema/beans http://www.springframework.org/schema/beans/spring-
    beans.xsd
    http://www.springframework.org/schema/context http://www.springframework.org/schema/context/
    spring-context-4.0.xsd">

  <context:component-scan base-package="com.apress.isf.spring"/>
```

```xml
<!-- Active MQ -->
<bean id="activemqConnectionFactory" class="org.apache.activemq.ActiveMQConnectionFactory"
        p:brokerURL="tcp://localhost:61616"/>

<!-- JMS Listener -->
<jms:listener-container connection-factory="activemqConnectionFactory"
        acknowledge="auto" container-type="default">
    <jms:listener destination="mydocumentsQueue" ref="JMSConsumer"
                method="onMessage"/>
</jms:listener-container>

<!-- JDBC -->
<jdbc:embedded-database id="dataSource">
  <jdbc:script location="classpath:/META-INF/data/schema.sql" />
  <jdbc:script location="classpath:/META-INF/data/data.sql" />
</jdbc:embedded-database>

<!-- SQL Queries Omitted -->

</beans>
```

In Listing 11-5, the ActiveMQConnectionFactory class was added because it will help to connect to the Apache ActiveMQ broker. Normally it will only require the broker's URL. However, in this case, because you are running it locally, it will be tcp://localhost:6161. Then a new <xmlns:jms/>namespace was also added; with this namespace you can add the <jms:listener-container/>tag that makes a reference to the connection factory and where you are referencing the JMSConsumer class (Listing 11-2) by using the <jms:listener/>tag. The <jms:listener/>tag has a reference to the name of the queue, mydocumentsQueue. This tag will start listening to the mydocumentsQueue for any new incoming message and they will be delivered to the onMessage method.

Next, let's see the test class (see Listing 11-6) and run it.

Listing 11-6. MyDocumentsTest.java

```java
package com.apress.isf.spring.test;

import static org.junit.Assert.assertEquals;
import static org.junit.Assert.assertNotNull;

import org.junit.Ignore;
import org.junit.Test;
import org.junit.runner.RunWith;
import org.slf4j.Logger;
import org.slf4j.LoggerFactory;
import org.springframework.beans.factory.annotation.Autowired;
import org.springframework.test.context.ContextConfiguration;
import org.springframework.test.context.junit4.SpringJUnit4ClassRunner;

import com.apress.isf.java.model.Document;
import com.apress.isf.java.model.Type;
import com.apress.isf.java.service.SearchEngine;
import com.apress.isf.java.utils.XmlUtils;
import com.apress.isf.spring.amqp.RabbitMQProducer;
import com.apress.isf.spring.jms.JMSProducer;
```

```
@RunWith(SpringJUnit4ClassRunner.class)
@ContextConfiguration("classpath:META-INF/spring/mydocuments-context.xml")
public class MyDocumentsTest {
        private static final Logger log = LoggerFactory.getLogger(MyDocumentsTest.class);
        //Based on the META-INF/data/jms.txt - only one record
        private static final int MAX_ALL_DOCS = 5;
        private static final int MAX_WEB_DOCS = 2;

        @Autowired
        private SearchEngine engine;

        @Test
        public void testSpringJMS() throws InterruptedException {
                log.debug("Testing Spring JMS Listener/Insert...");
                assertNotNull(engine);

                //Waiting a least 5 seconds so the message is consumed.
                Thread.sleep(5000);
                //After the JMS message and insert, must be 5 Documents
                assertEquals(MAX_ALL_DOCS, engine.listAll().size());

                Type documentType = new Type("WEB",".url");
                assertEquals(MAX_WEB_DOCS, engine.findByType(documentType).size());
        }

}
```

If you run this test (using `gradle :ch11:test`), it will work as long as you have an XML message sitting on the queue; in other words, if you run the test again, it will fail because there are no messages. Then you need to do the same as before: copy and paste the XML (Listing 11-1) and send it to the queue.

Maybe you are wondering why this test will fail. Based on the `data.sql` file that is loaded as an embedded database in memory, you have only four records; after the consumer consumes the XML document and saves it into the database, you will have five documents and the assertion will fail (`assertEquals(MAX_ALL_DOCS, engine.listAll().size())`) because it is comparing the documents number in the database with the MAX_ALL_DOCS variable that is set to 5. If you decide to run this test over and over, it will become tedious to manually send a message into the ActiveMQ web page, right?

The Spring Framework also provides a template, the `org.springframework.jms.core.JmsTemplate` class, to help you to send messages to any JMS broker so you can avoid copying and pasting messages manually into the ActiveMQ web page. So let's create a producer that will send messages through the broker. Listing 11-7 shows the producer.

Listing 11-7. JMSProducer.java

```
package com.apress.isf.spring.jms;

import java.io.IOException;
import java.io.InputStream;
import java.util.Scanner;

import javax.jms.JMSException;
import javax.jms.Message;
import javax.jms.Session;
```

```java
import org.springframework.beans.factory.annotation.Autowired;
import org.springframework.beans.factory.annotation.Value;
import org.springframework.core.io.Resource;
import org.springframework.jms.core.JmsTemplate;
import org.springframework.jms.core.MessageCreator;
import org.springframework.stereotype.Component;

@Component("jmsProducer")
public class JMSProducer {

        @Value("classpath:META-INF/data/jms.txt")
        private Resource jmstxt;
        @Autowired
        private JmsTemplate jmsTemplate;

        public void send(){
                jmsTemplate.send(new MessageCreator() {
                        @Override
                        public Message createMessage(Session session) throws JMSException {
                                return session.createTextMessage(getMessage());
                        }
                });
        }

        private String getMessage(){
                StringBuilder str = new StringBuilder();
                try{
                  InputStream stream = jmstxt.getInputStream();
                  Scanner scanner = new Scanner(stream);
                  while (scanner.hasNext()) {
                          str.append(scanner.nextLine());
                  }
                  scanner.close();
                  stream.close();
                }catch(IOException e){
                        e.printStackTrace();
                }
                return str.toString();
        }
}
```

Listing 11-7 shows you how easy it is to send messages using the Spring's JmsTemplate class to any JMS container. In Listing 11-7, you are calling the jmsTemplate.send method; this method has a MessageCreator implementation as a parameter and you are creating an instance of it by implementing the Message createMessage(Session session) method.

Listing 11-8 shows the XML configuration with the new jmsTemplate bean that defines the helper that will send the message to the Apache ActiveMQ container.

Listing 11-8. mydocuments-context.xml

```xml
<?xml version="1.0" encoding="UTF-8"?>
<beans xmlns="http://www.springframework.org/schema/beans"
        xmlns:xsi="http://www.w3.org/2001/XMLSchema-instance"
        xmlns:jms="http://www.springframework.org/schema/jms"
        xmlns:context="http://www.springframework.org/schema/context"
        xmlns:jdbc="http://www.springframework.org/schema/jdbc"
        xsi:schemaLocation="
http://www.springframework.org/schema/jdbc http://www.springframework.org/schema/jdbc/spring-jdbc-
4.0.xsd
    http://www.springframework.org/schema/jms http://www.springframework.org/schema/jms/spring-jms-
        4.0.xsd
    http://www.springframework.org/schema/beans http://www.springframework.org/schema/beans/spring-
        beans.xsd
    http://www.springframework.org/schema/context http://www.springframework.org/schema/context/
        spring-context-4.0.xsd">

  <context:component-scan base-package="com.apress.isf.spring"/>

  <!-- Active MQ -->
  <bean id="activemqConnectionFactory" class="org.apache.activemq.ActiveMQConnectionFactory"
        p:brokerURL="tcp://localhost:61616"/>

  <!-- JMS Template -->
  <bean id="jmsTemplate" class="org.springframework.jms.core.JmsTemplate">
    <constructor-arg name="connectionFactory" ref="activemqConnectionFactory"/>
    <property name="defaultDestinationName" value="mydocumentsQueue" />
  </bean>

  <!-- JMS Listener -->
  <jms:listener-container connection-factory="activemqConnectionFactory"
        acknowledge="auto" container-type="default">
    <jms:listener destination="mydocumentsQueue" ref="JMSConsumer"
                method="onMessage"/>
  </jms:listener-container>

  <!-- JDBC -->
  <jdbc:embedded-database id="dataSource">
    <jdbc:script location="classpath:/META-INF/data/schema.sql" />
    <jdbc:script location="classpath:/META-INF/data/data.sql" />
  </jdbc:embedded-database>

  <!-- SQL Queries omitted -->

</beans>
```

Listing 11-8 shows you the jmsTemplate bean that references the org.springframework.jms.core.JmsTemplate class. The JmsTemplate has a constructor where it's being referenced to the activemqConnectionFactory bean and it has a property that will be the name of the queue, mydocumentsQueue. This will help the template to send messages to the correct destination queue. Listing 11-9 shows the modification of the previous test.

Listing 11-9. MyDocumentTest.java

```java
package com.apress.isf.spring.test;

import static org.junit.Assert.assertEquals;
import static org.junit.Assert.assertNotNull;

import org.junit.Ignore;
import org.junit.Test;
import org.junit.runner.RunWith;
import org.junit.runners.MethodSorters;
import org.junit.FixMethodOrder;
import org.slf4j.Logger;
import org.slf4j.LoggerFactory;
import org.springframework.beans.factory.annotation.Autowired;
import org.springframework.test.context.ContextConfiguration;
import org.springframework.test.context.junit4.SpringJUnit4ClassRunner;

import com.apress.isf.java.model.Document;
import com.apress.isf.java.model.Type;
import com.apress.isf.java.service.SearchEngine;
import com.apress.isf.java.utils.XmlUtils;
import com.apress.isf.spring.amqp.RabbitMQProducer;
import com.apress.isf.spring.jms.JMSProducer;

@RunWith(SpringJUnit4ClassRunner.class)
@ContextConfiguration("classpath:META-INF/spring/mydocuments-context.xml")
@FixMethodOrder(MethodSorters.NAME_ASCENDING)
public class MyDocumentsTest {
        private static final Logger log = LoggerFactory.getLogger(MyDocumentsTest.class);
        //Based on the META-INF/data/jms.txt - only one record
        private static final int MAX_ALL_DOCS = 5;
        private static final int MAX_WEB_DOCS = 2;

        @Autowired
        private SearchEngine engine;

        @Test
        public void testSpringJMS_1(){
                log.debug("Testing Spring JMS Producer...");
                jmsProducer.send();
        }

        @Test
        public void testSpringJMS_2() throws InterruptedException {
                log.debug("Testing Spring JMS Listener/Insert...");
                assertNotNull(engine);
```

```
        //Waiting a least 5 seconds so the message is consumed.
        Thread.sleep(5000);
        //After the JMS message and insert, must be 5 Documents
        assertEquals(MAX_ALL_DOCS, engine.listAll().size());

        Type documentType = new Type("WEB",".url");
        assertEquals(MAX_WEB_DOCS, engine.findByType(documentType).size());
    }

}
```

Listing 11-9 shows how to run the producer and consumer. There are two methods: testSpringJMS_1 for your producer and testSpringJMS_2 for your consumer. Note that at some point you need to run the tests in order, and JUnit has no guarantee of doing that. That's why the @FixMethodOrder annotation was added and the test methods were renamed so you can run this test and the methods will be executed in order.

RabbitMQ and Spring Rabbit

Now let's do the next part where your other friend is waiting for you to send an XML message, but in this case using a AMQP (Advance Message Queue Protocol), and he or she is using the RabbitMQ broker.

RabbitMQ is a messaging broker that uses AMQP, which is a wired protocol, meaning that it is not based on any API implementation like JMS (only Java can run JMS). RabbitMQ provides a platform for your application to send and receive messages and has several features, such as speed and reliability; a persistence mechanism for your messages; clustering; high availability; multiple Client APIs in different programming languages; the ability to run in many platforms, and other features.

Now for your Spring application, you need to install RabbitMQ and run it (for more information about how to install RabbitMQ, see Appendix A). Make sure RabbitMQ is running by going to http://localhost:15672 in your browser. See Figure 11-6.

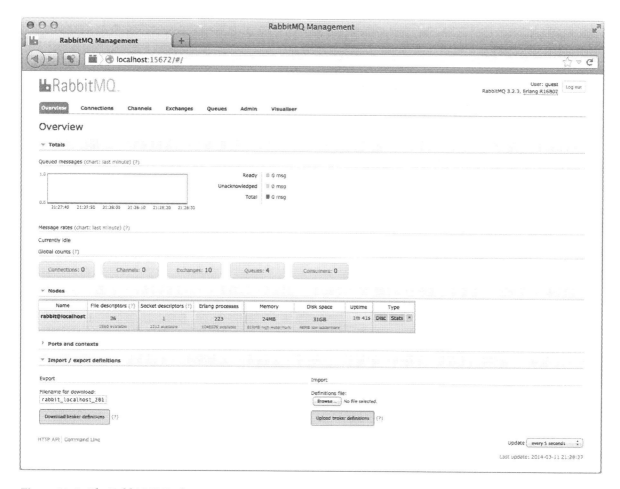

Figure 11-6. *The RabbitMQ Broker Main Page*

Next, you need to create the producer that will send messages to RabbitMQ. But how are you going to send AMQP messages? That's right; by using Spring! The Spring Framework has Spring AMQP and Spring Rabbit modules that know how to talk AMQP and know how to communicate to RabbitMQ. Listing 11-10 shows the RabbitMQ producer.

Listing 11-10. RabbitMQProducer.java

```
package com.apress.isf.spring.amqp;

import org.springframework.amqp.core.Message;
import org.springframework.amqp.core.MessageProperties;
import org.springframework.amqp.rabbit.core.RabbitTemplate;
import org.springframework.beans.factory.annotation.Autowired;
import org.springframework.stereotype.Component;

import com.apress.isf.java.model.Document;
import com.apress.isf.java.utils.XmlUtils;
```

```
@Component("rabbitmqProducer")
public class RabbitMQProducer {

        @Autowired
        private RabbitTemplate rabbitTemplate;

        public void send(Document document){
                MessageProperties messageProperties = new MessageProperties();
                messageProperties.setContentType("text/xml");
                byte[] body = XmlUtils.toXML(document).getBytes();
                Message message = new Message(body, messageProperties);
                rabbitTemplate.send(message);
        }
}
```

Listing 11-10 shows the producer; here you are using the `org.springframework.amqp.rabbit.core.`
`RabbitTemplate` class (provided by the Spring Rabbit module) that allows you to send messages through the AMQP
to the RabbitMQ broker. Also, you are creating an instance of the `org.springframework.amqp.core.Message` class,
a `Message` class that takes two parameters. The first parameter is the body of the message; in this case the `Document`
object is converted into an array of bytes by using the `XmlUtil` class (see Listing 11-3). The second parameter will be
a `MessageProperties` instance that only indicates that the message will be in XML. Then you send the message by
calling the `rabbitTemplate.send` method.

Listing 11-11 shows the XML configuration and the use of the `<xmlns:rabbit/>`namespace to declare some of
the elements needed to connect to the RabbitMQ broker. This is necessary for the Spring container to know about the
RabbitMQ broker.

Listing 11-11. mydocuments-context.xml

```
<?xml version="1.0" encoding="UTF-8"?>
<beans xmlns="http://www.springframework.org/schema/beans"
        xmlns:xsi="http://www.w3.org/2001/XMLSchema-instance"
        xmlns:jms="http://www.springframework.org/schema/jms"
        xmlns:rabbit="http://www.springframework.org/schema/rabbit"
        xmlns:p="http://www.springframework.org/schema/p"
        xmlns:context="http://www.springframework.org/schema/context"
        xmlns:jdbc="http://www.springframework.org/schema/jdbc"
        xsi:schemaLocation="
          http://www.springframework.org/schema/jdbc http://www.springframework.org/schema/jdbc/
spring-jdbc-4.0.xsd
    http://www.springframework.org/schema/jms http://www.springframework.org/schema/jms/spring-jms-
        4.0.xsd
    http://www.springframework.org/schema/rabbit http://www.springframework.org/schema/rabbit/
        spring-rabbit-1.2.xsd
    http://www.springframework.org/schema/beans http://www.springframework.org/schema/beans/spring-
        beans.xsd
```

```
    http://www.springframework.org/schema/context http://www.springframework.org/schema/context/
        spring-context-4.0.xsd">

  <context:component-scan base-package="com.apress.isf.spring"/>

  <!-- Active MQ -->
  <bean id="activemqConnectionFactory" class="org.apache.activemq.ActiveMQConnectionFactory"
        p:brokerURL="tcp://localhost:61616"/>

  <!-- JMS Template -->
  <bean id="jmsTemplate" class="org.springframework.jms.core.JmsTemplate">
    <constructor-arg name="connectionFactory" ref="activemqConnectionFactory"/>
    <property name="defaultDestinationName" value="mydocumentsQueue" />
  </bean>

  <!-- JMS Listener -->
  <jms:listener-container connection-factory="activemqConnectionFactory"
          acknowledge="auto" container-type="default">
      <jms:listener destination="mydocumentsQueue" ref="JMSConsumer"
                    method="onMessage"/>
  </jms:listener-container>

  <!-- RabbitMQ -->
  <rabbit:connection-factory id="rabbitConnectionFactory" host="localhost"/>
  <rabbit:admin connection-factory="rabbitConnectionFactory"/>
  <rabbit:template id="rabbitTemplate" connection-factory="rabbitConnectionFactory"
      routing-key="mydocumentsQueue"/>
  <rabbit:queue name="mydocumentsQueue"/>

  <!-- JDBC -->
  <jdbc:embedded-database id="dataSource">
    <jdbc:script location="classpath:/META-INF/data/schema.sql" />
    <jdbc:script location="classpath:/META-INF/data/data.sql" />
  </jdbc:embedded-database>

  <!-- SQL queries omitted -->
</beans>
```

Listing 11-11 contains several RabbitMQ tags. But let's take a moment to review them. Table 11-1 shows the tags used in the XML.

Table 11-1. *RabbitMQ Namespace Definitions*

Tag	Description
<rabbit:connection-factory />	This tag will handle the connections to the RabbitMQ broker; it can accept multiple properties such as username, password, virtual host, etc.
<rabbit:admin />	This tag will help to create queues, exchanges and bindings; this is necessary to create the queue you are using, mydocumentsQueue.
<rabbit:template />	This tag will send messages to the RabbitMQ broker using the routing key, which in this case is the same as the queue, mydocumentsQueue. This template also is capable of receiving and converting messages, but in your case you already took care to serialize the message into an XML format by using the XMLUtils class in the producer.
<rabbit:queue />	This tag will help to create the mydocumentsQueue; the Spring Rabbit module will attempt to create the queue only if the queue doesn't exist.
<rabbit:listener-container/>	This tag will help to create a container that will be connected to the RabbitMQ broker. This tag has an embedded tag, the <rabbit:listener/> tag. This tag will be used at the end of the chapter.
<rabbit:listener />	This tag declares the class that will be used as an actual listener for a message; in other words, every new message from RabbitMQ will be handled by the referenced class. This tag will be used at the end of the chapter.

Next, you need to create the unit test so you can start sending messages to RabbitMQ. Listing 11-12 shows the unit test.

Listing 11-12. MyDocumentsTest.java

```java
package com.apress.isf.spring.test;

import static org.junit.Assert.assertEquals;
import static org.junit.Assert.assertNotNull;

import java.util.Date;
import java.util.UUID;

import org.junit.FixMethodOrder;
import org.junit.Ignore;
import org.junit.Test;
import org.junit.runner.RunWith;
import org.junit.runners.MethodSorters;
import org.slf4j.Logger;
import org.slf4j.LoggerFactory;
import org.springframework.beans.factory.annotation.Autowired;
import org.springframework.test.context.ContextConfiguration;
import org.springframework.test.context.junit4.SpringJUnit4ClassRunner;

import com.apress.isf.java.model.Document;
import com.apress.isf.java.model.Type;
import com.apress.isf.java.service.SearchEngine;
import com.apress.isf.java.utils.XmlUtils;
```

```java
import com.apress.isf.spring.amqp.RabbitMQProducer;
import com.apress.isf.spring.jms.JMSProducer;

@RunWith(SpringJUnit4ClassRunner.class)
@ContextConfiguration("classpath:META-INF/spring/mydocuments-context.xml")
@FixMethodOrder(MethodSorters.NAME_ASCENDING)
public class MyDocumentsTest {
        private static final Logger log = LoggerFactory.getLogger(MyDocumentsTest.class);
        //Based on the META-INF/data/jms.txt - only one record
        private static final int MAX_ALL_DOCS = 5;
        private static final int MAX_WEB_DOCS = 2;
        private static final String DOCUMENT_ID = "df569fa4-a513-4252-9810-818cade184ca";

        @Autowired
        private SearchEngine engine;

        @Autowired
        JMSProducer jmsProducer;

        @Test
        public void testSpringJMS_1(){
                log.debug("Testing Spring JMS Producer...");
                jmsProducer.send();
        }

        @Test
        public void testSpringJMS_2() throws InterruptedException {
                log.debug("Testing Spring JMS Listener/Insert...");
                assertNotNull(engine);

                //Waiting a least 5 seconds so the message is consumed.
                Thread.sleep(5000);
                //After the JMS message and insert, must be 5 Documents
                assertEquals(MAX_ALL_DOCS, engine.listAll().size());

                Type documentType = new Type("WEB",".url");
                assertEquals(MAX_WEB_DOCS, engine.findByType(documentType).size());
        }

        @Autowired
        RabbitMQProducer rabbitmqProducer;

        @Test
        public void testSpringRabbitMQ_1(){
                log.debug("Testing RabbitMQ producer...");
                assertNotNull(rabbitmqProducer);

                Document document = engine.findById(DOCUMENT_ID);
                assertNotNull(document);
                rabbitmqProducer.send(document);
        }

}
```

Listing 11-12 shows the `rabbitmqProducer` instance and the `testSpringRabbitMQ_1()` method. When this method is executed, it will send a document to the RabbitMQ broker by calling the `rabbitmqProducer.send` method. If you run Listing 11-12 with `gradle :ch11:test`, then you should have a message in the RabbitMQ broker. Figure 11-7 shows the queue and the message that is ready to be consumed.

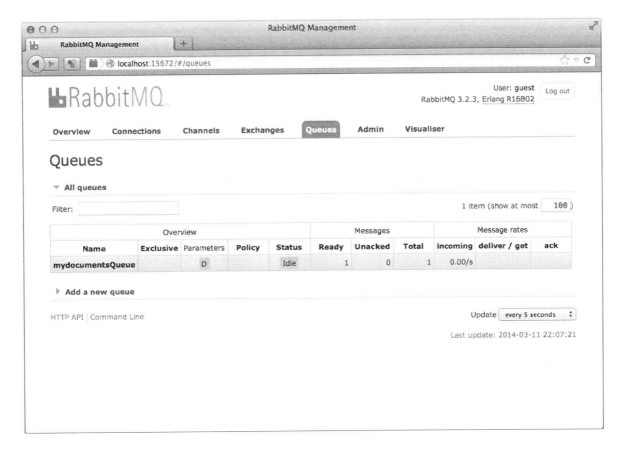

Figure 11-7. *RabbitMQ: Queues*

Remember that you are pretending to be your friend that uses RabbitMQ, so how can you consume the messages from RabbitMQ? Listing 11-13 shows the XML configuration that will help you start consuming from RabbitMQ.

Listing 11-13. mydocuments-context.xml

```xml
<?xml version="1.0" encoding="UTF-8"?>
<beans xmlns="http://www.springframework.org/schema/beans"
       xmlns:xsi="http://www.w3.org/2001/XMLSchema-instance"
       xmlns:jms="http://www.springframework.org/schema/jms"
       xmlns:rabbit="http://www.springframework.org/schema/rabbit"
       xmlns:p="http://www.springframework.org/schema/p"
       xmlns:context="http://www.springframework.org/schema/context"
       xmlns:jdbc="http://www.springframework.org/schema/jdbc"
```

```
        xsi:schemaLocation="
          http://www.springframework.org/schema/jdbc http://www.springframework.org/schema/jdbc/
                spring-jdbc-4.0.xsd
      http://www.springframework.org/schema/jms http://www.springframework.org/schema/jms/spring-jms-
          4.0.xsd
      http://www.springframework.org/schema/rabbit http://www.springframework.org/schema/rabbit/
          spring-rabbit-1.2.xsd
      http://www.springframework.org/schema/beans http://www.springframework.org/schema/beans/spring-
          beans.xsd
      http://www.springframework.org/schema/context http://www.springframework.org/schema/context/
          spring-context-4.0.xsd">

  <context:component-scan base-package="com.apress.isf.spring"/>

  <!-- Active MQ -->
  <bean id="activemqConnectionFactory" class="org.apache.activemq.ActiveMQConnectionFactory"
          p:brokerURL="tcp://localhost:61616"/>

  <!-- JMS Template -->
  <bean id="jmsTemplate" class="org.springframework.jms.core.JmsTemplate">
    <constructor-arg name="connectionFactory" ref="activemqConnectionFactory"/>
    <property name="defaultDestinationName" value="mydocumentsQueue" />
  </bean>

  <!-- JMS Listener -->
  <jms:listener-container connection-factory="activemqConnectionFactory"
          acknowledge="auto" container-type="default">
      <jms:listener destination="mydocumentsQueue" ref="JMSConsumer"
                  method="onMessage"/>
  </jms:listener-container>

  <!-- RabbitMQ -->
  <rabbit:connection-factory id="rabbitConnectionFactory" host="localhost"/>
  <rabbit:admin connection-factory="rabbitConnectionFactory"/>
  <rabbit:template id="rabbitTemplate" connection-factory="rabbitConnectionFactory" routing-
key="mydocumentsQueue"/>
  <rabbit:listener-container connection-factory="rabbitConnectionFactory">
    <rabbit:listener ref="rabbitmqConsumer" queues="mydocumentsQueue"/>
  </rabbit:listener-container>
  <rabbit:queue name="mydocumentsQueue"/>

  <!-- JDBC -->
  <jdbc:embedded-database id="dataSource">
    <jdbc:script location="classpath:/META-INF/data/schema.sql" />
    <jdbc:script location="classpath:/META-INF/data/data.sql" />
  </jdbc:embedded-database>

  <!-- SQL queries omitted -->
</beans>
```

Listing 11-13 shows the `<jms:listener-container/>` tag that allows you to consume messages from RabbitMQ through the rabbitmqConsumer component. Listing 11-14 shows the RabbitMQ consumer.

Listing 11-14. RabbitMQConsumer.java

```
package com.apress.isf.spring.amqp;

import org.slf4j.Logger;
import org.slf4j.LoggerFactory;
import org.springframework.amqp.core.Message;
import org.springframework.amqp.core.MessageListener;
import org.springframework.stereotype.Component;

import com.apress.isf.java.model.Document;
import com.apress.isf.java.utils.XmlUtils;

@Component("rabbitmqConsumer")
public class RabbitMQConsumer implements MessageListener {
        private static final Logger log = LoggerFactory.getLogger(RabbitMQConsumer.class);

        @Override
        public void onMessage(Message message) {
                Document document = XmlUtils.fromXML(new String(message.getBody()),Document.class);
                log.debug("Document received: " + document);
        }

}
```

In Listing 11-14, you are using the **org.springframework.amqp.core.MessageListener** class by implementing its method **onMessage(Message message)**, so every time there is a new message on RabbitMQ and in the mydocumentsQueue, this method will receive the message. Take a look at this method; its parameter is a org.springframework.amqp.core.Message class, so it will be necessary to convert it back from the array of bytes[ ] to XML String and from XML String to a Document object. Now if you run Listing 11-12 again, you should get output saying Document received!

▓ **Note**   The book's companion source code contains all the dependencies (through gradle) used in this chapter.

Summary

In this chapter, you saw how you can interact and integrate your application between external systems. The Spring Framework provides useful extensions to do these integrations: the JMS and the AMQP. But that's not all; Spring also provides the Spring Integration module that facilitates even more of the integration between systems, requiring minimal or even zero code! Apress has an excellent book called *Pro Spring Integration* written by the creators of this extension.

In the next chapter, you are going to expose a REST API for your **My Documents** Spring application so that other developers can add documents to your application.

CHAPTER 12

■ ■ ■

Exposing a REST API

Nowadays most of the big social network companies like Facebook and Twitter expose some services through REST API calls, making them easy to integrate with other applications. In this chapter, you are going to extend your code by adding some new functionality. You are going to expose a RESTful API so other people can easily send, receive, update, and remove documents from your Spring application over the HTTP protocol. And yes, this is a web application too!

RESTful

Before you start coding, let's start designing the RESTful calls. I'll also review what this RESTful thing is. Roy Fielding introduced the Representational State Transfer (REST) in 2000 as a doctoral dissertation, and it has been adopted for exposing a new architectural style for the Web with a set of constraints that are applied to components and data elements, simplifying implementations, reducing the complexity, and helping to improve performance. Table 12-1 shows how these architectural constraints describe a uniform interface for accessing different resources over HTTP.

Table 12-1. *Representation for Resources*

Representation	Description
GET	Gets the resource
POST	Creates a new resource
PUT	Updates a new resource
DELETE	Deletes the resource

Table 12-1 shows the HTTP standard methods that are also applied to Web Service APIs as an alternative to SOAP (Simple Object Access Protocol). The RESTful APIs have the following features:

- They use an internet media type for the data, like JSON, XML, Images, Atom, etc.
- A base URI such as `http://mydocuments.com/resources/`
- Hyperlinks to reference state
- Hyperlinks to reference resources
- They use HTTP standard methods: GET, POST, PUT, DELETE, TRACE, OPTIONS, CONNECT, PATCH.

Table 12-2 shows the RESTful calls for the Spring application. You are going to use and extend the DocumentService and create the DocumentController class. Your base URI will be http://localhost:8080/mydocuments/<PATH>.

Table 12-2. *My Documents RESTful Design Over HTTP (http://localhost:8080/ch12/mydocuments/) - DocumentController*

HTTP Method	PATH	Description	DocumentController Method Call
GET	/documents	Gets all the documents in the repository	getDocuments
GET	/documents/**{id}**	Finds a document, providing the ID	findDocument
POST	/documents	Creates a new document, will accept a Json format document	addDocument
PUT	/documents/**{id}**	Updates an existing document, passing an ID and a Json format document	updateDocument
DELETE	/documents/**{id}**	Deletes an existing document, passing an ID	removeDocument

Let's review the classes that will be refactored and modified by starting with the DocumentService class in Listing 12-1.

Listing 12-1. DocumentService.java

```java
package com.apress.isf.java.service;

import java.util.List;

import com.apress.isf.java.model.Document;

public interface DocumentService {
        public List<Document> getAllDocuments();
        public Document findDocumentById(String id);
        public Document saveDocument(String id, Document document);
        public Document removeDocumentById(String id);
        public boolean updateLocationFromDocumentId(String documentId, String location);
}
```

In Listing 12-1, you added some new methods to the DocumentService class. This class exposes an entire CRUD (Create-Read-Update-Delete) of the documents. You also added the saveDocument method that you use to insert or update a document; you added a getAllDocuments method that will get all the documents available, you added the removeDocumentById that will delete a document. Next, Listing 12-2 shows the implementation of the DocumentService class.

Listing 12-2. DocumentServiceFacade.java

```java
package com.apress.isf.spring.service;

import java.util.List;

import org.springframework.beans.factory.annotation.Autowired;
import org.springframework.stereotype.Component;

import com.apress.isf.java.model.Document;
import com.apress.isf.java.service.DocumentService;
import com.apress.isf.spring.data.DocumentDAO;

@Component("documentFacade")
public class DocumetServiceFacade implements DocumentService {

        @Autowired
        DocumentDAO documentDAO;

        public List<Document> getAllDocuments(){
                return documentDAO.getAll();
        }

        public Document saveDocument(String id, Document document) {
                return documentDAO.save(id, document);
        }

        public Document removeDocumentById(String id) {
                return documentDAO.removeById(id);
        }

        public Document findDocumentById(String id){
                return documentDAO.findById(id);
        }

        public boolean updateLocationFromDocumentId(String documentId, String location) {
                Document document = documentDAO.findById(documentId);
                if(null == document)
                        return false;
                document.setLocation(location);
                saveDocument(documentId, document);
                return true;
        }

}
```

Listing 12-2 shows the DocumentServiceFacade class. This class is using the DocumentDAO implementation that takes care of persistence because it has direct access to the database. Listing 12-3 shows the DocumentDAO implementation class that needs to be modified as well.

Listing 12-3. DocumentRepository.java

```java
package com.apress.isf.spring.data;

import java.util.Date;
import java.util.List;
import java.util.Map;

import javax.annotation.Resource;
import javax.sql.DataSource;

import org.springframework.beans.factory.annotation.Autowired;
import org.springframework.dao.EmptyResultDataAccessException;
import org.springframework.jdbc.core.JdbcTemplate;
import org.springframework.stereotype.Repository;

import com.apress.isf.java.model.Document;

@Repository("documentDAO")
public class DocumentRepository implements DocumentDAO {

        @Autowired
        private DataSource dataSource;

        @Resource
        private Map<String,String> sql;

        public List<Document> getAll() {
                return new JdbcTemplate(dataSource).query(sql.get("query"),
                                new DocumentRowMapper());
        }

        public Document findById(String id) {
                Document document = null;
                JdbcTemplate template = new JdbcTemplate(dataSource);

                try {
                        document = template.queryForObject(sql.get("find"),
                                        new Object[] { id },
                                        new DocumentRowMapper());
                } catch (EmptyResultDataAccessException ex) {}
                return document;
        }

        public Document save(String id, Document document) {
                try {
                        JdbcTemplate template = new JdbcTemplate(dataSource);
                        Document _document = findById(id);
```

```
                if (null == _document)
                        template.update(
                                     sql.get("insert"),
                                     new Object[] { id,
                                             document.getName(), document.getLocation(),
                                             document.getDescription(),
                                             document.getType().getTypeId(),
                                             document.getCreated(), document.getModified() });
                else{
    _document.setName((null==document.getName())?_document.getName():document.getName());
    _document.setLocation((null==document.getLocation())?_document.getLocation():document.
    getLocation());
    _document.setDescription((null==document.getDescription())?_document.
    getDescription():document.getDescription());
    _document.setType((null==document.getType())?_document.getType():document.getType());
    _document.setModified(new Date());
                        template.update(
                                     sql.get("update"),
                                     new Object[] { _document.getName(),
                                             _document.getLocation(),
                                             _document.getDescription(),
                                             _document.getType().getTypeId(), new
                                             Date(),
                                             id });
                        document = _document;
                }
        } catch (Exception ex) {
                ex.printStackTrace();
        }

        return document;
}

public Document removeById(String id){
        Document document = findById(id);
        if(null != document){
                try{
                        JdbcTemplate template = new JdbcTemplate(dataSource);
                        int rows  = template.update(sql.get("delete"), new Object[] { id});
                        if(rows <= 0)
                                document = null;
                }catch (Exception ex) {
                        ex.printStackTrace();
                }
        }
        return document;
    }
}
```

Listing 12-3 shows the DocumentRespository class, which implements the DocumentDAO interface. Before you had only three defined methods in the DocumentDAO interface, and its implementation had very specific properties to hold each SQL statement. Now you modified it by adding the removeById method, adding a map that will now hold the SQL statements. Also, you refined the save method because now you are taking care of some null values.

Let's see how the DocumentController will expose those resources over HTTP, as described in Table 12-2. Listing 12-4 shows your DocumentController class.

Listing 12-4. DocumentController.java

```java
package com.apress.isf.spring.web;

import java.util.List;

import org.springframework.beans.factory.annotation.Autowired;
import org.springframework.stereotype.Controller;
import org.springframework.web.bind.annotation.PathVariable;
import org.springframework.web.bind.annotation.RequestBody;
import org.springframework.web.bind.annotation.RequestMapping;
import org.springframework.web.bind.annotation.RequestMethod;
import org.springframework.web.bind.annotation.ResponseBody;

import com.apress.isf.java.model.Document;
import com.apress.isf.java.service.DocumentService;

@Controller
@RequestMapping("/documents")
public class DocumentController {

        @Autowired
        DocumentService documentFacade;

        @RequestMapping(method=RequestMethod.GET)
        public @ResponseBody List<Document> getDocuments(){
                return documentFacade.getAllDocuments();
        }

        @RequestMapping(value="/{id}",method=RequestMethod.GET)
        public @ResponseBody Document findDocument(@PathVariable String id){
                return documentFacade.findDocumentById(id);
        }

        @RequestMapping(method=RequestMethod.POST)
        public @ResponseBody Document addDocument(@RequestBody Document document){
                String id = document.getDocumentId();
                return documentFacade.saveDocument(id,document);
        }

        @RequestMapping(value="/{id}",method=RequestMethod.PUT)
        public @ResponseBody Document updateDocument(
                @RequestBody Document document, @PathVariable String id){
                return documentFacade.saveDocument(id,document);
        }
```

```
        @RequestMapping(value="/{id}",method=RequestMethod.DELETE)
        public @ResponseBody Document removeDocument(@PathVariable String id){
                return documentFacade.removeDocumentById(id);
        }
}
```

Remember Chapter 10? You are doing the same thing here, defining the controller through the different annotations. The Spring Framework MVC extension facilitates the way you expose these resources or web services. The difference now is that you are using the @ResponseBody and @RequestBody annotations. The Spring MVC extension uses JSON (JavaScript Object Notation, a readable text format with key-value pairs) as the default format for the RESTful resources, so @ResponseBody will convert the result in a JSON format and @RequestBody will accept a Content-Type:"application/json" format. Also, you are using the @PathVariable that will match the variable name between curly braces and the name of the parameter within the method call.

Listing 12-5 shows the XML configuration that you will use in the unit test. The web.xml is the same as the one in Chapter 10.

Listing 12-5. WEB-INF/mydocuments-servlet.xml

```xml
<?xml version="1.0" encoding="UTF-8"?>
<beans xmlns="http://www.springframework.org/schema/beans"
  xmlns:xsi="http://www.w3.org/2001/XMLSchema-instance"
  xmlns:context="http://www.springframework.org/schema/context"
  xmlns:jdbc="http://www.springframework.org/schema/jdbc"
  xmlns:mvc="http://www.springframework.org/schema/mvc"
  xmlns:p="http://www.springframework.org/schema/p"
  xsi:schemaLocation="http://www.springframework.org/schema/jdbc http://www.springframework.org/
    schema/jdbc/spring-jdbc-4.0.xsd
    http://www.springframework.org/schema/mvc http://www.springframework.org/schema/mvc/spring-mvc-
    4.0.xsd
    http://www.springframework.org/schema/beans http://www.springframework.org/schema/beans/spring-
    beans.xsd
    http://www.springframework.org/schema/context http://www.springframework.org/schema/context/
    spring-context-4.0.xsd">

<context:component-scan base-package="com.apress.isf.spring"/>
<mvc:annotation-driven />

<mvc:interceptors>
  <bean class="org.springframework.web.servlet.i18n.LocaleChangeInterceptor" p:paramName="lang" />
</mvc:interceptors>

<bean id="messageSource" class="org.springframework.context.support.
  ReloadableResourceBundleMessageSource"
  p:basenames="WEB-INF/i18n/messages" p:fallbackToSystemLocale="false"/>
<bean id="localeResolver" class="org.springframework.web.servlet.i18n.CookieLocaleResolver"
  p:cookieName="locale"/>

<bean class="org.springframework.web.servlet.view.InternalResourceViewResolver">
  <property name="prefix" value="/WEB-INF/views/"/>
  <property name="suffix" value=".jspx"/>
</bean>
```

```xml
<jdbc:embedded-database id="dataSource">
  <jdbc:script location="classpath:/META-INF/data/schema.sql" />
  <jdbc:script location="classpath:/META-INF/data/data.sql" />
</jdbc:embedded-database>

<bean id="sql" class="java.util.HashMap">
  <constructor-arg>
    <map>
      <entry key="query">
        <value>
      select d.documentId, d.name, d.location, d.description as doc_desc,
      d.typeId, d.created, d.modified,
      t.name as type_name, t.description as type_desc, t.extension from
      documents d
      join types t
      on d.typeId = t.typeId
        </value>
      </entry>
      <entry key="find">
        <value>
      select d.documentId, d.name, d.location, d.description as doc_desc,
      d.typeId, d.created, d.modified,
      t.name as type_name, t.description as type_desc, t.extension from
      documents d
      join types t
      on d.typeId = t.typeId
      where d.documentId = ?
        </value>
      </entry>
      <entry key="insert">
        <value>
      insert into documents (documentId,name,location,description, typeId, created, modified)
      values (?,?,?,?,?,?,?)
        </value>
      </entry>
      <entry key="update">
        <value>
      update documents set name = ?, location = ?, description = ?, typeId = ?,modified = ?
      where documentId = ?
        </value>
      </entry>
      <entry key="delete">
        <value>
      delete from documents
      where documentId = ?
        </value>
      </entry>
    </map>
  </constructor-arg>
</bean>
</beans>
```

The only modification you made in the Listing 12-5 was adding the `sql` bean as a `HashMap`. Remember that instead of using individual properties for each SQL statement, now you're going to use a map. Now, you can test the web application. You need to run the following command:

```
gradle :ch12:jettyEclipseRun
```

After you execute the preceding command, you can start testing each RESTful call.

▓ **Note** In Chapter 10 you used the `gradle :ch10:jettyRun` command. But here you are using a more robust plugin for gradle that supports the latest version of the Jetty container. This is the `jettyEclipse` plugin that uses the latest servlet specification, version 3.0. You can find more information about how to define it in the book's source code companion.

HTTP-GET

First, let's go with HTTP-GET for the /documents resource. Figure 12-1 shows the result of executing the `http://localhost:8080/mydocuments/documents` URL. You need to remember that this data is located in the `META-INF/data/` folder and is loaded in memory (using the HSQL) when the server is starting up.

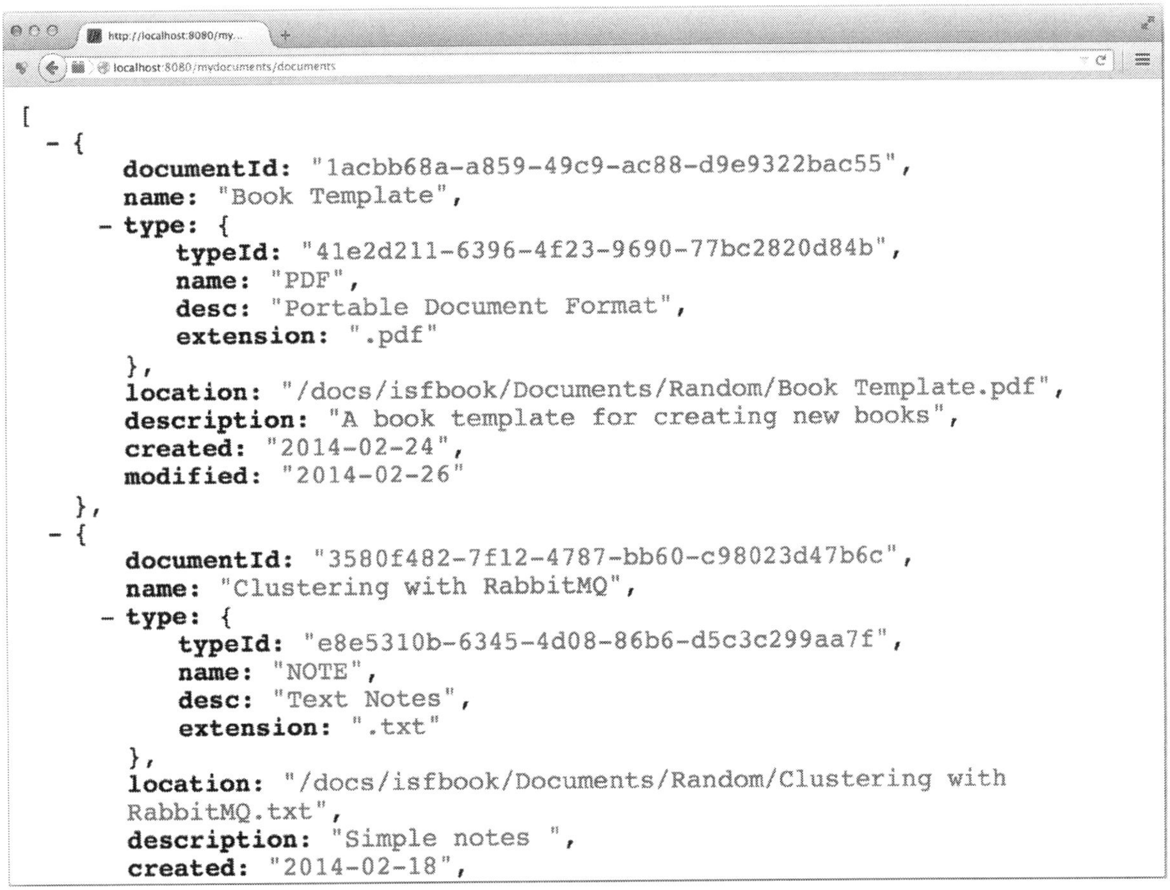

Figure 12-1. Response of the HTTP GET Method from `http://localhost:8080/mydocuments/documents`

Next, find a document. You can use the following ID: 431cddbf-f3c0-4076-8c1c-564e7dce16c9. Go to the browser and use the following URL: http://localhost:8080/mydocuments/documents/431cddbf-f3c0-4076-8c1c-564e7dce16c9. Figure 12-2 shows the result.

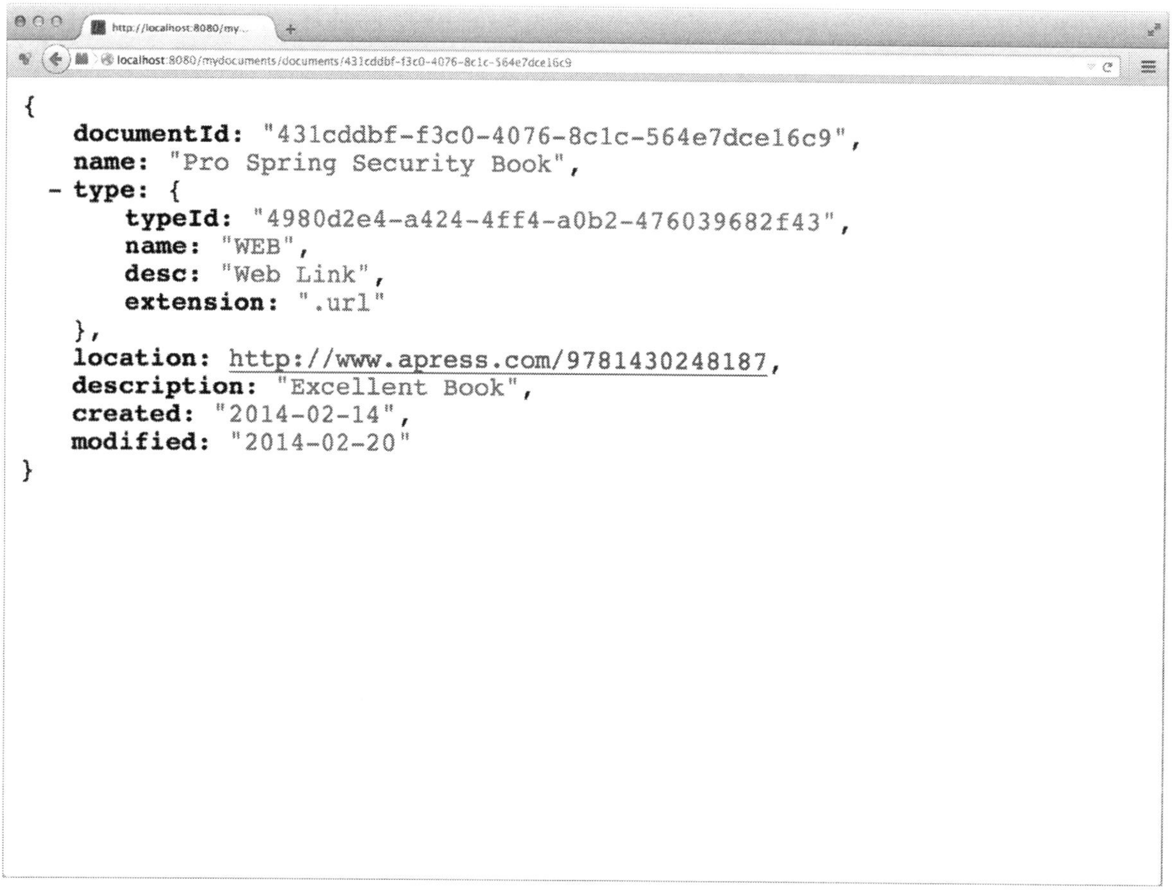

```
{
    documentId: "431cddbf-f3c0-4076-8c1c-564e7dce16c9",
    name: "Pro Spring Security Book",
  - type: {
        typeId: "4980d2e4-a424-4ff4-a0b2-476039682f43",
        name: "WEB",
        desc: "Web Link",
        extension: ".url"
    },
    location: http://www.apress.com/9781430248187,
    description: "Excellent Book",
    created: "2014-02-14",
    modified: "2014-02-20"
}
```

Figure 12-2. *http://localhost:8080/mydocuments/documents/431cddbf-f3c0-4076-8c1c-564e7dce16c9*

HTTP-POST

Next, you need to add a new document. The REST call will use the HTTP-POST method and it is necessary to indicate that you are going to send a Content-Type:"application/json" on the header, and then pass the document as a JSON format. The following JSON can be used as a new document:

```
{
    "documentId": "03b94c89-c4e0-4144-90ce-a64ebaaea8b5",
    "name": "Spring Recipes.pdf",
    "type": {
        "typeId": "41e2d211-6396-4f23-9690-77bc2820d84b",
        "name": "PDF",
        "desc": "Portable Document Format",
        "extension": ".pdf"
    },
```

```
    "location": "/docs/isfbook/Documents/Books/Spring Recepies.pdf",
    "description": "A Spring Recipes from Apress",
    "created": "2014-02-24",
    "modified": "2014-02-26"
}
```

But how can you post this data? Well, there are different ways. One is using the CURL command line, like so:

```
curl -X POST -H "Content-Type: application/json" -d '{"documentId": "03b94c89-c4e0-4144-90ce-
a64ebaaea8b5","name":e": {"typeId": "41e2d211-6396-4f23-9690-77bc2820d84b","name": "PDF","desc":
"Portable Document Format","extension": ".pdf"},"location": "/docs/isfbook/Documents/Books/Spring
recipes.pdf","description": "A Spring recipes from Apress","created": "2014-02-24","modified":
"2014-02-26"}' http://localhost:8080/mydocuments/documents
```

Another way is using an add-on from Firefox or any other browser that can do RESTful calls. Figure 12-3 shows the RESTClient add-on for Firefox and how to add a new document using the HTTP-POST method.

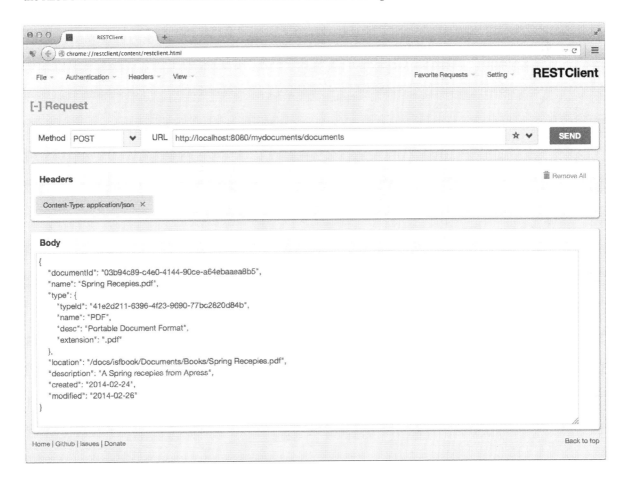

Figure 12-3. *RESTClient*

Once you press the Send button, it will POST your JSON document and it will insert it into the database. Regardless of which method you choose to POST the document, you can test it using the same method as Figure 12-1.

HTTP-PUT

Next, let's use the HTTP-PUT method to update a record. Again, you can use the CURL or the RESTClient add-on. Figure 12-4 shows the use of the RESTClient. Remember that for this you need to pass the ID and the JSON document.

```
ID: 1acbb68a-a859-49c9-ac88-d9e9322bac55
{
    "name": "Book Template 2.pdf",
    "location": "/docs/isfbook/Documents/Random/Book Template 2.pdf",
    "description": "A Book Template version 2"
}
```

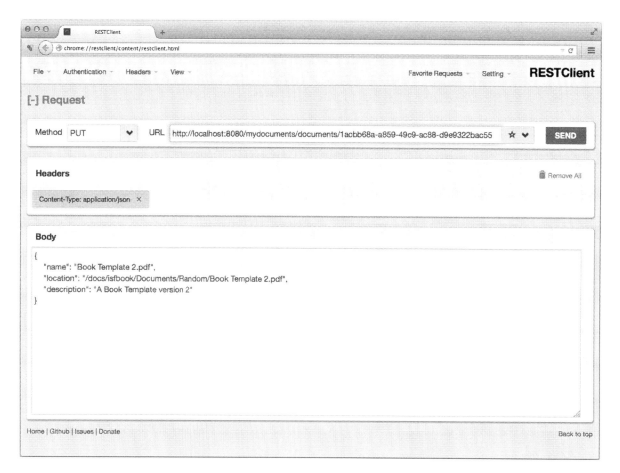

Figure 12-4. *RESTClient - http://localhost:8080/mydocuments/documents/1acbb68a-a859-49c9-ac88-d9e9322bac55*

After you press the Send button, you can test if it works by doing the same as Figure 12-2 and passing the ID 1acbb68a-a859-49c9-ac88-d9e9322bac55.

HTTP-DELETE

Lastly, you are going to test the HTTP-DELETE method, and for this you are going to need the ID. You can use the previous ID, 1acbb68a-a859-49c9-ac88-d9e9322bac55. And again you can use either the CURL command or the RESTClient add-on. Figure 12-5 shows the RESTClient.

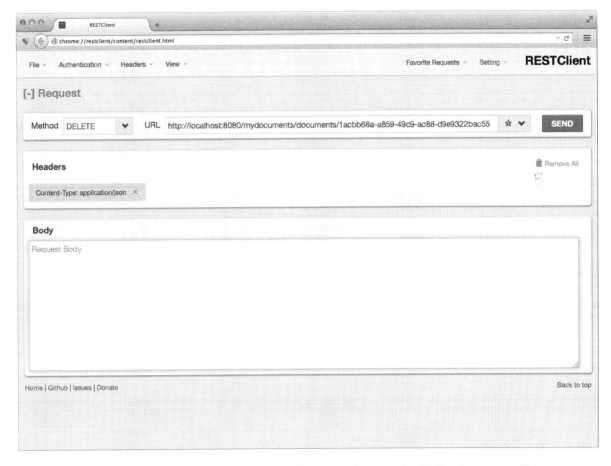

Figure 12-5. *HTTP-DELETE - http://localhost:8080/mydocuments/documents/1acbb68a-a859-49c9-ac88-d9e9322bac55*

If you execute the HTTP-GET method at `http://localhost:8080/mydocuments/documents`, you will see that the document with ID 1acbb68a-a859-49c9-ac88-d9e9322bac55 was removed.

Summary

In this chapter, you exposed some RESTful calls from your Spring application. You created the controller to expose some of the most common RESTful calls, and you learned how easy it is to use the Spring MVC module to expose these web services.

In the next chapter, you will add more services to your Spring application. You will add an e-mail service and schedule some tasks that will help you to check out if the data is accurate.

CHAPTER 13

■ ■ ■

Adding E-mail and Scheduling Tasks

In this chapter, you are going to incorporate new features into your Spring application. Let's imagine that you have some users that like your **My Documents** application and they want to subscribe to an e-mail to receive the latest documents that are inserted. Let's also add some logic that verifies the location of all of the documents (remember that the location is a physical path where the document's type is a note or PDF and the location for a book type is a URL); if the location is wrong or unavailable, the application will alert you to take some action about it.

Let's start by creating your first e-mail example code.

Sending E-mails

The Spring Framework provides some libraries for sending e-mails in a very easy way. Listing 13-1 is an EmailService class that just contains a send method. This method will have four parameters: *from* (the e-mail address where the e-mail is being sent from), *to* (the recipient's e-mail), *subject* (the e-mail's subject), and the *message* (the e-mail's message).

Listing 13-1. EmailService.java

```
package com.apress.isf.spring.email;

import org.springframework.beans.factory.annotation.Autowired;
import org.springframework.mail.MailSender;
import org.springframework.mail.SimpleMailMessage;
import org.springframework.stereotype.Service;

@Service
public class EmailService {

    @Autowired
    private MailSender mailSender;

    public void send(String from, String to, String subject, String message) {
        sendEmail(from,to,subject,message);
    }

    private void sendEmail(String from, String to, String subject, String message){
        SimpleMailMessage mailMessage = new SimpleMailMessage();
        mailMessage.setFrom(from);
        mailMessage.setTo(to);
```

```
                mailMessage.setSubject(subject);
                mailMessage.setText(message);
                mailSender.send(mailMessage);
        }
}
```

Listing 13-1 shows a `MailSender` and a `SimpleMailMessage` class; these helpers will send an e-mail passing the To recipients, the subject, and the message. So easy! Now you need to tell the Spring container what credentials you are going to use in order to send an e-mail. You can use any external e-mail account like Hotmail, Gmail, or Yahoo. This example will use the Gmail settings. See Listing 13-2 for the XML configuration.

Listing 13-2. mydocuments-context.xml

```xml
<?xml version="1.0" encoding="UTF-8"?>
<beans xmlns="http://www.springframework.org/schema/beans"
       xmlns:xsi="http://www.w3.org/2001/XMLSchema-instance"
       xmlns:context="http://www.springframework.org/schema/context"
       xmlns:task=http://www.springframework.org/schema/task
       xmlns:jdbc="http://www.springframework.org/schema/jdbc"
       xsi:schemaLocation="http://www.springframework.org/schema/task http://www.springframework.
       org/schema/task/spring-task-4.0.xsd
               http://www.springframework.org/schema/jdbc http://www.springframework.org/schema/
               jdbc/spring-jdbc-4.0.xsd
               http://www.springframework.org/schema/beans http://www.springframework.org/schema/
               beans/spring-beans.xsd
               http://www.springframework.org/schema/context

        <context:component-scan base-package="com.apress.isf.spring" />

        <context:property-placeholder location="email.properties" />

        <!-- EMAIL -->
        <bean id="email" class="org.springframework.mail.javamail.JavaMailSenderImpl">
                <property name="host" value="${email.host}" />
                <property name="port" value="${email.port}" />
                <property name="username" value="${email.username}" />
                <property name="password" value="${email.password}" />

                <property name="javaMailProperties">
                        <props>
                                <prop key="mail.smtp.auth">true</prop>
                                <prop key="mail.smtp.starttls.enable">true</prop>
                        </props>
                </property>
        </bean>

        <!-- Omitted JDBC and Queries -->
</beans>
```

Listing 13-2 shows your XML configuration. As you can see, you are using the property placeholder to read the `email.properties` file. Also, you are creating a `mailSender` bean that references the `org.springframework.mail.javamail.JavaMailSenderImpl` class. This class is the Spring's e-mail helper class and it has several setters like host, port, username, password, and a `javaMailProperties`. You are setting these property values by putting in placeholders. Listing 13-3 shows the e-mail properties file.

Listing 13-3. email.properties

```
email.host=smtp.gmail.com
email.port=587
email.username=username
email.password=password
```

■ **Note** If you are using a different e-mail provider such as Hotmail or Yahoo, you can check out their help pages to find servers, ports, and more advance settings so you can configure the properties file and the `javaMailProperties` setters accordingly.

Now let's see Listing 13-4, the unit test. You are going to add some time measurement to see how long it will take to send an e-mail. Why? This is because the `JavaMailSenderImpl` has a synchronous call for sending a message to the server, meaning it must wait until the server accepts and responds that the e-mail was successfully sent.

Listing 13-4. MyDocumentsTest.java

```java
package com.apress.isf.spring.test;

import static org.junit.Assert.assertNotNull;

import java.util.Date;

import org.junit.Ignore;
import org.junit.Test;
import org.junit.runner.RunWith;
import org.slf4j.Logger;
import org.slf4j.LoggerFactory;
import org.springframework.beans.factory.annotation.Autowired;
import org.springframework.test.context.ContextConfiguration;
import org.springframework.test.context.junit4.SpringJUnit4ClassRunner;

import com.apress.isf.spring.email.EmailService;

@RunWith(SpringJUnit4ClassRunner.class)
@ContextConfiguration("classpath:META-INF/spring/mydocuments-context.xml")
public class MyDocumentsTest {
        private static final Logger log = LoggerFactory.getLogger(MyDocumentsTest.class);

        @Autowired
        EmailService email;
```

```
        @Test
        public void testEmail() throws InterruptedException{
                log.debug("Testing Email...");
                assertNotNull(email);

                long start = new Date().getTime();
                email.send("user@gmail.com", "user@gmail.com", "New Document Add",
                                    "A new document was added to the collection.");
                long end = new Date().getTime();
                long time = (end - start)/1000;
                log.debug("Sending email done. Took: " + time + " seconds.");
        }

}
```

Listing 13-4 shows the start and end time that will be use to calculate how long it takes to send an e-mail to the server. After running the unit test with

gradle :ch13:test

you should see something similar to the following output:

```
2014-03-19 21:29:28,567 DEBUG [main] Testing Email...
2014-03-19 21:29:38,147 DEBUG [main] Sending email done. Took: 10 seconds.
```

■ **Note**   If by some reason you get some errors, review the server, port, password, and other e-mail settings that go with your e-mail server provider.

You have just sent an e-mail and it took 10 seconds (in this example) to do so. Now, let's imagine that you have 1,000 subscribers, and they want an e-mail per document, and you have 1,000 documents. It would take forever to send all those e-mails to your subscribers! There must be a better way to do this. Of course the Spring Framework provides some nice features for this. Let's see how in the next section.

Let's Talk About Asynchronous Tasks

The Spring Framework provides an annotation called @Async to call methods asynchronously using the Tasks and Scheduling classes. These classes are a great way to solve the problem of sending many e-mails and waiting too long to get a response for every message sent. Let's review Listing 13-5, the EmailService and its modification.

Listing 13-5. EmailService.java

```
package com.apress.isf.spring.email;

import org.springframework.beans.factory.annotation.Autowired;
import org.springframework.mail.MailSender;
import org.springframework.mail.SimpleMailMessage;
import org.springframework.scheduling.annotation.Async;
import org.springframework.stereotype.Service;
```

```java
@Service
public class EmailService {

        @Autowired
        private MailSender mailSender;

        public void send(String from, String to, String subject, String message) {
                sendEmail(from,to,subject,message);
        }

        @Async
        public void sendAsync(String from, String to, String subject, String message) {
                sendEmail(from,to,subject,message);
        }

        private void sendEmail(String from, String to, String subject, String message){
                SimpleMailMessage mailMessage = new SimpleMailMessage();
                mailMessage.setFrom(from);
                mailMessage.setTo(to);
                mailMessage.setSubject(subject);
                mailMessage.setText(message);
                mailSender.send(mailMessage);
        }
}
```

Listing 13-5 shows another method named sendAsync, which is actually the same as the send method; the only difference is that it is annotated with the @Async annotation. This will tell the Spring container to treat this method asynchronously when it's called. But how do you tell the Spring container that you are going to use this Async annotation? Take a look at Listing 13-6, which shows the new namespace you are going to use: <task:annotation-drive/>.

Listing 13-6. mydocuments-context.xml

```xml
<?xml version="1.0" encoding="UTF-8"?>
<beans xmlns="http://www.springframework.org/schema/beans"
       xmlns:xsi="http://www.w3.org/2001/XMLSchema-instance"
       xmlns:context="http://www.springframework.org/schema/context"
       xmlns:task=http://www.springframework.org/schema/task
       xmlns:jdbc="http://www.springframework.org/schema/jdbc"
       xsi:schemaLocation="❶
               http://www.springframework.org/schema/jdbc http://www.springframework.org/schema/
               jdbc/spring-jdbc-4.0.xsd
               http://www.springframework.org/schema/beans http://www.springframework.org/schema/
               beans/spring-beans.xsd
               http://www.springframework.org/schema/context http://www.springframework.org/schema/
               context/spring-context-4.0.xsd">

        <context:component-scan base-package="com.apress.isf.spring" />
        <context:property-placeholder location="email.properties" />

        <!-- Task Scheduling -->
        <task:annotation-driven/>
```

```xml
        <!-- EMAIL -->
        <bean id="mailSender" class="org.springframework.mail.javamail.JavaMailSenderImpl">
                <property name="host" value="${email.host}" />
                <property name="port" value="${email.port}" />
                <property name="username" value="${email.username}" />
                <property name="password" value="${email.password}" />

                <property name="javaMailProperties">
                        <props>
                                <prop key="mail.smtp.auth">true</prop>
                                <prop key="mail.smtp.starttls.enable">true</prop>
                        </props>
                </property>
        </bean>

        <!-- Omitted the JDBC and Queries -->
</beans>
```

Listing 13-6 shows that adding the `<task:annotation-driven/>` tag will let the container know when a method call will be asynchronous because it will have the @Async annotation on it. Listing 13-7 contains the unit test; let's see how long it will take to send the e-mail.

Listing 13-7. MyDocumentsTest.java

```java
package com.apress.isf.spring.test;

import static org.junit.Assert.assertNotNull;

import java.util.Date;

import org.junit.Ignore;
import org.junit.Test;
import org.junit.runner.RunWith;
import org.slf4j.Logger;
import org.slf4j.LoggerFactory;
import org.springframework.beans.factory.annotation.Autowired;
import org.springframework.test.context.ContextConfiguration;
import org.springframework.test.context.junit4.SpringJUnit4ClassRunner;

import com.apress.isf.spring.email.EmailService;

@RunWith(SpringJUnit4ClassRunner.class)
@ContextConfiguration("classpath:META-INF/spring/mydocuments-context.xml")
public class MyDocumentsTest {
        private static final Logger log = LoggerFactory.getLogger(MyDocumentsTest.class);

        @Autowired
        EmailService email;

        @Test
        @Ignore
```

```
    public void testAsyncEmail() throws InterruptedException{
        log.debug("Testing Async Email...");
        assertNotNull(email);
        long start = new Date().getTime();
        email.sendAsync("user@gmail.com", "user@gmail.com", "New Document Add",
                        "A new document was added to the collection.");

        long end = new Date().getTime();
        long time = (end - start)/1000;
        log.debug("Sending Async email done. Took: " + time + " seconds.");
    }

}
```

Running the test with

gradle :ch13:test

you should have the following output:

```
2014-03-19 22:19:33,567 DEBUG [main] Testing Async Email...
2014-03-19 22:19:33,568 DEBUG [main] Sending Async email done. Took: 0 seconds.
```

It returns immediately! Now you can take care of more business logic, and let those heavy tasks run in the background.

Let's Schedule

Another feature you need to add to your Spring application is to periodically check out if any document's location (on the hard drive or on the Web) is still valid. Because you have some web document types, you need to check this often for any broken resource links.

The Spring Framework provides Schedulers classes that can help you with these tasks. Let's create a simple example and see how easy it is to schedule a task every three seconds. Listing 13-8 shows the example.

Listing 13-8. DocumentScheduler.java

```
package com.apress.isf.spring.scheduler;

import org.slf4j.Logger;
import org.slf4j.LoggerFactory;
import org.springframework.scheduling.annotation.Scheduled;
import org.springframework.stereotype.Component;

@Component
public class DocumentScheduler {
    private static Logger log = LoggerFactory.getLogger(DocumentScheduler.class);

    @Scheduled(fixedRate=3000)
    public void sampleCronMethod(){
        log.debug("Running every 3 seconds...");
    }
}
```

Listing 13-8 shows the @Scheduled annotation that takes a parameter called fixedRate, which is a long value in milliseconds. This will make the method sampleCronMethod run every three seconds. To test this class, let's create a small Test method in your unit test class. See Listing 13-9.

Listing 13-9. MyDocumentsTest.java

```java
package com.apress.isf.spring.test;

import org.junit.Test;
import org.junit.runner.RunWith;
import org.slf4j.Logger;
import org.slf4j.LoggerFactory;
import org.springframework.beans.factory.annotation.Autowired;
import org.springframework.test.context.ContextConfiguration;
import org.springframework.test.context.junit4.SpringJUnit4ClassRunner;

@RunWith(SpringJUnit4ClassRunner.class)
@ContextConfiguration("classpath:META-INF/spring/mydocuments-context.xml")
public class MyDocumentsTest {
        private static final Logger log = LoggerFactory.getLogger(MyDocumentsTest.class);

        @Test
        public void testScheduler() throws InterruptedException{
                Thread.sleep(45000);
        }

}
```

The output of running Listing 13-9 should be the following:

```
2014-03-19 22:06:33,030 DEBUG [pool-1-thread-1] Running every 3 seconds...
2014-03-19 22:06:36,000 DEBUG [pool-1-thread-1] Running every 3 seconds...
2014-03-19 22:06:39,001 DEBUG [pool-1-thread-1] Running every 3 seconds...
2014-03-19 22:06:42,000 DEBUG [pool-1-thread-1] Running every 3 seconds...
2014-03-19 22:06:45,001 DEBUG [pool-1-thread-1] Running every 3 seconds...
2014-03-19 22:06:48,000 DEBUG [pool-1-thread-1] Running every 3 seconds...
2014-03-19 22:06:51,000 DEBUG [pool-1-thread-1] Running every 3 seconds...
2014-03-19 22:06:54,000 DEBUG [pool-1-thread-1] Running every 3 seconds...
2014-03-19 22:06:57,001 DEBUG [pool-1-thread-1] Running every 3 seconds...
```

Now you know what to do for scheduling the logic to validate the document's location, right? Yes! You use the @Scheduled annotation in a method that runs every 2 hours perhaps to validate the location. But what happens if you need more granularity? In other words, what happens if you need to schedule this validation logic every Monday, every two months? Thanks to the Spring scheduling classes, the @Scheduled also can accept "cron-tab" expressions. (The cron is a tool used in Unix to execute commands periodically at specified date/time intervals). Listing 13-10 shows the final DocumentScheduler class.

Listing 13-10. DocumentScheduler.java

```java
package com.apress.isf.spring.scheduler;

import java.io.IOException;
import java.net.HttpURLConnection;
import java.net.URL;
import java.util.List;

import org.slf4j.Logger;
import org.slf4j.LoggerFactory;
import org.springframework.beans.factory.annotation.Autowired;
import org.springframework.scheduling.annotation.Scheduled;
import org.springframework.stereotype.Component;

import com.apress.isf.java.model.Document;
import com.apress.isf.java.model.Type;
import com.apress.isf.java.service.DocumentService;

@Component
public class DocumentScheduler {
        private static Logger log = LoggerFactory.getLogger(DocumentScheduler.class);
        private static int HTTP_NOT_FOUND_CODE = 404;
        private static int HTTP_OK_CODE = 200;

        @Autowired
        DocumentService documentService;

        private Type webType = new Type("WEB",".url");

        @Scheduled(cron="*/10 * * * * ?")
        public void urlCheck() throws IOException{
                log.debug("@@ Checking valid WEB type Document's URL...");
                URL url = null;
                HttpURLConnection connection = null;
                int responseCode = 0;
                List<Document> documents = documentService.findByType(webType);
                for(Document document : documents){
                        url = new URL(document.getLocation());
                        connection = (HttpURLConnection)url.openConnection();
                        connection.setRequestMethod("GET");
                            connection.connect();
                            responseCode = connection.getResponseCode();
                            log.debug("Name lookup: " + document.getName());
                            log.debug("Code: " + Integer.toString(responseCode));
                            if(HTTP_OK_CODE ==  responseCode)
                                        log.info("URL is still valid!!");
                            else
                                log.error("URL INVALID! Code: " + HTTP_NOT_FOUND_CODE + ". Please let
                                the Administrator know");
                }
        }

}
```

Listing 13-10 shows the urlCheck method that will run every 10 seconds. This method will get all the documents that are a web type; for every document found, it will use its location to send a request and get a response. If the response is good, it will log "URL is still valid"; if not, it will log "URL INVALID". It uses the java.net.URL class to send the request to the URL (the document's location).

For testing purposes, you are testing the web types; you can modify the code in order to verify that the location of a note, PDF, or any other type of document is still valid. Also, there are very good resources on the cron-tab expressions on the Web if you want to learn more.

You can use the same code in Listing 13-9 (MyDocumentTest.java) and run it with

```
gradle :ch13:test
```

and see results like the following:

```
2014-03-19 22:30:50,005 DEBUG [pool-1-thread-1] @@ Checking valid WEB type Document's URL...
2014-03-19 22:30:50,937 DEBUG [pool-1-thread-1] Name lookup: Pro Spring Security
2014-03-19 22:30:50,937 DEBUG [pool-1-thread-1] Code: 200
2014-03-19 22:30:50,937  INFO [pool-1-thread-1] URL is still valid!!
2014-03-19 22:30:51,717 DEBUG [pool-1-thread-1] Name lookup: Bad Book
2014-03-19 22:30:51,717 DEBUG [pool-1-thread-1] Code: 404
2014-03-19 22:30:51,717 ERROR [pool-1-thread-1] URL INVALID! Code: 404. Please let know the
AdministratorL
2014-03-19 22:30:51,935 DEBUG [pool-1-thread-1] Name lookup: Pro Spring 3
2014-03-19 22:30:51,935 DEBUG [pool-1-thread-1] Code: 200
2014-03-19 22:30:51,935  INFO [pool-1-thread-1] URL is still valid!!
```

Using the book's companion source code, you can find the data.sql. There are some new records that contain bad data. Those records are being checked by the document scheduler every 10 seconds.

Summary

In this chapter, you saw that sending e-mail is easy with the Spring Framework e-mail's helper classes. Also, you saw that the @Async annotation helps to call a method asynchronously.

You added a new feature to the Spring application that can validate the Location field and report back if it is still valid or not. As you can see, the Spring Framework offers very cool features for every task.

In the next chapter, you'll start using other languages besides Java, and you'll see how they interact with the Spring container.

PART III

Spring Framework Advanced

In Part III, you will learn about more advanced features via the newest technologies; you'll see how the Spring Framework makes it easy to develop and integrate your applications with them. You will also learn how to use dynamic languages and extensions such as Spring Data, Spring Social, and Spring AMQP within your Spring application.

You will start using Groovy, Ruby, and the Bean Shell to interact with your Spring application. You'll see how easy it is to create dynamic scripts, and you will use the persistence mechanism called NoSQL databases. You are going to use MongoDB and you will see how the Spring Data module will leverage and simplify development.

After that, you are going to learn more about AMQP (by using RabbitMQ). You'll see how to use the Spring AMQP module for sending and receiving messages, and finally you will use the Spring Social module to send tweets from within your Spring application.

■ ■ ■

CHAPTER 14

Using Dynamic Languages

Often you are required to do some business logic as fast as possible, such as a prototype that needs to work or a quick security authorization check or calculating some hash. In this chapter, you are going to see how the use of dynamic languages together with the Spring Framework can help you to do such tasks.

Get More Dynamic

The Spring Framework supports Groovy, JRuby, and BeanShell dynamic languages and you can interact with them like any other bean defined in the container. Remember the Login interface and Login implementation? Let's review them. See Listings 14-1 and 14-2.

Listing 14-1. Login.java

```
package com.apress.isf.java.service;

public interface Login {
        public boolean isAuthorized(String email, String pass);
}
```

Listing 14-1 shows the Login interface with only one method, isAuthorized, which takes two parameters, the e-mail and the password. Listing 14-2 shows its implementation.

Listing 14-2. LoginService.java

```
package com.apress.isf.spring.service;

import com.apress.isf.java.service.Login;

public class LoginService implements Login {

        private String username;
        private String password;

        public String getUsername() {
                return username;
        }

        public void setUsername(String username) {
                this.username = username;
        }
```

```
        public String getPassword() {
                return password;
        }

        public void setPassword(String password) {
                this.password = password;
        }

        public boolean isAuthorized(String email, String pass){
                if(username.equals(email) && password.equals(pass))
                        return true;
                return false;
        }

}
```

Listing 14-2 shows the LoginService implementation of the Login interface. It shows the isAuthorized method implementation, and it only verifies if the e-mail and password are equal to the ones set in the LoginService class.

For this chapter you are going to create a new class, a SecurityServiceFacade that will use the Login implementation. It will help you interact with the dynamic languages. Listing 14-3 shows the SecurityServiceFacade class.

Listing 14-3. SecurityServiceFacade.java

```
package com.apress.isf.spring.service;

import org.slf4j.Logger;
import org.slf4j.LoggerFactory;

import com.apress.isf.java.service.Login;

public class SecurityServiceFacade {
        private Logger log = LoggerFactory.getLogger(SecurityServiceFacade.class);

        private Login login;

        public void setLogin(Login login) {
                this.login = login;
        }

        public boolean areCredentialsValid(String email, String pass){
                log.debug("Validating Credentials > email:" + email + ", pass:" + pass);
                return this.login.isAuthorized(email, pass);
        }
}
```

As you can see, Listing 14-3 has the Login interface ready to be injected by the Spring container.

Doing Something Groovy

Groovy is a dynamic language that sits on top of the Java virtual machine; it has powerful features inspired by Python, Ruby, and Smalltalk. Easy to create DSLs (domain-specific languages) increase the developer's productivity by eliminating all of Java's boilerplate code, and they integrate very well with existing Java libraries. In other words, Groovy is Java! But don't worry about it too much, Groovy has almost a zero learning curve. You have seen it in action in Chapter 1, and you are going to use it in later chapters too.

Now, back to your code. You are not going to use the existing implementation (see Listing 14-2); you are going to use the Groovy programming language as the implementation of the `Login` interface class. But how are you going to use a dynamic language for this? Well, because Groovy sits on top of the virtual machine, it will be easy to compile the Groovy class or script and then put it into your classpath so it can be used by your Spring application. But what happens if you need to change or add some more behavior to your Groovy class? First, you need to do the modification and compile it, then you need to re-deploy or change it for the new compiled class. That's a lot of trouble.

That is why the Spring Framework allows for the use of dynamic languages and changing them at runtime without even compiling them. Listing 14-4 shows the Groovy implementation of the `Login` interface.

Listing 14-4. META-INF/scripts/groovylogin.groovy

```groovy
import com.apress.isf.java.service.Login

class GroovyLoginService implements Login {

        String username
        String password

        boolean isAuthorized(String email, String pass) {
                if(username==email && password==pass)
                        return true
                return false
        }
}
```

As you can see, Listing 14-4 is very simple. You got rid of the setters and getters and all the Java clutter. Now let's see how the XML will look in order to use this Groovy script; see Listing 14-5.

Listing 14-5. mydocuments-context.xml

```xml
<?xml version="1.0" encoding="UTF-8"?>
<beans xmlns="http://www.springframework.org/schema/beans"
        xmlns:xsi="http://www.w3.org/2001/XMLSchema-instance"
        xmlns:context="http://www.springframework.org/schema/context"
        xmlns:jdbc="http://www.springframework.org/schema/jdbc"
        xmlns:lang="http://www.springframework.org/schema/lang"
        xsi:schemaLocation="http://www.springframework.org/schema/jdbc
http://www.springframework.org/schema/jdbc/spring-jdbc-4.0.xsd
                http://www.springframework.org/schema/beans
http://www.springframework.org/schema/beans/spring-beans.xsd
                http://www.springframework.org/schema/context
http://www.springframework.org/schema/context/spring-context-4.0.xsd
                http://www.springframework.org/schema/lang
http://www.springframework.org/schema/lang/spring-lang-4.0.xsd">
```

```
        <context:component-scan base-package="com.apress.isf.spring" />

    <lang:groovy id="groovyloginScript"
        refresh-check-delay="5000"
        script-source="classpath:META-INF/scripts/groovylogin.groovy">
      <lang:property name="username" value="john@email.com"/>
      <lang:property name="password" value="doe"/>
    </lang:groovy>

    <bean id="security" class="com.apress.isf.spring.service.SecurityServiceFacade">
      <property name="login" ref=" groovyloginScript "/>
    </bean>

</beans>
```

You can see in Listing 14-5 that you are using a new tag, the <lang:groovy/>namespace. This tag helps the Spring container identify the dynamic language to be used. You pass the path where your script is located with the script-source property, and then you set the refresh rate (if you want to change the script at runtime, it will load it again after 5 seconds) with the refresh-check-delay property. Lastly, you provide the two property values needed (the same as a regular Spring bean).

Also, you define the "security" bean that has a reference to your SecurityServiceFacade class, and you set the login property by referencing the groovyloginScript id. Now let's see Listing 14-6, the unit test.

Listing 14-6. MyDocumentsTest.java

```java
package com.apress.isf.spring.test;

import static org.junit.Assert.assertNotNull;
import static org.junit.Assert.assertTrue;

import org.junit.Ignore;
import org.junit.Test;
import org.junit.runner.RunWith;
import org.slf4j.Logger;
import org.slf4j.LoggerFactory;
import org.springframework.beans.factory.annotation.Autowired;
import org.springframework.test.context.ContextConfiguration;
import org.springframework.test.context.junit4.SpringJUnit4ClassRunner;

import com.apress.isf.spring.service.SecurityServiceFacade;

@RunWith(SpringJUnit4ClassRunner.class)
@ContextConfiguration("classpath:META-INF/spring/mydocuments-context.xml")
public class MyDocumentsTest {
        private static final Logger log = LoggerFactory.getLogger(MyDocumentsTest.class);
        private static String EMAIL = "john@email.com";
        private static String PASSWORD = "doe";

        @Autowired
        SecurityServiceFacade security;
```

```
    @Test
    public void testSecurity(){
            log.debug("Testing Security...");
            assertNotNull(security);

            assertTrue(security.areCredentialsValid(EMAIL,PASSWORD));
    }

}
```

Listing 14-6 shows you that the only assertion here will be just to verify that the credentials are valid by calling the areCredentialsValid method. So, after you run the test (Listing 14-6) with

```
gradle :ch14:test
```

you should see the following output:

```
2014-03-20 00:11:59,835 DEBUG [Test worker] Testing Security...
2014-03-20 00:11:59,854 DEBUG [Test worker] Validating Credentials > email:john@email.com, pass:doe
com.apress.isf.spring.test.MyDocumentsTest > testBeanShell PASSED
```

It worked! Now you know how to use Groovy if you want to implement or add some dynamic business logic to your Spring application. But wait, there's more! The Spring Framework also allows you to add inline scripting in the XML configuration. Listing 14-7 shows that.

Listing 14-7. mydocuments-context.xml

```xml
<?xml version="1.0" encoding="UTF-8"?>
<beans xmlns="http://www.springframework.org/schema/beans"
       xmlns:xsi="http://www.w3.org/2001/XMLSchema-instance"
       xmlns:context="http://www.springframework.org/schema/context"
       xmlns:jdbc="http://www.springframework.org/schema/jdbc"
       xmlns:lang="http://www.springframework.org/schema/lang"
       xsi:schemaLocation="http://www.springframework.org/schema/jdbc
http://www.springframework.org/schema/jdbc/spring-jdbc-4.0.xsd
               http://www.springframework.org/schema/beans
http://www.springframework.org/schema/beans/spring-beans.xsd
               http://www.springframework.org/schema/context
http://www.springframework.org/schema/context/spring-context-4.0.xsd
               http://www.springframework.org/schema/lang
http://www.springframework.org/schema/lang/spring-lang-4.0.xsd">

       <context:component-scan base-package="com.apress.isf.spring" />

<lang:groovy id="groovyloginScript" refresh-check-delay="5000">
    <lang:inline-script>
      import com.apress.isf.java.service.Login

      class GroovyLoginService implements Login {

              String username
              String password
```

```
                boolean isAuthorized(String email, String pass) {
                        if(username==email &amp;&amp; password==pass)
                                return true
                        return false
                }

        }
    </lang:inline-script>
    <lang:property name="username" value="john@email.com"/>
    <lang:property name="password" value="doe"/>
</lang:groovy>

  <bean id="security" class="com.apress.isf.spring.service.SecurityServiceFacade">
    <property name="login" ref=" groovyloginScript "/>
  </bean>

</beans>
```

Listing 14-7 shows you the same Groovy script but now within the XML configuration. If you run the same unit test (see Listing 14-6), you should get the same result:

```
2014-05-18 00:10:59,835 DEBUG [Test worker] Testing Security...
2014-05-18 00:10:59,854 DEBUG [Test worker] Validating Credentials > email:john@email.com, pass:doe
com.apress.isf.spring.test.MyDocumentsTest > testBeanShell PASSED
```

Using JRuby and Bean Shell

Next, let's see how the JRuby and Bean shell works. Listings 14-8 and 14-9 contain the declaration of the other two dynamic languages.

Listing 14-8. mydocuments-context.xml

```
<?xml version="1.0" encoding="UTF-8"?>
<beans xmlns="http://www.springframework.org/schema/beans"
       xmlns:xsi="http://www.w3.org/2001/XMLSchema-instance"
       xmlns:context="http://www.springframework.org/schema/context"
       xmlns:jdbc="http://www.springframework.org/schema/jdbc"
       xmlns:lang="http://www.springframework.org/schema/lang"
       xsi:schemaLocation="http://www.springframework.org/schema/jdbc
http://www.springframework.org/schema/jdbc/spring-jdbc-4.0.xsd
              http://www.springframework.org/schema/beans
http://www.springframework.org/schema/beans/spring-beans.xsd
              http://www.springframework.org/schema/context
http://www.springframework.org/schema/context/spring-context-4.0.xsd
              http://www.springframework.org/schema/lang
http://www.springframework.org/schema/lang/spring-lang-4.0.xsd">

    <context:component-scan base-package="com.apress.isf.spring" />
```

```
<lang:jruby id="jrubyloginScript" script-interfaces="com.apress.isf.java.service.Login">
  <lang:inline-script>
    class GroovyLoginService

        def setUsername(email)
          @username = email
        end
        def setPassword(pass)
          @password = pass
        end

        def isAuthorized(email,pass)
          if @username == email and @password == pass
            return true
          else
            return false
          end
        end
    end
  </lang:inline-script>
  <lang:property name="username" value="john@email.com"/>
  <lang:property name="password" value="doe"/>
</lang:jruby>

<bean id="security" class="com.apress.isf.spring.service.SecurityServiceFacade">
    <property name="login" ref=" jrubyloginScript "/>
  </bean>

</beans>
```

Listing 14-8 shows you the <lang:jruby/>tag; here you are putting Ruby code inline, and it will work the same as the Groovy language. Listing 14-9 shows the Bean Shell language.

Listing 14-9. mydocuments-context.xml

```
<?xml version="1.0" encoding="UTF-8"?>
<beans xmlns="http://www.springframework.org/schema/beans"
       xmlns:xsi="http://www.w3.org/2001/XMLSchema-instance"
       xmlns:context="http://www.springframework.org/schema/context"
       xmlns:jdbc="http://www.springframework.org/schema/jdbc"
       xmlns:lang="http://www.springframework.org/schema/lang"
       xsi:schemaLocation="http://www.springframework.org/schema/jdbc
http://www.springframework.org/schema/jdbc/spring-jdbc-4.0.xsd
            http://www.springframework.org/schema/beans
http://www.springframework.org/schema/beans/spring-beans.xsd
            http://www.springframework.org/schema/context
http://www.springframework.org/schema/context/spring-context-4.0.xsd
            http://www.springframework.org/schema/lang
http://www.springframework.org/schema/lang/spring-lang-4.0.xsd">

        <context:component-scan base-package="com.apress.isf.spring" />
```

```
<lang:bsh id="bshloginScript" script-interfaces="com.apress.isf.java.service.Login">
    <lang:inline-script>
        String username;
        String password;

        void setUsername(String _username){
            username = _username;
        }

        void setPassword(String _password){
            password = _password;
        }

        boolean isAuthorized(String email,String pass){
          if(username.equals(email) &amp;&amp; password.equals(pass))
            return true;
          return false;
        }
    </lang:inline-script>
    <lang:property name="username" value="john@email.com"/>
    <lang:property name="password" value="doe"/>
 </lang:bsh>

 <bean id="security" class="com.apress.isf.spring.service.SecurityServiceFacade">
   <property name="login" ref="bshloginScript"/>
 </bean>
</beans>
```

Listing 14-9 shows the inline Bean Shell script. If you run the same unit test one time for each XML configuration, you will have the same results:

```
2014-05-19 00:12:59,835 DEBUG [Test worker] Testing Security...
2014-05-19 00:12:59,844 DEBUG [Test worker] Validating Credentials > email:john@email.com, pass:doe
com.apress.isf.spring.test.MyDocumentsTest > testBeanShell PASSED
```

Summary

In this chapter, you saw how to use dynamic languages and how they can help you do quick and easy tasks, like creating a Groovy script to validate the URL or to validate the location of your documents in a filesystem (something similar to what you did in Chapter 13). If you want, you can extend this and take advantage of the Groovy or JRuby programming languages by using their own features such as metaprogramming.

In the next chapter, you will use a new persistent mechanism. Instead of using a JDBC with SQL, now you are going to use a new paradigm that has been getting stronger over the past few years: a NoSQL databases. You will use MongoDB.

CHAPTER 15

■ ■ ■

Spring Data Within Your Spring Application

So far your Spring application has some basic features, enough to demonstrate the capabilities of the Spring Framework. But imagine for a moment that you need to add more attributes to the model, maybe something like tags or keywords to the documents. It should be easy enough to add the attributes and modify the DAOs and/or SQL statements, right? For easy attributes, maybe it is, but what happens if you require more complicated relationships or more attributes every week? It would be a tedious job to change it all the time.

Fortunately, there are NoSQL databases, which provide features like adding more attributes to a persistence object without adding or modifying schemas. In this chapter, you are going to add a NoSQL database: MongoDB.

Using NoSQL Databases

MongoDB is a document-oriented database system that makes the integration of data very easy; it persists objects using a JSON-like style and creates collections of this data. Let's add this new feature to your Spring application.

The Spring Framework provides a module for NoSQL databases: Spring Data. Before you continue, you need to make sure you have installed the MongoDB server on your computer. (For more information about how to install MongoDB, see Appendix A.) See Listing 15-1 for the modification of the Document class.

Listing 15-1. Document.java

```
package com.apress.isf.java.model;

import java.util.Date;

import org.springframework.data.annotation.Id;
import org.springframework.data.mongodb.core.mapping.DBRef;

@org.springframework.data.mongodb.core.mapping.Document(collection="docs")
public class Document {
        @Id
        private String documentId;
        private String name;
        @DBRef
        private Type type;
        private String location;
        private String description;
```

```java
    private Date created;
    private Date modified;

    //Constructors Omitted

    public String getDocumentId() {
            return documentId;
    }

    public void setDocumentId(String documentId) {
            this.documentId = documentId;
    }

    public String getName() {
            return name;
    }

    public void setName(String name) {
            this.name = name;
    }

    public Type getType() {
            return type;
    }

    public void setType(Type type) {
            this.type = type;
    }

    public String getLocation() {
            return location;
    }

    public void setLocation(String location) {
            this.location = location;
    }

    public String getDescription() {
            return description;
    }

    public void setDescription(String description) {
            this.description = description;
    }

    public Date getCreated() {
            return created;
    }

    public void setCreated(Date created) {
            this.created = created;
    }
```

```java
    public Date getModified() {
            return modified;
    }

    public void setModified(Date modified) {
            this.modified = modified;
    }

    public String toString(){
            StringBuilder builder = new StringBuilder("Document(");
            builder.append("id: ");
            builder.append(documentId);
            builder.append(", name: ");
            builder.append(name);
            builder.append(", type: ");
            builder.append(type);
            builder.append(", location: ");
            builder.append(location);
            builder.append(", created: ");
            builder.append(created);
            builder.append(", modified: ");
            builder.append(modified);
            builder.append(")");
            return builder.toString();
    }
}
```

Listing 15-1 shows you the modified model, the Document class. It uses three annotations. The @Id that will help to identify the object saved, the @DBRef that will add a reference to another collection (remember that Mongo uses collections for saving objects), and finally the @Document annotation that identifies a domain object to be persisted into a collection.

Listing 15-2 shows you another domain model, the Type class.

Listing 15-2. Type.java

```java
package com.apress.isf.java.model;

import org.springframework.data.annotation.Id;

@org.springframework.data.mongodb.core.mapping.Document(collection="types")
public class Type {

    @Id
    private String typeId;
    private String name;
    private String desc;
    private String extension;

    //Constructors Omitted

    public String getTypeId() {
            return typeId;
    }
```

```java
        public void setTypeId(String typeId) {
                this.typeId = typeId;
        }

        public String getName() {
                return name;
        }

        public void setName(String name) {
                this.name = name;
        }

        public String getDesc() {
                return desc;
        }

        public void setDesc(String desc) {
                this.desc = desc;
        }

        public String getExtension() {
                return extension;
        }

        public void setExtension(String extension) {
                this.extension = extension;
        }

        public String toString(){
                StringBuilder builder = new StringBuilder("Type(");
                builder.append("id: ");
                builder.append(typeId);
                builder.append(", name: ");
                builder.append(name);
                builder.append(", description: ");
                builder.append(desc);
                builder.append(", extension: ");
                builder.append(extension);
                builder.append(")");
                return builder.toString();
        }
}
```

As you can see in Listings 15-1 and 15-2, you are using the annotations @Document, @Id, and the @DBRef; the Spring Data module provides these annotations and it will know what to do to persist the document and its type. Next, take a look at the build.gradle in the book's companion source code to get more detail of what library you are using. Using the @Document annotation, you are telling the Spring Data module that the collection used will be docs and types.

Implementing the DocumentDAO

Now let's implement a DocumentDAO class. This class will have the same behavior as its counterpart (the JDBC implementation). Here you need to implement all the DocumentDAO interface methods (see Listing 15-3).

Listing 15-3. MongoDocumentRepository.java

```java
package com.apress.isf.spring.mongo;

import static org.springframework.data.mongodb.core.query.Criteria.where;
import static org.springframework.data.mongodb.core.query.Query.query;

import java.util.Date;
import java.util.List;

import org.springframework.beans.factory.annotation.Autowired;
import org.springframework.data.mongodb.core.MongoOperations;
import org.springframework.data.mongodb.core.query.Query;
import org.springframework.data.mongodb.core.query.Update;
import org.springframework.stereotype.Repository;

import com.apress.isf.java.model.Document;
import com.apress.isf.spring.data.DocumentDAO;

@Repository("mongoDocumentDAO")
public class MongoDocumentRespository implements DocumentDAO{

        @Autowired
        private MongoOperations mongoTemplate;

        public List<Document> getAll() {
                return mongoTemplate.findAll(Document.class);
        }

        public Document save(String id, Document document) {
                Document _documentUpdate = findById(id);
                if(null==_documentUpdate){
                        mongoTemplate.insert(document);
                }else{
                        Query query = query(where("documentId").is(id));
                        Update update = new Update();
                        update.set("name",null == document.getName() ?
                                        _documentUpdate.getName():document.getName());
                        update.set("location",null == document.getLocation() ?
                                        _documentUpdate.getLocation():document.getLocation());
                        update.set("description",null == document.getDescription() ?
                                        _documentUpdate.getDescription() : document.getDescription());
                        update.set("type",null == document.getType() ?
                                        _documentUpdate.getType() : document.getType());
                        update.set("modified", new Date());
```

```
                        mongoTemplate.updateFirst(query, update, Document.class);
                        document = findById(id);
                }
                return document;
        }

        public Document findById(String id) {
                Query query = query(where("documentId").is(id));
                return mongoTemplate.findOne(query, Document.class);
        }

        public Document removeById(String id) {
                Document document = findById(id);
                if(document!=null)
                        mongoTemplate.remove(document);
                return document;
        }

        public List<Document> findByTypeName(String name) {
                Query query = query(where("documentId.type.name").is(name));
                return mongoTemplate.find(query, Document.class);
        }

}
```

Listing 15-3 shows the DocumentDAO implementation. Now instead of using a jdbcTemplate (like you did in Chapter 9) you are using a mongoTemplate that is an instance of the MongoOperations class. Next is the implementation of the TypeDAO interface, as shown in Listing 15-4.

Listing 15-4. MongoTypeRepository.java

```
package com.apress.isf.spring.mongo;

import static org.springframework.data.mongodb.core.query.Criteria.where;
import static org.springframework.data.mongodb.core.query.Query.query;

import java.util.List;

import org.springframework.beans.factory.annotation.Autowired;
import org.springframework.data.mongodb.core.MongoOperations;
import org.springframework.data.mongodb.core.query.Query;
import org.springframework.stereotype.Repository;

import com.apress.isf.java.model.Type;
import com.apress.isf.spring.data.TypeDAO;

@Repository("mongoTypeDAO")
public class MongoTypeRepository implements TypeDAO {

        @Autowired
        private MongoOperations mongoTemplate;
```

```
        @Override
        public List<Type> getAll() {
                return mongoTemplate.findAll(Type.class);
        }

        @Override
        public Type findById(String id) {
                Query query = query(where("typeId").is(id));
                return mongoTemplate.findOne(query, Type.class);
        }

        @Override
        public Type save(Type type) {
                mongoTemplate.insert(type);
                return type;
        }

}
```

Listings 15-3 and Listing 15-4 show your implementation of the DocumentDAO and TypeDAO interfaces. As you can see, you are using the MongoOperations class. This class is a template that provides functionality to operate with MongoDB. The Spring Data-Mongo provides a set of templates and annotations that help to talk with a MongoDB server, making it easy to interact with it.

Here you don't need to map any class or go row by row. The document will be saved, as is, in a Mongo format, something similar to JSON. Next, let's see the XML configuration, shown in Listing 15-5, and how to interact with the MongoDB server.

Listing 15-5. mydocuments-context.xml

```
<?xml version="1.0" encoding="UTF-8"?>
<beans xmlns="http://www.springframework.org/schema/beans"
       xmlns:xsi="http://www.w3.org/2001/XMLSchema-instance"
       xmlns:context="http://www.springframework.org/schema/context"
       xmlns:mongo="http://www.springframework.org/schema/data/mongo"
       xmlns:jdbc="http://www.springframework.org/schema/jdbc"
       xsi:schemaLocation="http://www.springframework.org/schema/jdbc http://www.springframework.
org/schema/jdbc/spring-jdbc-4.0.xsd
                http://www.springframework.org/schema/beans http://www.springframework.org/schema/
beans/spring-beans.xsd
                http://www.springframework.org/schema/context http://www.springframework.org/schema/
context/spring-context-4.0.xsd
                http://www.springframework.org/schema/data/mongo http://www.springframework.org/
schema/data/mongo/spring-mongo-1.4.xsd">

        <context:component-scan base-package="com.apress.isf.spring" />

  <!-- MongoDB -->
  <mongo:mongo id="mongo" host="127.0.0.1" port="27017" />
  <mongo:db-factory id="mongoDbFactory" dbname="mydocuments" />
```

```
    <bean id="mongoTemplate" class="org.springframework.data.mongodb.core.MongoTemplate">
    <constructor-arg name="mongoDbFactory" ref="mongoDbFactory" />
  </bean>

  <!-- JDBC Omitted -->

</beans>
```

Listing 15-5 shows the XML configuration file and the use of a new <xmlns:mongo/>namespace. This tag tells the Spring Data module how to connect to the MongoDB server and what database to use, in this case mydocuments. Now you need to start testing your application.

Testing MongoDB

You are going to start testing the new DocumentDAO and TypeDAO implementations, so you need to have the MongoDB up and running. See the "Install Mongo DB" section in Appendix A. See Listing 15-6 for the unit test.

Listing 15-6. MyDocumentsTest.java

```java
package com.apress.isf.spring.test;

import static org.junit.Assert.assertEquals;
import static org.junit.Assert.assertNotNull;
import static org.junit.Assert.assertNull;

import java.util.List;

import org.junit.Ignore;
import org.junit.Test;
import org.junit.runner.RunWith;
import org.slf4j.Logger;
import org.slf4j.LoggerFactory;
import org.springframework.beans.factory.annotation.Autowired;
import org.springframework.test.context.ContextConfiguration;
import org.springframework.test.context.junit4.SpringJUnit4ClassRunner;

import com.apress.isf.java.model.Document;
import com.apress.isf.java.model.Type;
import com.apress.isf.java.service.DocumentService;
import com.apress.isf.java.service.TypeService;
import com.apress.isf.spring.data.DocumentDAO;
import com.apress.isf.spring.data.TypeDAO;


@RunWith(SpringJUnit4ClassRunner.class)
@ContextConfiguration("classpath:META-INF/spring/mydocuments-context.xml")
public class MyDocumentsTest {
        private static final Logger log = LoggerFactory.getLogger(MyDocumentsTest.class);
```

```java
@Autowired
DocumentDAO mongoDocumentDAO;
@Autowired
TypeDAO mongoTypeDAO;

@Autowired
DocumentService documentFacade;
@Autowired
TypeService typeFacade;

@Test
public void testMongoDBMigration(){
        log.debug("Testing Spring Data MongoDB - Migration (Run only once)...");
        assertNotNull(mongoDocumentDAO);
        assertNotNull(documentFacade);
        assertNotNull(typeFacade);
        assertNotNull(mongoTypeDAO);

        List<Type> types = typeFacade.getAllDefinedTypes();
        assertNotNull(types);
        assertEquals(4, types.size());

        for(Type type: types){
                mongoTypeDAO.save(type);
        }

        List<Document> documents = documentFacade.getAllDocuments();
        assertNotNull(documents);
        assertEquals(6, documents.size());

        for(Document document : documents){
                mongoDocumentDAO.save(document.getDocumentId(), document);
        }
    }
}
```

Reviewing the logic in your unit test (see Listing 15-6), you are going to start by migrating the JDBC into the MongoDB server; here you are using the two implementations of the DocumentDAO interface. And you are going to begin by adding the types that should be in the types collection, and then the documents that should be in the docs collection. After running the unit test you can open a new terminal (DOS or Unix) and connect to the MongoDB server to see if the data is there.

Figure 15-1 shows the databases and the collections created.

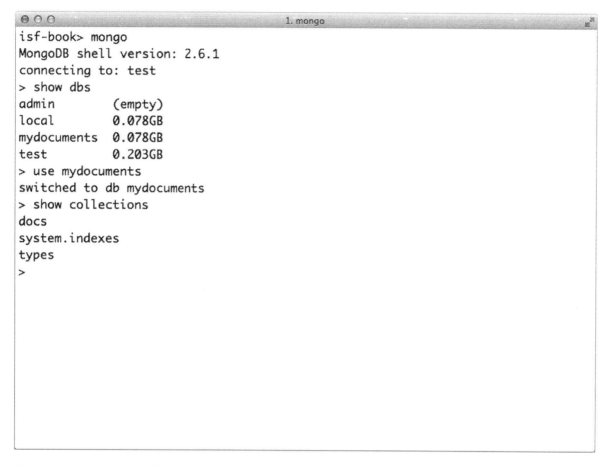

Figure 15-1. *MongoDB Shell Shows the mydocuments Database and the Two Collections, Docs and Types*

Figure 15-1 shows the invocation of the MongoDB server with the command mongo. This command will enter into the MongoDB shell, and by default the MongoDB server will set the test database as a default. To list the available databases, use the show dbs command. In your case, you should have the mydocuments database. To switch to the mydocuments database, use the use mydocuments command. Then you can see the collection that belongs to the database with the show collections command; you should see the docs and the types collections.

Figures 15-2 and 15-3 show the results of the unit test.

```
● ○ ○                              1. mongo                                    ⬚
> db.types.find()
{ "_id" : "41e2d211-6396-4f23-9690-77bc2820d84b", "_class" : "com.apress.isf.java.model.Type"
, "name" : "PDF", "desc" : ".pdf", "extension" : "Portable Document Format" }
{ "_id" : "4980d2e4-a424-4ff4-a0b2-476039682f43", "_class" : "com.apress.isf.java.model.Type"
, "name" : "WEB", "desc" : ".url", "extension" : "Web Link" }
{ "_id" : "c9f1a16d-852d-4132-b4b8-ead20aafc6ef", "_class" : "com.apress.isf.java.model.Type"
, "name" : "WORD", "desc" : ".doc?", "extension" : "Microsoft Word" }
{ "_id" : "e8e5310b-6345-4d08-86b6-d5c3c299aa7f", "_class" : "com.apress.isf.java.model.Type"
, "name" : "NOTE", "desc" : ".txt", "extension" : "Text Notes" }
> █
```

Figure 15-2. *MongoDB Shell Shows the Types Collections*

```
● ○ ○                              1. mongo                                    ⬚
> db.docs.find()
{ "_id" : "1acbb68a-a859-49c9-ac88-d9e9322bac55", "_class" : "com.apress.isf.java.model.Document", "name"
: "Book Template", "location" : "/docs/isfbook/Documents/Random/Book Template.pdf", "description" : "A boo
k template for creating new books", "created" : ISODate("2014-02-24T07:00:00Z"), "modified" : ISODate("201
4-02-26T07:00:00Z"), "type" : DBRef("types", "41e2d211-6396-4f23-9690-77bc2820d84b") }
{ "_id" : "3580f482-7f12-4787-bb60-c98023d47b6c", "_class" : "com.apress.isf.java.model.Document", "name"
: "Clustering with RabbitMQ", "location" : "/docs/isfbook/Documents/Random/Clustering with RabbitMQ.txt",
"description" : "Simple notes ", "created" : ISODate("2014-02-18T07:00:00Z"), "modified" : ISODate("2014-0
2-20T07:00:00Z"), "type" : DBRef("types", "e8e5310b-6345-4d08-86b6-d5c3c299aa7f") }
{ "_id" : "431cddbf-f3c0-4076-8c1c-564e7dce16c9", "_class" : "com.apress.isf.java.model.Document", "name"
: "Pro Spring Security", "location" : "http://www.apress.com/9781430248187", "description" : "Excellent Bo
ok", "created" : ISODate("2014-02-14T07:00:00Z"), "modified" : ISODate("2014-02-20T07:00:00Z"), "type" : D
BRef("types", "4980d2e4-a424-4ff4-a0b2-476039682f43") }
{ "_id" : "65c28c5a-ce8c-4446-84da-9e44e1525bd0", "_class" : "com.apress.isf.java.model.Document", "name"
: "Bad Book", "location" : "http://bad.url.com/bad", "description" : "Bad URL", "created" : ISODate("2014-
02-14T07:00:00Z"), "modified" : ISODate("2014-02-20T07:00:00Z"), "type" : DBRef("types", "4980d2e4-a424-4f
f4-a0b2-476039682f43") }
{ "_id" : "bb633530-20dc-4b46-b320-ff98dc5c3e49", "_class" : "com.apress.isf.java.model.Document", "name"
: "Pro Spring 3", "location" : "http://www.apress.com/9781430241072", "description" : "Spring 3 Book", "cr
eated" : ISODate("2014-02-14T07:00:00Z"), "modified" : ISODate("2014-02-20T07:00:00Z"), "type" : DBRef("ty
pes", "4980d2e4-a424-4ff4-a0b2-476039682f43") }
{ "_id" : "cf7fec3e-55bf-426d-8a6f-2ca752ae34ac", "_class" : "com.apress.isf.java.model.Document", "name"
: "Sample Contract", "location" : "/docs/isfbook/Documents/Contracts/Sample Contract.pdf", "description" :
 "Just a Contract", "created" : ISODate("2014-02-24T07:00:00Z"), "modified" : ISODate("2014-02-28T07:00:00
Z"), "type" : DBRef("types", "41e2d211-6396-4f23-9690-77bc2820d84b") }
> █
```

Figure 15-3. *MongoDB Shell Shows the Docs Collections*

Figure 15-2 shows how you can execute the db.types.find() command in order to see the contents of the types collections. Figure 15-3 shows the contents of the docs collection.

To see the docs collection data, execute the db.docs.find() command as shown in Figure 15-3.

A Complete DocumentDAO Test

Now you can complete the unit test with the rest of the DocumentDAO implementation. Remember that you have just migrated the existing data from JDBC to the MongoDB. So now it's time to test the other methods from the DocumentDAO implementation—that is find, update, and remove from MongoDB. Listing 15-7 shows the completed unit test.

Listing 15-7. MyDocumentsTest.java – Complete

```java
package com.apress.isf.spring.test;

import static org.junit.Assert.assertEquals;
import static org.junit.Assert.assertNotNull;
import static org.junit.Assert.assertNull;

import java.util.List;

import org.junit.Ignore;
import org.junit.Test;
import org.junit.runner.RunWith;
import org.slf4j.Logger;
import org.slf4j.LoggerFactory;
import org.springframework.beans.factory.annotation.Autowired;
import org.springframework.test.context.ContextConfiguration;
import org.springframework.test.context.junit4.SpringJUnit4ClassRunner;

import com.apress.isf.java.model.Document;
import com.apress.isf.java.model.Type;
import com.apress.isf.java.service.DocumentService;
import com.apress.isf.java.service.TypeService;
import com.apress.isf.spring.data.DocumentDAO;
import com.apress.isf.spring.data.TypeDAO;

@RunWith(SpringJUnit4ClassRunner.class)
@ContextConfiguration("classpath:META-INF/spring/mydocuments-context.xml")
public class MyDocumentsTest {
        private static final Logger log = LoggerFactory.getLogger(MyDocumentsTest.class);
        private static final String ID = "1acbb68a-a859-49c9-ac88-d9e9322bac55";
        private static final String NAME = "Book Template";
        private static final String NAME_UPDATED = "My Book";

        @Autowired
        DocumentDAO mongoDocumentDAO;
        @Autowired
        TypeDAO mongoTypeDAO;

        @Autowired
        DocumentService documentFacade;
        @Autowired
        TypeService typeFacade;
```

```java
@Test
@Ignore
public void testMongoDBMigration(){
        log.debug("Testing Spring Data MongoDB - Migration (Run only once)...");
        assertNotNull(mongoDocumentDAO);
        assertNotNull(documentFacade);
        assertNotNull(typeFacade);
        assertNotNull(mongoTypeDAO);

        List<Type> types = typeFacade.getAllDefinedTypes();
        assertNotNull(types);
        assertEquals(4, types.size());

        for(Type type: types){
                mongoTypeDAO.save(type);
        }

        List<Document> documents = documentFacade.getAllDocuments();
        assertNotNull(documents);
        assertEquals(6, documents.size());

        for(Document document : documents){
                mongoDocumentDAO.save(document.getDocumentId(), document);
        }
}

@Test
@Ignore
public void testMongoDBFind(){
        log.debug("Testing Spring Data MongoDB... [ FIND ]");
        assertNotNull(mongoDocumentDAO);
        Document document = mongoDocumentDAO.findById(ID);
        assertNotNull(document);
        assertEquals(NAME,document.getName());
        log.debug(document.toString());
}

@Test
@Ignore
public void testMongoDBUpdate(){
        log.debug("Testing Spring Data MongoDB... [ UPDATE ]");
        assertNotNull(mongoDocumentDAO);
        Document document = new Document(ID,NAME_UPDATED);
        assertNotNull(document);
        Document updatedDocument = mongoDocumentDAO.save(ID, document);
        assertNotNull(updatedDocument);
        log.debug(updatedDocument.toString());
}
```

```
@Test
@Ignore
public void testMongoDBRemove(){
        log.debug("Testing Spring Data MongoDB... [ REMOVE ]");
        assertNotNull(mongoDocumentDAO);
        Document document = mongoDocumentDAO.removeById(ID);
        assertNotNull(document);
        Document removedDocument = mongoDocumentDAO.findById(ID);
        assertNull(removedDocument);
    }
}
```

Listing 15-7 shows the complete list of methods. In some cases, you are using the @Ignore of the unit test to test one by one and see the results on the Mongo shell. Also, you can use the @FixMethodOrder(MethodSorters.NAME_ASCENDING) that you used in previous chapters to keep the order of the execution of the test methods; this is because the unit test doesn't guarantee any order, so maybe you will run into doing a remove before the find method.

Now you can add any other property to your domain model without modifying the rest of the implementation, making this more reliable than drastic changes. For example, you can add an author property or a likes property (for how many likes the document has), and only change your Document class, and the rest of the application will be the same.

Summary

In this chapter, you saw how to use a NoSQL database using the MongoDB and the Spring Data module via the MongoOperations template. The Spring Framework offers more options not only for NoSQL but for graph databases like Neo4J. Of course the JPA (Java Persistence API) is another way to use relational databases.

In the next chapter, you will go deeper into messaging and use even more features of the RabbitMQ broker.

■ ■ ■

CHAPTER 16

Messaging with Your Spring Application

In Chapter 11, you integrated your Spring application with JMS and RabbitMQ servers. In this chapter, I'll talk more about RabbitMQ and the Spring AMQP (Advance Message Queue Protocol) module. Imagine for a moment that you are going to receive a lot of new documents and at some point you will want to classify them by extension.

An easy way to do this classification by extension is to create a RabbitMQ queue. Once the message arrives to the consumer, they get the Type and the Extension, and then based on these two properties, do some processing. Well, that sounds like the right way to do it. But you are going to want to process as many documents as you can, and if you do, this solution might become overwhelming.

So how are you going to solve this problem? The good news is that you can take advantage of a nice set of features from RabbitMQ that differs from other brokers. RabbitMQ provides a routing mechanism for free. I'll explain the RabbitMQ's routing features in the following paragraphs, but first you need to do some coding.

Using RabbitMQ

Let's start by creating the producer that will emulate all the documents that will be sent to you. See Listing 16-1 for the RabbitMQProducer class.

Listing 16-1. RabbitMQProducer.java

```java
package com.apress.isf.spring.amqp;

import org.springframework.amqp.rabbit.core.RabbitTemplate;
import org.springframework.beans.factory.annotation.Autowired;
import org.springframework.stereotype.Component;

import com.apress.isf.java.model.Document;

@Component("rabbitmqProducer")
public class RabbitMQProducer {
        private static final String EXCHANGE = "mydocuments";

        @Autowired
        private RabbitTemplate rabbitTemplate;
```

```
        public void send(Document document){

                rabbitTemplate.convertAndSend(EXCHANGE,document.getType().getExtension(),document);
        }
}
```

Listing 16-1 shows the new producer. You can see that you are using a variable named Exchange with the value of mydocuments, and you are still using the RabbitTemplate, but now you are using a different method to publish the document. If you remember in Chapter 11, I never mentioned any exchange; you used a Message object and you converted the document into an XML format. But wait! What does that exchange do?

RabbitMQ: Exchanges, Bindings, and Queues

Let's review the basic RabbitMQ messaging architecture. RabbitMQ is based on the AMQP (Advance Message Queue Protocol) and it offers *routing* capabilities through exchanges. You can see an exchange as an entry point for the message, and the exchange is in charge of delivering the message to the correct queue based on the routing key provided by the bindings. Figure 16-1 shows the basic architecture based on the direct exchange.

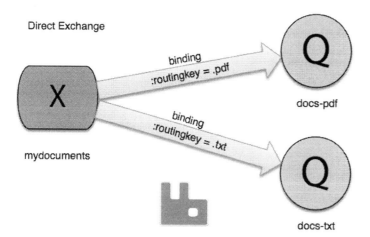

Figure 16-1. *The RabbitMQ Direct Exchange Routes the Messages Based on the Routing Key to the Correct Queue*

As you can see in Figure 16-1, a producer sends a message to the mydocuments exchange; this message has a routing key of either .pdf or .txt. Then, based on the binding, the exchange will put the message in the corresponding queue, either docs-pdf or docs-txt.

RabbitMQ also has Topic, Headers, and Fanout exchanges, and each one offers different routing mechanisms. In Listing 16-1, you are using the convertAndSend method that accepts three parameters. The first parameter is the name of the exchange, in this case, mydocuments; the second parameter is the routing key, in this case the document's extension (either .pdf, .txt, or .url); and the last parameter is the document itself. The convertAndSend method is one of several methods that allows you to publish using the org.springframework.amqp.rabbit.core.RabbitTemplate class. This class is part of the Spring-AQMP extension. You can take a look at the Spring-AMQP extension to explore more about the API at http://docs.spring.io/spring-amqp/docs/latest-ga/api/.

As you can see in Figure 16-1, there is a queue per extension, so you need to create a consumer for every queue; in your case, it will be one consumer for the PDF, one for the text, and one for the web documents. In other words, a consumer will be listening from the docs-pdf queue, another consumer will be listening from the docs-txt queue, and the last consumer will be listening from the docs-web queue. Listings 16-2, 16-3, 16-4, and 16-5 show your consumers.

Listing 16-2. RabbitMQConsumer.java

```
package com.apress.isf.spring.amqp;

import com.apress.isf.java.model.Document;

public interface RabbitMQConsumer{
        public void process(Document document);
}
```

Listing 16-2 shows the RabbitMQConsumer interface; this interface will be the base for your three consumers (remember, one per queue). Next, Listing 16-3 shows the first consumer, the PdfDocumentConsumer class.

Listing 16-3. PdfDocumentsConsumer.java

```
package com.apress.isf.spring.amqp;

import org.slf4j.Logger;
import org.slf4j.LoggerFactory;
import org.springframework.stereotype.Component;

import com.apress.isf.java.model.Document;

@Component("pdfConsumer")
public class PdfDocumentsConsumer implements RabbitMQConsumer{
        private static final Logger log = LoggerFactory.getLogger(PdfDocumentsConsumer.class);

        public void process(Document document) {
                log.debug("PDF Document received: " + document);
        }

}
```

Listing 16-3 shows the consumer that will be listening from the docs-pdf queue. Next, the TextDocumentsConsumer class is shown in Listing 16-4.

Listing 16-4. TextDocumentsConsumer.java

```
package com.apress.isf.spring.amqp;

import org.slf4j.Logger;
import org.slf4j.LoggerFactory;
import org.springframework.stereotype.Component;

import com.apress.isf.java.model.Document;

@Component("textConsumer")
public class TextDocumentsConsumer implements RabbitMQConsumer{
        private static final Logger log = LoggerFactory.getLogger(TextDocumentsConsumer.class);

        public void process(Document document) {
                log.debug("Text Document received: " + document);
        }

}
```

Listing 16-4 shows the consumer that will be listening from the docs-txt queue. Next, the WebDocumentsConsumer class is shown in Listing 16-5.

Listing 16-5. WebDocumentsConsumer.java

```java
package com.apress.isf.spring.amqp;

import org.slf4j.Logger;
import org.slf4j.LoggerFactory;
import org.springframework.stereotype.Component;

import com.apress.isf.java.model.Document;

@Component("webConsumer")
public class WebDocumentsConsumer implements RabbitMQConsumer{
        private static final Logger log = LoggerFactory.getLogger(WebDocumentsConsumer.class);

        public void process(Document document) {
                log.debug("Web Document received: " + document);
        }

}
```

Listing 16-5 shows the consumer that will be listening from the docs-web queue. As you can see, in every consumer you only log the document received. Of course, here you can add more processing; perhaps you need to send an e-mail to your subscribers or maybe you want to create a statistic of how many messages you received from each type. For now just the log will do.

Also, if you look very carefully, every consumer is different from the one you did in Chapter 11. First, you used a Message object, then you needed to convert the body of the message from an array of bytes to String, and then you needed to convert it into an object using the Utils class, remember?

Using a XML Marshaller for Message Conversion

So how is RabbitMQ capable of understanding that you are sending a Document object and converting it into an array of bytes back and forth?

The Spring Framework has some built-in utilities that help you to do this kind of conversion (from object to XML and vice versa) and you are going to use them. You will continue to use the XStream library (http://xstream.codehaus.org/) and now you will be using a Spring Framework Marshaller that will marshal the document into XML and un-marshal when you need to get it from String XML to object.

Let's take a look at the XML configurations, as shown in Listing 16-6. These configurations are the key to the solution.

Listing 16-6. mydocuments-context.xml

```xml
<?xml version="1.0" encoding="UTF-8"?>
<beans xmlns="http://www.springframework.org/schema/beans"
        xmlns:xsi="http://www.w3.org/2001/XMLSchema-instance"
        xmlns:context="http://www.springframework.org/schema/context"
        xmlns:jdbc="http://www.springframework.org/schema/jdbc"
        xmlns:rabbit="http://www.springframework.org/schema/rabbit"
        xmlns:util="http://www.springframework.org/schema/util"
        xsi:schemaLocation="http://www.springframework.org/schema/jdbc
```

```
http://www.springframework.org/schema/jdbc/spring-jdbc-4.0.xsd
                http://www.springframework.org/schema/beans
http://www.springframework.org/schema/beans/spring-beans.xsd
                http://www.springframework.org/schema/context
http://www.springframework.org/schema/context/spring-context-4.0.xsd
                http://www.springframework.org/schema/rabbit
http://www.springframework.org/schema/rabbit/spring-rabbit-1.2.xsd
                http://www.springframework.org/schema/util
http://www.springframework.org/schema/util/spring-util-4.0.xsd">

        <context:component-scan base-package="com.apress.isf.spring" />

  <!-- Import Resources -->
  <import resource="mydocuments-rabbitmq-context.xml"/>
  <import resource="mydocuments-jdbc-context.xml"/>

</beans>
```

As you can see in Listing 16-6, you have split the context into two more resources so you don't clutter your main configuration. It is important to know that at some point you are going to have many beans defined in your XML configurations, and one easy practice will be to separate them to better organize your concerns. In this example, you are separating a file for a RabbitMQ configuration and another for a JDBC.

Listing 16-7 shows the JDBC that you are going to use to send some documents to RabbitMQ using the RabbitMQProducer class.

Listing 16-7. mydocuments-jdbc-context.xml

```
<?xml version="1.0" encoding="UTF-8"?>
<beans xmlns="http://www.springframework.org/schema/beans"
       xmlns:xsi="http://www.w3.org/2001/XMLSchema-instance"
       xmlns:jdbc="http://www.springframework.org/schema/jdbc"
       xsi:schemaLocation="http://www.springframework.org/schema/jdbc
http://www.springframework.org/schema/jdbc/spring-jdbc-4.0.xsd
                http://www.springframework.org/schema/beans
http://www.springframework.org/schema/beans/spring-beans.xsd">

  <!-- JDBC -->
  <jdbc:embedded-database id="dataSource">
    <jdbc:script location="classpath:/META-INF/data/schema.sql" />
    <jdbc:script location="classpath:/META-INF/data/data.sql" />
  </jdbc:embedded-database>

  <bean id="sql" class="java.util.HashMap">
    <constructor-arg>
      <map>
        <entry key="query">
          <value>
            select d.documentId, d.name, d.location, d.description as doc_desc,
            d.typeId, d.created, d.modified,
            t.name as type_name, t.description as type_desc, t.extension from
            documents d
```

```xml
            join types t
            on d.typeId = t.typeId
          </value>
        </entry>
        <entry key="find">
          <value>
            select d.documentId, d.name, d.location, d.description as doc_desc,
            d.typeId, d.created, d.modified,
            t.name as type_name, t.description as type_desc, t.extension from
            documents d
            join types t
            on d.typeId = t.typeId
            where d.documentId = ?
          </value>
        </entry>
        <entry key="type-name">
          <value>
            select d.documentId, d.name, d.location, d.description as doc_desc,
            d.typeId, d.created, d.modified,
            t.name as type_name, t.description as type_desc, t.extension from
            documents d
            join types t
            on d.typeId = t.typeId
            where t.name = ?
          </value>
        </entry>
        <entry key="insert">
          <value>
            insert into documents (documentId,name,location,description, typeId,
            created, modified)
            values (?,?,?,?,?,?,?)
          </value>
        </entry>
        <entry key="update">
          <value>
            update documents set name = ?, location = ?, description = ?, typeId =
            ?,modified = ?
            where documentId = ?
          </value>
        </entry>
        <entry key="delete">
          <value>
            delete from documents
            where documentId = ?
          </value>
        </entry>
      </map>
    </constructor-arg>
  </bean>

</beans>
```

Listing 16-7 shows you the JDBC XML configuration, but why are you using this JDBC if you are going to use the RabbitMQ anyway? Well, you need to have some documents to send, right? So you are going to use the ones either in the in-memory database using JDBC or the documents in the MongoDB server. So let's also see the MongoDB XML configuration in Listing 16-8.

Listing 16-8. mydocuments-mongo-context.xml

```xml
<?xml version="1.0" encoding="UTF-8"?>
<beans xmlns="http://www.springframework.org/schema/beans"
        xmlns:xsi="http://www.w3.org/2001/XMLSchema-instance"
        xmlns:mongo="http://www.springframework.org/schema/data/mongo"
        xsi:schemaLocation="http://www.springframework.org/schema/beans
http://www.springframework.org/schema/beans/spring-beans.xsd
                http://www.springframework.org/schema/data/mongo
http://www.springframework.org/schema/data/mongo/spring-mongo-1.4.xsd">

  <!-- MongoDB -->
  <mongo:mongo id="mongo" host="127.0.0.1" port="27017" />
  <mongo:db-factory id="mongoDbFactory" dbname="mydocuments" />

  <bean id="mongoTemplate" class="org.springframework.data.mongodb.core.MongoTemplate">
    <constructor-arg name="mongoDbFactory" ref="mongoDbFactory" />
  </bean>

</beans>
```

In Listings 16-7 and Listing 16-8, you are going to just take the documents from the in-memory database and the MongoDB server.

Next, let's see the Marshaller bean definition, shown in Listing 16-9. This XML configuration has the beans that will help to convert your documents into XML and vice versa.

Listing 16-9. mydocuments-oxm-context.xml

```xml
<?xml version="1.0" encoding="UTF-8"?>
<beans xmlns="http://www.springframework.org/schema/beans"
        xmlns:xsi="http://www.w3.org/2001/XMLSchema-instance"
        xsi:schemaLocation="http://www.springframework.org/schema/beans
http://www.springframework.org/schema/beans/spring-beans.xsd">

  <!-- OXM -->
  <bean id="xstreamMarshaller" class="org.springframework.oxm.xstream.XStreamMarshaller">
        <property name="aliases">
            <props>
                <prop key="document">com.apress.isf.java.model.Document</prop>
            </props>
        </property>
        <property name="mode" value="1001"/> <!-- XStream.NO_REFERENCES -->
  </bean>
</beans>
```

Listing 16-9 shows the `xstreamMarshaller` bean that is a reference to the Spring's `org.springframework.oxm.xstream.XStreamMarshaller` class that you are going to use as a helper, and it is being imported in the RabbitMQ XML context. You can also see that you are using some features that the XStream library provides, like the aliases, so instead of your XML starting with `<com.apress.isf.java.model.Document />`, it will alias to `<document />`. You can check out the "Alias Tutorial" from the XStream web site at `http://xstream.codehaus.org/alias-tutorial.html`. Also, the book's companion source code includes a unit test of the OXM Marshaller.

Now, let's take a look at the special XML configuration, the RabbitMQ, shown in Listing 16-10.

Listing 16-10. mydocuments-rabbitmq-context.xml

```xml
<?xml version="1.0" encoding="UTF-8"?>
<beans xmlns="http://www.springframework.org/schema/beans"
       xmlns:xsi="http://www.w3.org/2001/XMLSchema-instance"
       xmlns:rabbit="http://www.springframework.org/schema/rabbit"
       xsi:schemaLocation="http://www.springframework.org/schema/beans
http://www.springframework.org/schema/beans/spring-beans.xsd
             http://www.springframework.org/schema/rabbit
http://www.springframework.org/schema/rabbit/spring-rabbit-1.2.xsd">

  <import resource="mydocuments-oxm-context.xml"/>

  <!-- RabbitMQ -->
  <rabbit:connection-factory id="rabbitConnectionFactory"
                             host="localhost"/>

  <rabbit:admin connection-factory="rabbitConnectionFactory"/>

  <!-- RabbitMQ  Template-->
  <rabbit:template id="rabbitTemplate"
   connection-factory="rabbitConnectionFactory"
   message-converter="messageConverter"/>

  <!-RabbitMQ Exchange and Binding Definition -->
  <rabbit:direct-exchange name="mydocuments">
     <rabbit:bindings>
        <rabbit:binding key=".pdf" queue="docs-pdf"/>
        <rabbit:binding key=".txt" queue="docs-txt"/>
        <rabbit:binding key=".url" queue="docs-web"/>
     </rabbit:bindings>
  </rabbit:direct-exchange>

  <!-- RabbitMQ  Queues Definitions-->
  <rabbit:queue name="docs-pdf"/>
  <rabbit:queue name="docs-txt"/>
  <rabbit:queue name="docs-web"/>

  <!-- Listeners -->
  <rabbit:listener-container id="listener" connection-factory="rabbitConnectionFactory">
     <rabbit:listener  ref="pdfAdapter" queues="docs-pdf" />
     <rabbit:listener ref="textAdapter" queues="docs-txt"/>
     <rabbit:listener ref="webAdapter" queues="docs-web"/>
  </rabbit:listener-container>
```

```xml
<!-- Message Listener Adapters -->
<bean id="pdfAdapter" class="org.springframework.amqp.rabbit.listener.adapter.MessageListenerAdapter">
  <constructor-arg name="delegate" ref="pdfConsumer"/>
  <constructor-arg name="messageConverter" ref="messageConverter"/>
  <property name="defaultListenerMethod" value="process"/>
</bean>

<bean id="textAdapter" class="org.springframework.amqp.rabbit.listener.adapter.MessageListenerAdapter">
  <constructor-arg name="delegate" ref="textConsumer"/>
  <constructor-arg name="messageConverter" ref="messageConverter"/>
  <property name="defaultListenerMethod" value="process"/>
</bean>

<bean id="webAdapter" class="org.springframework.amqp.rabbit.listener.adapter.MessageListenerAdapter">
  <constructor-arg name="delegate" ref="webConsumer"/>
  <constructor-arg name="messageConverter" ref="messageConverter"/>
  <property name="defaultListenerMethod" value="process"/>
</bean>

<!-- Message Converter -->
<bean id="messageConverter"
class="org.springframework.amqp.support.converter.MarshallingMessageConverter">
    <constructor-arg ref="xstreamMarshaller"/>
</bean>

</beans>
```

Listing 16-10 shows all the necessary information (like the location of the RabbitMQ server; the name of queues and their bindings with the exchange; the message converter and the consumers) that RabbitMQ needs in order to start sending, converting, and receiving messages. This configuration can be done using the RabbitMQ web console or it can be done programmatically, offering more control depending on certain business rules, but here you are going to use the Spring XML configuration, the declarative way. If you want to see how you can do all of this configuration programmatically, you can take a look at the RabbitMQ reference at http://docs.spring.io/spring-amqp/docs/latest-ga/reference/html/.

This configuration (see Listing 16-10) has several sections; let's take a look at each one of them. Remember that you are using the `<xmlns:rabbit/>` namespace.

<rabbit:connection-factory/>

The `<rabbit:connection-factory/>` tag will create a caching connection to the RabbitMQ broker and you can pass some extra information like username, password, host, vhost, and port.

The `<rabbit:admin/>` tag will create all the necessary exchanges, bindings, and queues, and it is necessary to pass the ID of the connection (`rabbitConnectionFactory`).

<rabbit:template/>

The `<rabbit:template/>` tag is an implementation of the Template pattern, and this will help to send and convert messages to the RabbitMQ broker. You need to specify what connection you are going to use to pass the ID of the `connection-factory` (`rabbitConnectionFactory`) and the converter that you are going to use (`messageConverter`); in this case, it's the Marshaller defined in Listing 16-9.

<rabbit:direct-exchange/> and <rabbit:binding/>

The <rabbit:direct-exchange/> tag defines a direct exchange, passing in the name (in your case mydocuments). By default, the exchange will be durable=true and autoDelete=false. The <rabbit:bindings/> tags are a collection that contains one or more <rabbit:binding/> tag. The <rabbit:binding/> tag defines the bindings that are attached to that exchange—in other words, the rules that the exchange will follow after a message is sent to it. These tags accept the routing key and the name of the queue attributes. Even an exchange can be bound to another exchange!

<rabbit:queue/>

The <rabbit:queue/> tag creates a queue with the name provided; by default the queue has some properties that can be overridden, specifying their attributes. By default, your queues will be durable=true, autoDelete=false, and exclusive=false.

<rabbit:listener-container/> and <rabbit:listener/>

The listeners are your consumers and the <rabbit:listener-container/> tag will create a SimpleMessageListener instance that will point to several adapters that will receive the document. These adapters now are your own implementation of a consumer and they don't depend on implementing the MessageListener as before in Chapter 11. Every adapter points to your classes defined previously; in this case it's your three consumers.

Test the Rabbit

Now let's see the unit test, as shown in Listing 16-11.

Listing 16-11. MyDocumentsTest.java

```
package com.apress.isf.spring.test;

import static org.junit.Assert.assertNotNull;

import org.junit.Test;
import org.junit.runner.RunWith;
import org.slf4j.Logger;
import org.slf4j.LoggerFactory;
import org.springframework.beans.factory.annotation.Autowired;
import org.springframework.test.context.ContextConfiguration;
import org.springframework.test.context.junit4.SpringJUnit4ClassRunner;

import com.apress.isf.java.model.Document;
import com.apress.isf.java.service.DocumentService;
import com.apress.isf.spring.amqp.RabbitMQProducer;

@RunWith(SpringJUnit4ClassRunner.class)
@ContextConfiguration({"classpath:META-INF/spring/mydocuments-context.xml",
"classpath:META-INF/spring/mydocuments-mongo-context.xml"})
public class MyDocumentsTest {
        private static final Logger log = LoggerFactory.getLogger(MyDocumentsTest.class);
```

```
    @Autowired
    RabbitMQProducer rabbitmqProducer;

    @Autowired
    DocumentService documentFacade;

    @Test
    public void testProducer(){
            log.debug("Testing RabbitMQ Producer...");
            assertNotNull(rabbitmqProducer);
            assertNotNull(documentFacade);
            for(Document document : documentFacade.getAllDocuments())
                    rabbitmqProducer.send(document);
    }

    @Test
    public void testJustWait() throws InterruptedException{
            Thread.sleep(5000);
    }
}
```

Listing 16-11 shows the unit test. You are using the same DocumentServiceFacade to pull some documents from the HSQLDB in-memory database; just send them through the RabbitMQProducer class. Also, you can get documents from the MongoDB server (by using the mongoDocumentDAO) and as you can see by the @ContextConfiguration annotation, you can add more XML configurations. Another way is to include or import more bean definitions.

And of course, you need to remember that the RabbitMQ server needs to be up and running, so you can run the unit test (see Listing 16-11 and the "Install RabbitMQ" section in Appendix A).

To run the test, use

```
gradle :ch16:test
```

While running the test, you should see the console and see that your mydocuments exchange and the docs-pdf, docs-txt, and docs-web queues were created as shown in Figures 16-2 and 16-3.

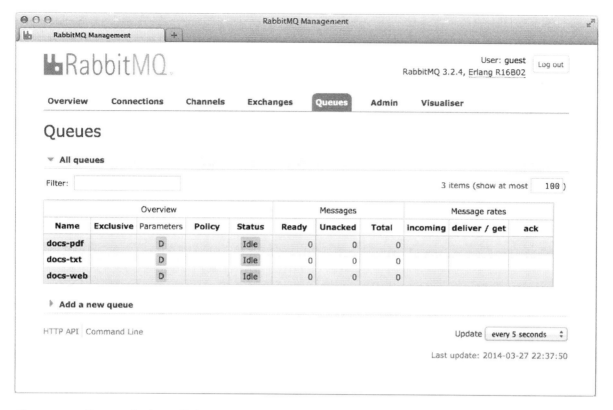

Figure 16-2. *Showing the docs-pdf, docs-txt, docs-web Queues Created Based on the rabbitmq Context File*

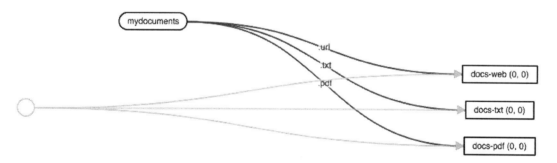

Figure 16-3. *Showing the Bindings Between the mydocuments Exchange and the Queues Showing Each Binding*

Figure 16-2 shows you the RabbitMQ web console (`http://localhost:15672/#/queues`) and how the queues were created based on the XML configuration (see Listing 16-9).

Figure 16-3 shows you the bindings that were created by the XML configuration (see Listing 16-9). Remember that the bindings are the routing keys and you are setting these to match the document's extension.

The result of running Listing 16-11 will be the following output (the documents sent and received by the consumers):

```
2014-03-27 22:46:21,328 DEBUG [main] Testing RabbitMQ Producer...
2014-03-27 22:46:21,539 DEBUG [SimpleAsyncTaskExecutor-1] Web Document received: Document(id:
431cddbf-f3c0-4076-8c1c-564e7dce16c9, name: Pro Spring Security, type: Type(id: 4980d2e4-a424-4ff4-
a0b2-476039682f43, name: WEB, description: Web Link, extension: .url), location:
http://www.apress.com/9781430248187, created: 2014-02-14, modified: 2014-02-20)
2014-03-27 22:46:21,539 DEBUG [SimpleAsyncTaskExecutor-1] Text Document received: Document(id:
3580f482-7f12-4787-bb60-c98023d47b6c, name: Clustering with RabbitMQ, type: Type(id: e8e5310b-6345-
4d08-86b6-d5c3c299aa7f, name: NOTE, description: Text Notes, extension: .txt), location: /docs/
isfbook/Documents/Random/Clustering with RabbitMQ.txt, created: 2014-02-18, modified: 2014-02-20)
2014-03-27 22:46:21,539 DEBUG [SimpleAsyncTaskExecutor-1] PDF Document received: Document(id:
1acbb68a-a859-49c9-ac88-d9e9322bac55, name: Book Template, type: Type(id: 41e2d211-6396-4f23-9690-
77bc2820d84b, name: PDF, description: Portable Document Format, extension: .pdf), location: /docs/
isfbook/Documents/Random/Book Template.pdf, created: 2014-02-24, modified: 2014-02-26)
2014-03-27 22:46:21,607 DEBUG [SimpleAsyncTaskExecutor-1] Web Document received: Document(id:
65c28c5a-ce8c-4446-84da-9e44e1525bd0, name: Bad Book, type: Type(id: 4980d2e4-a424-4ff4-a0b2-
476039682f43, name: WEB, description: Web Link, extension: .url), location:
http://bad.url.com/bad, created: 2014-02-14, modified: 2014-02-20)
2014-03-27 22:46:21,609 DEBUG [SimpleAsyncTaskExecutor-1] Web Document received: Document(id:
bb633530-20dc-4b46-b320-ff98dc5c3e49, name: Pro Spring 3, type: Type(id: 4980d2e4-a424-4ff4-a0b2-
476039682f43, name: WEB, description: Web Link, extension: .url), location:
http://www.apress.com/9781430241072, created: 2014-02-14, modified: 2014-02-20)
2014-03-27 22:46:21,989 DEBUG [SimpleAsyncTaskExecutor-1] PDF Document received: Document(id:
cf7fec3e-55bf-426d-8a6f-2ca752ae34ac, name: Sample Contract, type: Type(id: 41e2d211-6396-4f23-9690-
77bc2820d84b, name: PDF, description: Portable Document Format, extension: .pdf), location: /docs/
isfbook/Documents/Contracts/Sample Contract.pdf, created: 2014-02-24, modified: 2014-02-28)
```

Summary

In this chapter, you saw how the RabbitMQ works in detail, using exchanges, bindings, and queues. Also, you learned about RabbitMQ's routing capabilities and the direct exchange to route based on the routing key to the desired queue, a one-to-one relationship.

You also saw how to configure the Spring container so it can automatically create the exchanges, bindings, and queues in a declarative form. Now you are ready to do any type of messaging within your Spring application, such as adding messaging capabilities for users that only need to receive e-mail about the most recent books. Then you can create a specialized queue called a publish/subscribe scenario so your users can subscribe to it.

In the next chapter, you are going to Tweet messages through the Twitter REST API using the Spring Social module.

■ ■ ■

CHAPTER 17

Be Social and Go Mobile

Nowadays most applications expose some connectivity to social networks like Facebook, Twitter, and LinkedIn in order to allow users to post status messages or to get the latest news. Other applications offer some enhancements like connectivity to DropBox for storage or for sharing pictures and videos to Instagram or Tumblr.

In this chapter, you are going to use Twitter to tweet about new documents that you have created in your repository. But how are you going to do this? The answer is easy. By using Spring, of course!

Using Spring Social

The Spring Framework offers an extension called Spring Social that helps you to connect your applications with SaaS (Software-as-a-Service) API providers like Facebook, Twitter, LinkedIn, GitHub, and Tripit. There are also some community projects that use the Spring Social core module to connect to more of these providers like DropBox, Google, Tumblr, Instagram, and others.

The key features that Spring Social provides are the following:

- Bindings for APIs such as Facebook, Twitter, LinkedIn, Github, and Tripit.

- A simple way to connect a local user account to hosted provider accounts.

- Controllers that help with the authorization and authentication process.

- A high-level API that is easy to use.

So let's start integrating Twitter into your Spring application, **My Documents**.

Spring Social Twitter

Spring Social offers several modules, for example Spring Social Core, Spring Social FaceBook, and Spring Social Twitter. You will be using Spring Social Twitter, which offers an API binding for Twitter's REST API.

In order to interact with the REST API that Twitter offers, first it is necessary to have a Twitter account and then you need to register an application with Twitter. I'm assuming that you already have a Twitter account, so the next section will guide you through registering your application in Twitter. Why is this step necessary? Well, in order to perform actions with the Twitter API like post an update, read posts, getting all your friends' posts, etc., it is necessary to have some access keys to establish a secure and trustworthy communication between your application and Twitter's REST API.

Registering Your Application in Twitter

The following steps are required to register an application to use Twitter's REST API.

1. First, go to `https://apps.twitter.com` (see Figure 17-1) and sign in with your Twitter account (see Figure 17-2). If you don't have an account, you will need to create one.

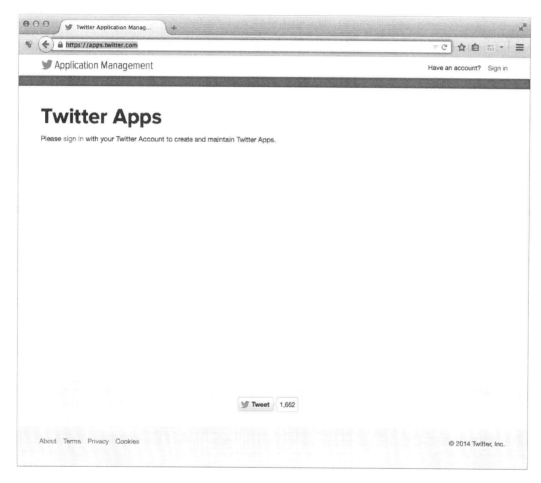

Figure 17-1. *Twitter Apps Web Page (`https://apps.twitter.com`)*

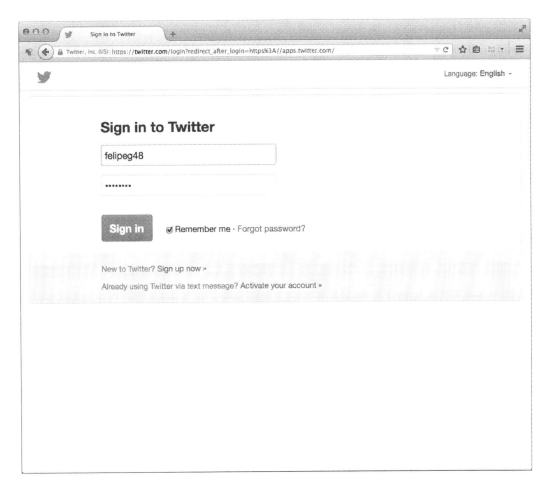

Figure 17-2. *Sign In Using Your Twitter Account*

Figure 17-2 shows the Twitter sign in page. After you sign in, you will see the web page shown in Figure 17-3.

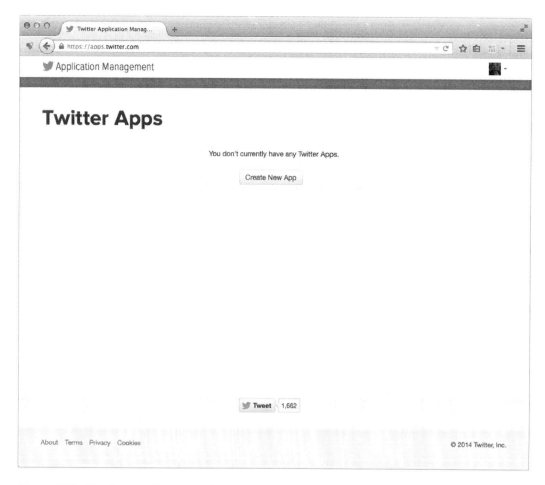

***Figure 17-3.** The Create a New App Web Page*

2. Next, click the "Create New App" button and complete the form with the specified fields. See Figure 17-4.

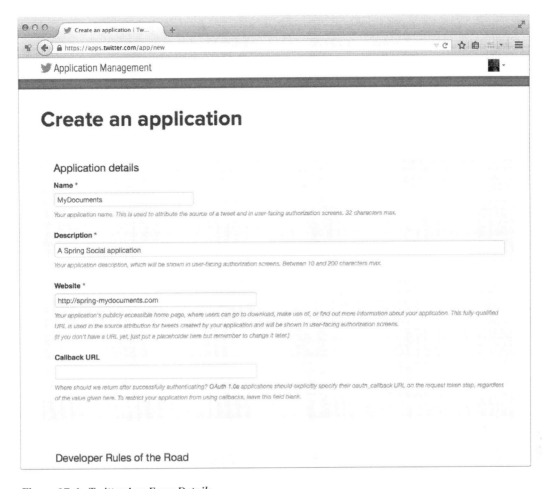

Figure 17-4. *Twitter App Form Details*

In Figure 17-4 you can enter any information you want, but note that the Name, Description, and Website fields are required. You can leave the Callback URL empty since you don't need it right now. You can also change this information later if needed.

3.   Next, on the same form, scroll to the bottom of the page and accept the "Developer Rules of the Road" section by checking the "Yes, I agree" check box. Then click the "Create your Twitter Application" button. See Figure 17-5.

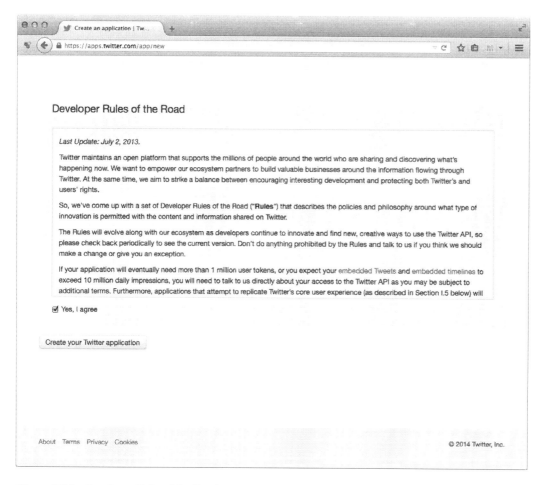

Figure 17-5. *Developer Rules of the Road*

Figure 17-5 shows some terms and conditions for you as developer. After you click the "Create your Twitter application" button, you will see the "My Documents" Twitter application information shown in Figure 17-6.

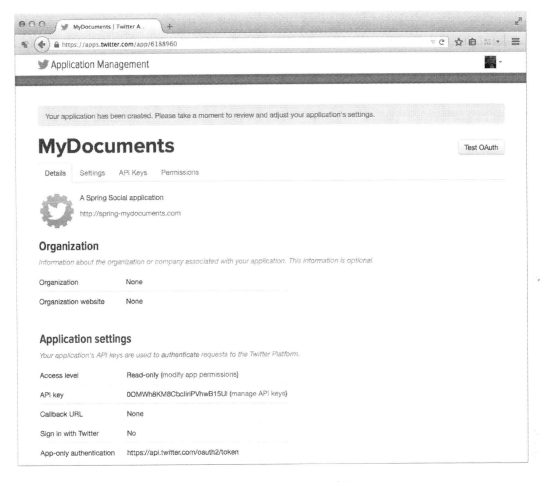

Figure 17-6. *My Documents Twitter Application Information Web Page*

Figure 17-6 shows the details about your application and the different tabs below your application's name.

4. Next, select the API Keys tab (these keys are important because you are going to use them later). See Figure 17-7.

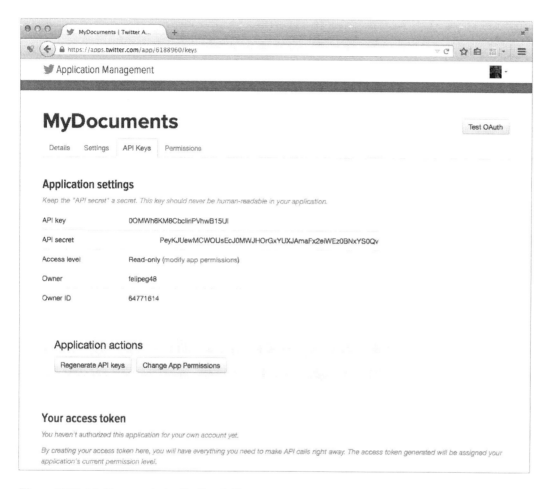

Figure 17-7. *My Documents Application Settings*

Figure 17-7 shows the application settings, like the API keys (which you will use later), the access level, the owner (your Twitter account), the owner ID, and a section where you are going to generate another key, the Access Token key (which you are also going to use later). By default, the access level of your Twitter application is read-only. See Figure 17-8.

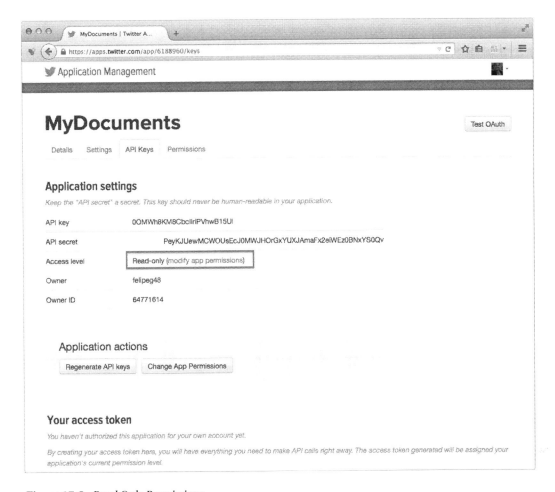

Figure 17-8. *Read Only Permissions*

Figure 18-8 shows in red that you by default have an access level of read-only permissions. You need to change this.

5. Click the "modify app permissions" link. The next screen will show you three options; click the "Read, Write and Access direct messages" option. Then click the "Update settings" button. See Figure 17-9.

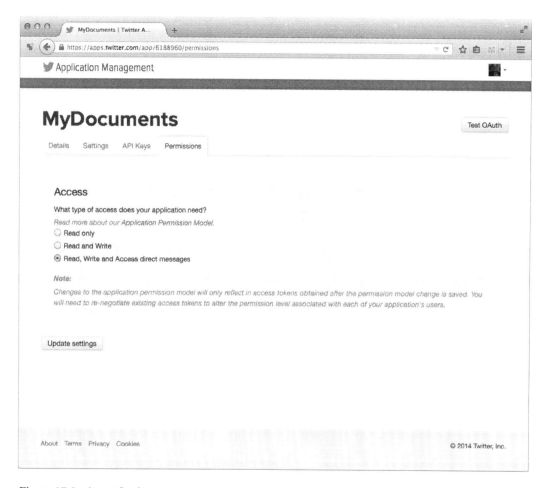

Figure 17-9. *Access Settings*

Figure 17-9 shows three options for the access level. Choose the last one and click the "Update settings" button. After that, you can go back to the previous page and see that your application access level has changed, as shown in Figure 17-10.

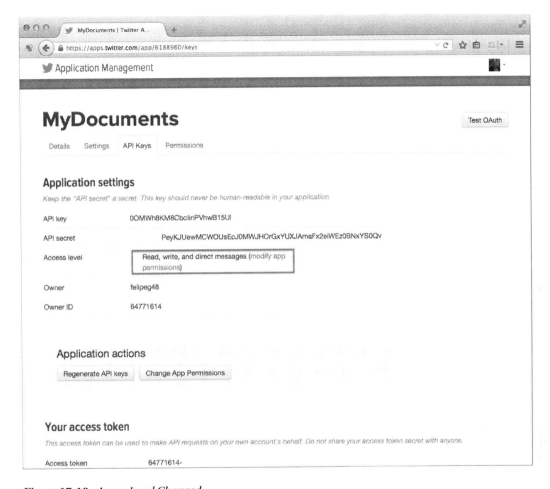

Figure 17-10. *Access Level Changed*

Figure 17-10 shows that the access level was successfully changed.

6. Next, scroll down to the bottom of the page and click the "Create my access token" button. See Figure 17-11.

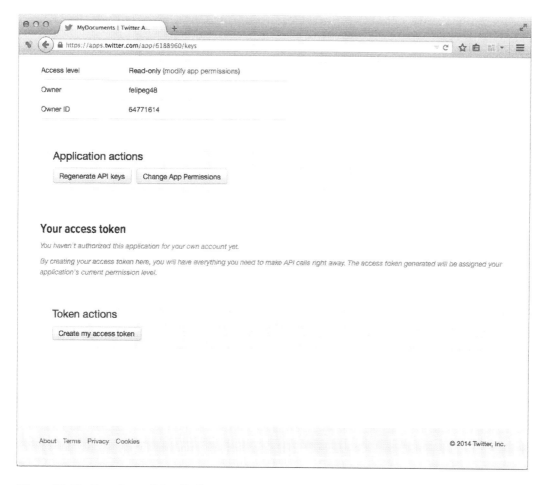

Figure 17-11. *Your Access Token Section*

Figure 17-11 shows that you need to generate your access token keys because you are going to use them later.

7. Next, click the "Create my access token" button; it will show your generated keys, as shown in Figure 17-12.

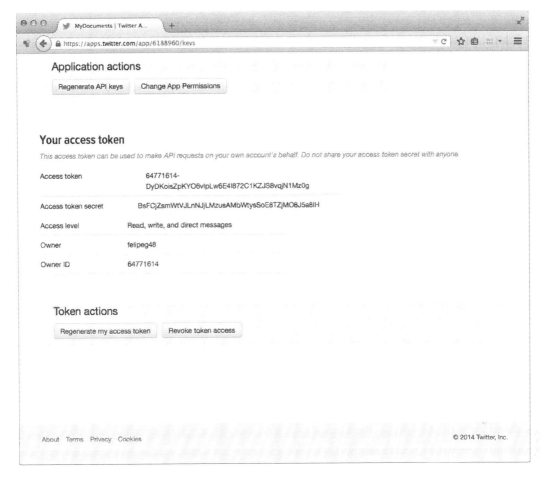

Figure 17-12. *Status After Token Access Created*

Figure 17-12 shows that the access token keys were generated successfully. Now you can see the keys you are going to need: the API key, API Secret, Access Token, and Access Token Secret (see Figure 17-13).

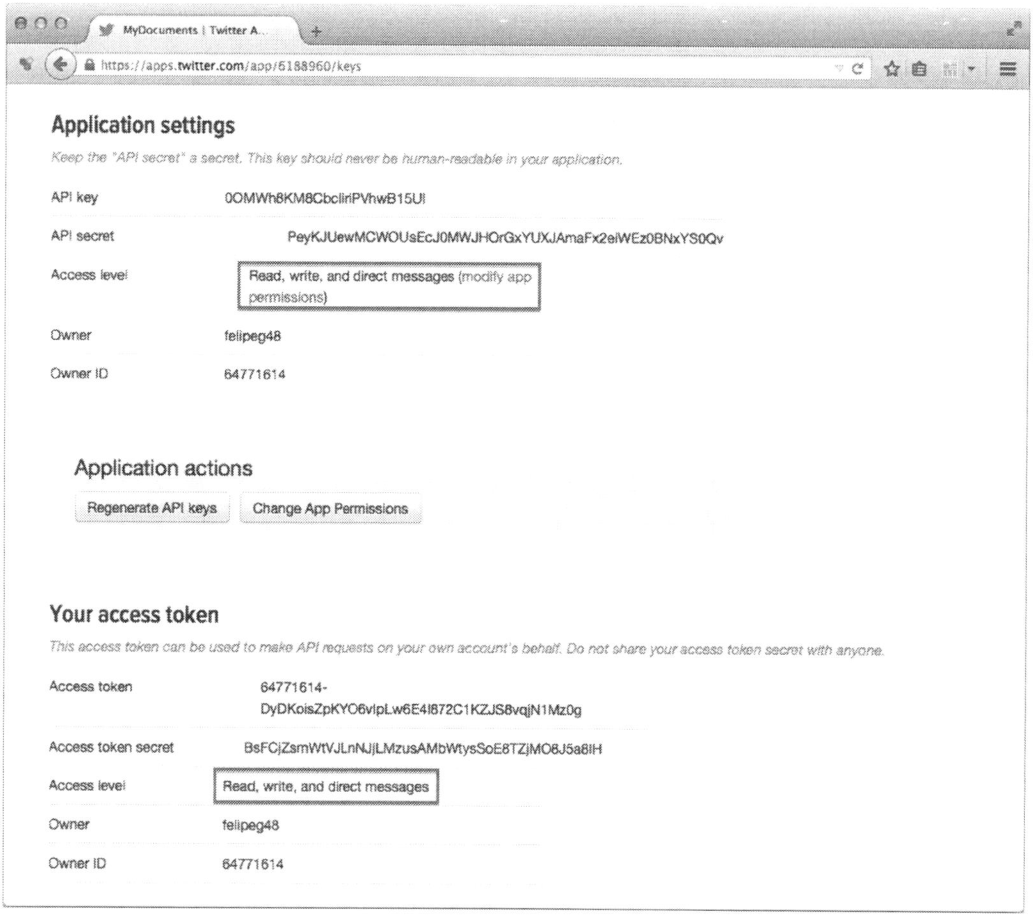

Figure 17-13. *Application Settings and the API, API Secret, Access Token, Access Token Secret keys with Read, Write and Direct Messages*

Figure 17-13 shows that all your keys have the access level required. This means that you can use the Twitter REST API to do several actions, such as posting a new status on Twitter.

Let's Tweet

Because you have your keys now, it is time to start coding. First, you are going to create the `twitter.properties` file as shown in Listing 17-1.

Listing 17-1. src/test/resources/twitter.properties

```
twitter.apiKey=OOMWh8KM8CbcIiriPVhwB15Ul
twitter.apiSecret=PeyKJUewMCWOUsEcJOMWJHOrGxYUXJAmaFx2eiWEz0BNxYS0Qv
twitter.accessToken=64771614-DyDKoisZpKYO6vIpLw6E4I872C1KZJS8vqjN1Mz0g
twitter.accessTokenSecret=BsFCjZsmWtVJLnNJjLMzusAMbWtysSoE8TZjMO8J5a8lH
```

In Listing 17-1, you need to add the four keys you created when you registered your Twitter application and when you generated your access token keys. These keys are needed in order to have a secure way to communicate between your application and Twitter's REST API. Next, you need to create the XML configuration for your **My Documents** Spring application, as shown in Listing 17-2.

Listing 17-2. mydocuments-context.xml

```xml
<?xml version="1.0" encoding="UTF-8"?>
<beans xmlns="http://www.springframework.org/schema/beans"
        xmlns:xsi="http://www.w3.org/2001/XMLSchema-instance"
        xmlns:context="http://www.springframework.org/schema/context"
        xmlns:jdbc="http://www.springframework.org/schema/jdbc"
        xmlns:rabbit="http://www.springframework.org/schema/rabbit"
        xmlns:util="http://www.springframework.org/schema/util"
        xsi:schemaLocation="http://www.springframework.org/schema/jdbc
http://www.springframework.org/schema/jdbc/spring-jdbc-4.0.xsd
                http://www.springframework.org/schema/beans
http://www.springframework.org/schema/beans/spring-beans.xsd
                http://www.springframework.org/schema/context
http://www.springframework.org/schema/context/spring-context-4.0.xsd
                http://www.springframework.org/schema/rabbit
http://www.springframework.org/schema/rabbit/spring-rabbit-1.2.xsd
                http://www.springframework.org/schema/util
http://www.springframework.org/schema/util/spring-util-4.0.xsd">

    <context:component-scan base-package="com.apress.isf.spring" />
    <context:property-placeholder location="twitter.properties" />

    <bean id="tweet" class="org.springframework.social.twitter.api.impl.TwitterTemplate">
        <constructor-arg name="consumerKey" value="${twitter.apiKey}"/>
        <constructor-arg name="consumerSecret" value="${twitter.apiSecret}"/>
        <constructor-arg name="accessToken" value="${twitter.accessToken}"/>
        <constructor-arg name="accessTokenSecret" value="${twitter.accessTokenSecret}"/>
    </bean>

    <!-- Import Resources -->
    <import resource="mydocuments-rabbitmq-context.xml"/>
    <import resource="mydocuments-jdbc-context.xml"/>

</beans>
```

Listing 17-2 shows the XML configuration that the Spring container will use in order to create the instances of your beans. First, you are creating a reference to the `twitter.properties` file. This reference will be a placeholder for your properties keys and their values. Then you are creating a "tweet" bean. This bean has a reference to the `org.springframework.social.twitter.api.impl.TwitterTemplate` class. This class has a constructor with four parameters: the `consumerKey`, the `consumerSecret`, the `accessToken`, and the `accessTokenSecret`. The values of these parameters will be the corresponding values of the placeholders you set (and that will match all the properties from the `twitter.properties` file).

Next, you are going to create the class that will use the `TwitterTemplate` bean, the `DocumentTweet` class (shown in Listing 17-3).

Listing 17-3. DocumentTweet.java

```java
package com.apress.isf.spring.social;

import org.springframework.beans.factory.annotation.Autowired;
import org.springframework.social.twitter.api.Twitter;
import org.springframework.stereotype.Component;

@Component("documentTweet")
public class DocumentTweet {

        @Autowired
        Twitter tweet;

        public void tweet(String text){
                tweet.timelineOperations().updateStatus(text);
        }
}
```

Listing 17-3 shows your DocumentTweet class that is using your "tweet" bean. You are creating a method tweet (String text) that will accept a String that will be the message posted to your Twitter account. To post the text, you need to call the timelineOperations that will give you the updateStatus.

Next, you need to create a unit test. See Listing 17-4.

Listing 17-4. MyDocumentsTest.java

```java
package com.apress.isf.spring.test;

import org.junit.Test;
import org.junit.runner.RunWith;
import static org.junit.Assert.assertNotNull;

import org.slf4j.Logger;
import org.slf4j.LoggerFactory;
import org.springframework.beans.factory.annotation.Autowired;
import org.springframework.test.context.ContextConfiguration;
import org.springframework.test.context.junit4.SpringJUnit4ClassRunner;

import com.apress.isf.spring.social.DocumentTweet;

@RunWith(SpringJUnit4ClassRunner.class)
@ContextConfiguration({"classpath:META-INF/spring/mydocuments-context.xml","classpath:META-INF/
spring/mydocuments-mongo-context.xml"})
public class MyDocumentsTest {
        private static final Logger log = LoggerFactory.getLogger(MyDocumentsTest.class);

        @Autowired
        DocumentTweet documentTweet;

        @Test
```

```
    public void testTwitter(){
            log.debug("Testing Spring Social....");
            assertNotNull(documentTweet);
            documentTweet.tweet("Playing with Spring Social!");
    }
}
```

Listing 17-4 shows the MyDocumentTest class that is using your DocumentTweet instance and the tweet method you defined. If you run this test with

```
gradle :ch17:test
```

you will see on your Twitter account the status "Playing with Spring Social!". See Figure 17-14.

Figure 17-14. *Showing the Result of Running the Unit Test*

Pretty cool! You have sent your first tweet! Next, you are going to integrate the DocumentTweet class into your **My Documents** Spring application.

Sending Tweets from My Spring Application

Now that you have everything in place, let's see how you are going to integrate sending tweets using your **My Documents** Spring application. You are going to update your DocumentFacade that implements the DocumentService interface, so after it saves or updates a Book document type you can tweet about it. In other words, you are going to reuse the DocumentTweet class. See Listing 17-5.

Listing 17-5. DocumentFacade.java

```
package com.apress.isf.spring.service;

import java.util.List;

import org.springframework.beans.factory.annotation.Autowired;
import org.springframework.stereotype.Service;

import com.apress.isf.java.model.Document;
import com.apress.isf.java.model.Type;
import com.apress.isf.java.service.DocumentService;
import com.apress.isf.spring.data.DocumentDAO;
import com.apress.isf.spring.social.DocumentTweet;
```

```
@Service("documentFacade")
public class DocumetServiceFacade implements DocumentService {

        @Autowired
        DocumentDAO documentDAO;

        @Autowired
        DocumentTweet documentTweet;

        public List<Document> getAllDocuments(){
                return documentDAO.getAll();
        }

        public Document saveDocument(String id, Document document) {
                Document documentResult = documentDAO.save(id, document);

                if("WEB".equals(documentResult.getType().getName())){
                        StringBuilder tweetText = new StringBuilder("My Documents App - A Book update: ");
                         tweetText.append(documentResult.getName());
                         tweetText.append(". Check it out: ");
                         tweetText.append(documentResult.getLocation());
                         documentTweet.tweet(tweetText.toString());
                }
                return documentResult;
        }

        public Document removeDocumentById(String id) {
                return documentDAO.removeById(id);
        }

        public Document findDocumentById(String id){
                return documentDAO.findById(id);
        }

        public boolean updateLocationFromDocumentId(String documentId, String location) {
                Document document = documentDAO.findById(documentId);
                if(null == document)
                        return false;
                document.setLocation(location);
                saveDocument(documentId, document);
                return true;
        }

        public List<Document> findByType(Type type) {
                return documentDAO.findByTypeName(type.getName());
        }
}

}
```

In Listing 17-5, you added the DocumentTweet class and added some code to the saveDocument method. You are adding logic that says if a document is a web type (note that so far you have three types of documents: PDF, note, and web), you are going to tweet about it.

Next, you are going to do the integration test, as shown in Listing 17-6.

Listing 17-6. MyDocumentsTest.java

```
package com.apress.isf.spring.test;

import org.junit.Test;
import org.junit.runner.RunWith;
import static org.junit.Assert.assertNotNull;

import org.slf4j.Logger;
import org.slf4j.LoggerFactory;
import org.springframework.beans.factory.annotation.Autowired;
import org.springframework.test.context.ContextConfiguration;
import org.springframework.test.context.junit4.SpringJUnit4ClassRunner;

import com.apress.isf.java.service.DocumentService;
import com.apress.isf.java.service.TypeService;
import com.apress.isf.java.model.Document;
import com.apress.isf.java.model.Type;

@RunWith(SpringJUnit4ClassRunner.class)
@ContextConfiguration({"classpath:META-INF/spring/mydocuments-context.xml",
"classpath:META-INF/spring/mydocuments-mongo-context.xml"})
public class MyDocumentsTest {
        private static final Logger log = LoggerFactory.getLogger(MyDocumentsTest.class);
        //The ID was taken from the src/main/resources/META-INF/data/data.sql
        private final String WEB_TYPE_ID = "4980d2e4-a424-4ff4-a0b2-476039682f43";

        @Autowired
        DocumentService documentFacade;

        @Autowired
        TypeService typeFacade;

        @Test
        public void testMyDocumentsTwitter(){
                log.debug("Testing My Documents with Spring Social....");
                assertNotNull(documentTweet);
                assertNotNull(typeFacade);

                Document document = new Document();
                document.setName("Beginning Blender");
                document.setType(typeFacade.getTypeById(WEB_TYPE_ID));
                document.setDescription("");
                document.setLocation("http://www.apress.com/9781430262237");

                documentFacade.saveDocument(document.getDocumentId(),document);
        }
}
```

In Listing 17-6, you are using the DocumentService and TypeService implementations. The TypeService implementation is used just to retrieve the web type because it is required when you create a new document. Then you create a new document and call the saveDocument method; this will save the document into the database and you can tweet about it.

Now if you run the test (see Listing 17-6) with

```
gradle :ch17:test
```

you should get the following output:

```
com.apress.isf.spring.test.MyDocumentsTest > testMyDocumentsTwitter STARTED
Test: test testMyDocumentsTwitter(com.apress.isf.spring.test.MyDocumentsTest) produced standard
out/err: 2014-05-17 17:09:37,253 DEBUG [Test worker] Testing My Documents with Spring Social....
com.apress.isf.spring.test.MyDocumentsTest > testMyDocumentsTwitter PASSED
```

You should also see in your Twitter account something similar to Figure 17-15.

Figure 17-15. *A Tweet Using the My Documents Spring Application*

Summary

In this chapter, you learned about Spring Social and how easy it is to integrate your **My Documents** Spring application with Twitter. You also learned how to register an application on Twitter in order to use Twitter's REST API.

In the next chapter, you will discover more features about the Spring Framework, such as a way to create an entire application with the Groovy programming language and Spring.

PART IV

Spring I/O

Spring I/O is not a new technology; it is a new way to see the whole Spring Framework stack by introducing the technologies new to version 4—technologies such as Spring Boot, Spring XD, Spring Hadoop, and Spring Data for NoSQL and Graph databases.

You will see how the new Spring Framework plays very nicely with Groovy and its new Spring DSL for your beans container configuration. Then, you'll dig deeper into Spring Boot and see how easy it is to develop with it, thereby reducing time and effort.

And finally, you will learn about the newest technology from the Spring Framework team: Spring XD. You'll see how to get real-time analytics for your Spring application.

■ ■ ■

CHAPTER 18

Spring and Groovy

So far, your Spring application has been dealing with XML files in order to help the Spring container create and instantiate your classes. In this chapter, you are going to change that by using Groovy to see how the new Spring Framework 4 plays nicely with it.

Grails, a web framework that uses Groovy as its primary language, is based on the Spring Framework, making it robust, extensible, and very easy to use. Because Spring is the foundation of this framework, the Grails team did a great job introducing a new Spring DSL (domain-specific language) based entirely on Groovy.

One of the most powerful features of the Groovy programming language is the ability to create a DSL easily and with minimal effort. So it was time to bring that powerful feature into the Spring Framework.

The Spring team developed a new way of exposing beans through a Groovy DSL and incorporating it in the new Spring 4 release through several classes, such as the GenericGroovyApplicationContext that can accept a Groovy script defining the beans in a DSL.

In this chapter, you are going to translate the beans definitions in your Spring application from XML to the new Spring DSL.

Let's Code Groovy

You are going to start by creating all the Spring DSL files that will be translated from the XML configuration into the new Spring DSL in Groovy. See Listing 18-1 for the XML that you are going to translate.

Listing 18-1. mydocuments-context.xml

```
<?xml version="1.0" encoding="UTF-8"?>
<beans xmlns="http://www.springframework.org/schema/beans"
       xmlns:xsi="http://www.w3.org/2001/XMLSchema-instance"
       xmlns:context="http://www.springframework.org/schema/context"
       xmlns:jdbc="http://www.springframework.org/schema/jdbc"
       xmlns:rabbit="http://www.springframework.org/schema/rabbit"
       xmlns:util="http://www.springframework.org/schema/util"
       xsi:schemaLocation="http://www.springframework.org/schema/jdbc
http://www.springframework.org/schema/jdbc/spring-jdbc-4.0.xsd
            http://www.springframework.org/schema/beans
http://www.springframework.org/schema/beans/spring-beans.xsd
            http://www.springframework.org/schema/context
http://www.springframework.org/schema/context/spring-context-4.0.xsd
            http://www.springframework.org/schema/rabbit
http://www.springframework.org/schema/rabbit/spring-rabbit-1.2.xsd
            http://www.springframework.org/schema/util
http://www.springframework.org/schema/util/spring-util-4.0.xsd">
```

```
        <context:component-scan base-package="com.apress.isf.spring" />

        <!-- Import Resources -->
        <import resource="mydocuments-rabbitmq-context.xml"/>
        <import resource="mydocuments-jdbc-context.xml"/>
        <import resource="mydocuments-mongo-context.xml"/>

</beans>
```

Listing 18-1 shows the XML that you have been using in the past chapters. Now it's time to make it more Groovy! Let's take a look at Listing 18-2, and don't worry too much about mastering it now. I will explain in detail what you doing are and the syntax.

Listing 18-2. mydocuments.groovy

```
beans {
        xmlns context:"http://www.springframework.org/schema/context"

        context.'component-scan'('base-package': "com.apress.isf.spring")

        importBeans("classpath:META-INF/groovy/mydocumentsJDBC.groovy")
        importBeans("classpath:META-INF/groovy/mydocumentsRabbitMQ.groovy")
        importBeans("classpath:META-INF/groovy/mydocumentsMongo.groovy")

}
```

Listing 18-2 shows the new Spring DSL (which is equivalent to Listing 18-1). You are removing all of the clutter from the XML! Very Groovy! Next, let me explain what every part means.

You need to start with a beans keyword, followed by curly braces that will contain all of the bean definitions; this will be the equivalent of starting your <beans />tag.

```
beans {
        //your beans definitions here
}
```

Next, you are going to use some of the namespaces. You are going to use

```
xmlns context:http://www.springframework.org/schema/context
```

This namespace will be the first element after the curly brace for beans. This is equivalent to adding the first part in the XML. Next, you use the <component-scan/>tag to tell the Spring container to look for some annotations and classes beginning in the com.apress.isf.spring Java package. Also, you are importing other beans with the method importBeans.

▪ **Note**   The following listings show you only the Spring DSL. These listings are equivalent to the XML. So, if needed, you can review the book's companion source code to see the XML in detail and compare it with the new Spring DSL.

Next, Listing 18-3 shows the JDBC groovy DSL, the mydocumentsJDBC.groovy file.

Listing 18-3. mydocumentsJDBC.groovy

```groovy
beans{
        xmlns jdbc:"http://www.springframework.org/schema/jdbc"
        xmlns util:"http://www.springframework.org/schema/util"

        jdbc.'embedded-database' (id:"dataSource"){
                jdbc.script(location:"classpath:/META-INF/data/schema.sql")
                jdbc.script(location:"classpath:/META-INF/data/data.sql")
        }

        util.map(id:"sql"){
                entry(key:"query", value:
                        """
                        select d.documentId, d.name, d.location, d.description as doc_desc,
                d.typeId, d.created, d.modified,
                t.name as type_name, t.description as type_desc, t.extension from
                documents d
                join types t
                on d.typeId = t.typeId
                        """)
                entry(key:"find", value:"""
                        select d.documentId, d.name, d.location, d.description as doc_desc,
                d.typeId, d.created, d.modified,
                t.name as type_name, t.description as type_desc, t.extension from
                documents d
                join types t
                on d.typeId = t.typeId
                where d.documentId = ?
                        """)
        }

}
```

Listing 18-3 shows the use of the xmlns jdbc and xmlns util namespaces, equivalent to the declarations at the beginning of the XML counterpart. Then, it shows the use of the jdbc.'embedded-database'. It's a common rule of the DSL syntax that if a name has a hyphen (-), it must be enclosed in single quotes. Then it shows the id between parentheses. In the Spring DSL, everything that is between parentheses is treat as a Map (key:value) syntax. Next, it shows the util.map where you define all the SQL statements.

Next, let's review the Mongo version of the XML. See Listing 18-4 for the mydocumentMongo.groovy file.

Listing 18-4. mydocumentsMongo.groovy

```groovy
import org.springframework.data.mongodb.core.MongoTemplate as MT

beans{

        xmlns mongo:"http://www.springframework.org/schema/data/mongo"

        mongo.'mongo'(id:"mongo",host:"127.0.0.1",port:27017)
        mongo.'db-factory'(id:"mongoDbFactory",dbname:"mydocuments")
        mongoTemplate(MT,ref("mongoDbFactory"))

}
```

Listing 18-4 shows the xmlns mongo namespace and its equivalent from the XML <mongo/>tag converted into the DSL and how to use it to create your beans. Another cool feature of the Groovy programming language and the Spring DSL is that you can import classes and give them an alias, like the MongoTemplate class with alias MT. This way you can avoid putting in the whole class.

Next, let's see the OXM that you used in Chapter 16 to convert from XML to object and vice versa. See Listing 18-5 for the mydocumentsOXM.groovy file.

Listing 18-5. mydocumentsOXM.groovy

```groovy
import org.springframework.amqp.support.converter.MarshallingMessageConverter as MMC
import org.springframework.oxm.xstream.XStreamMarshaller as XM
import com.apress.isf.java.model.Document

beans{

        messageConverter(MMC,ref("xstreamMarshaller"))
        xstreamMarshaller(XM){
                aliases = [document:Document]
                mode = 1001
        }
}
```

Listing 18-5 shows the OXM with the XStream Marshaller and the use of an alias for the imports. Also, it shows the import and alias feature that helps you avoid putting too much code in the definitions. Next, let's see Listing 18-6 for the RabbitMQ bean definitions.

Listing 18-6. mydocumentsRabbitMQ.groovy

```groovy
import org.springframework.amqp.rabbit.listener.adapter.MessageListenerAdapter as MLA

beans{

        xmlns rabbit:"http://www.springframework.org/schema/rabbit"

        importBeans("classpath:META-INF/groovy/mydocumentsOXM.groovy")

        rabbit.'connection-factory'(id:"rabbitConnectionFactory", host:"localhost")
        rabbit.admin('connection-factory':'rabbitConnectionFactory')
        rabbit.template(id:"rabbitTemplate",
                'connection-factory':"rabbitConnectionFactory",
                'message-converter':"messageConverter")

        rabbit.'direct-exchange'(name:"mydocuments"){
                rabbit.bindings{
                        rabbit.binding(key:".pdf", queue:"docs-pdf")
                        rabbit.binding(key:".txt", queue:"docs-txt")
                        rabbit.binding(key:".url", queue:"docs-web")
                }
        }
```

```
    rabbit.'listener-container'(id:"pdfListener", 'connection-factory':"rabbitConnectionFactory"){
            rabbit.listener(ref:"pdfAdapter", queues:"docs-pdf")
            rabbit.listener(ref:"textAdapter", queues:"docs-txt")
            rabbit.listener(ref:"webAdapter", queues:"docs-web")
    }

    rabbit.queue(name:"docs-pdf")
    rabbit.queue(name:"docs-txt")
    rabbit.queue(name:"docs-web")

    pdfAdapter(MLA,ref("pdfConsumer"),ref("messageConverter")){
            defaultListenerMethod = "process"
    }
    textAdapter(MLA,ref("textConsumer"),ref("messageConverter")){
            defaultListenerMethod = "process"
    }
    webAdapter(MLA,ref("webConsumer"),ref("messageConverter")){
            defaultListenerMethod = "process"
    }
}
```

Listing 18-6 shows the RabbitMQ bean definitions and the use of the xmlns rabbit namespace. Remember that you need to use your OXM Marshaller to convert the message. This is needed in the producers and consumers, so it shows the importBeans to import the OXM script. Next, it shows all the definitions needed to set up the RabbitMQ broker (rabbit.'connection-factory', rabbit.admin), producer (rabbit.template), consumer (rabbit.'listener-container'), queue (rabbit.queue), exchange (rabbit.'direct-exchange'), and binding (rabbit.binding).

Let's Test Groovy

You are going to start testing the new Spring DSL and see the difference between using the XML or using the Groovy way. Listing 18-7 shows the unit test written using Groovy.

Listing 18-7. MyDocumentsTest.groovy

```
package com.apress.isf.spring.test

import static org.junit.Assert.assertNotNull
import static org.junit.Assert.assertEquals

import org.junit.Test
import org.junit.Ignore
import org.slf4j.Logger
import org.slf4j.LoggerFactory
import org.springframework.context.support.GenericGroovyApplicationContext

import com.apress.isf.java.model.Document;
```

```groovy
class MyDocumentsTest {
        private static final Logger log = LoggerFactory.getLogger(MyDocumentsTest.class)
        private final RECORDS = 6
        private final ID = "1acbb68a-a859-49c9-ac88-d9e9322bac55"
        private final ctx = new GenericGroovyApplicationContext("classpath:META-INF/groovy/
        mydocuments.groovy")

        @Test
        @Ignore
        void testJDBC(){
                log.info "Testing JDBC..."
                assertNotNull ctx

                def documentFacade = ctx.getBean("documentFacade")
                assertNotNull documentFacade

                int size = documentFacade.allDocuments.size()
                assertEquals RECORDS,size

                assertNotNull documentFacade.findDocumentById(ID)
        }

        @Test
        public void testProducer(){
                log.debug("Testing RabbitMQ Producer...");
                def documentFacade = ctx.getBean("documentFacade")
                def rabbitmqProducer = ctx.getBean("rabbitmqProducer")

                assertNotNull(rabbitmqProducer)
                assertNotNull(documentFacade)

                documentFacade.allDocuments.each{
                        rabbitmqProducer.send it
                }
                sleep 5000
        }
}
```

Listing 18-7 shows the unit test. In this case, you wrote the unit test using Groovy, but you can use Java and still make the use of the Groovy scripts. So, what is the difference between this unit test versus the ones you did in previous chapters? The first big difference is that all your bean definitions are using the Spring DSL, and the second is that you are using the GenericGroovyApplicationContext class (that will load the groovy DSL files) instead of the ClassPathXmlApplicationContext class that loads only XML files.

Run this test with

```
gradle :ch18:test
```

You will have the same output as in Chapter 16 because you are using the same bean descriptions and doing RabbitMQ messaging (don't forget to have the RabbitMQ up and running).

Take a moment and do a last review of the unit test and the Spring DSL. You will find that you got rid of all the XML verbosity and simplified the bean definitions, thanks to the Groovy programing language.

DSL Syntax

Of course, you need to learn part of the syntax of the Spring DSL, right? This section will help you to understand the syntax.

First, you need to start with a beans keyword. Between curly braces, you'll place the bean definitions.

```
// Some imports

beans {

        //Beans here or even some logic

}
```

Every bean must have an Id and a class between the parentheses.

```
beanId ( class )
```

Example:

```
beans {
        helloWorldService ( com.mycompany.service.MyService)
}

//Equivalent to:
<bean id="helloWorldService" class="com.mycompany.service.MyService"/>
```

Every bean property must be enclosed between curly braces, then you add the name of the property = value.

```
beanId (class) {
        variable = value
        variable = ref('value')  //Reference to a another bean
}
```

Example:

```
beans {
        helloWorldService ( com.mycompany.service.MyService) {
                message = "Hello World"
                greeting = ref ("myGreeting")
        }

        myGreeting ( com.mycompany.service.CustomGreeting)
}

//Equivalent to:
<bean id="helloWorldService" class="com.mycompany.service.MyService">
        <property name="message" value="Hello World"/>
        <property name="greeting" ref="myGreeting"/>
</bean>
<bean id="myGreeting" class="com.mycompany.service.CustomGreeting"/>
```

If the property is a map or an array, use square brackets and separate the elements by a comma.

```
beanId (class) {
        name = [ value1, value2, ...]
        name = [ key1:value, key2:value]
}
```

```
//Example:
  beans {
        helloWorldService ( com.mycompany.service.MyService) {
                title = ["Sr.", "Jr.", "Ms.", "Mrs."]
                gender = [male: "Hi", female: "Hello"]
        }
  }
```

```
//Equivalent to:
<bean id="helloWorldService" class="com.mycompany.service.MyService">
      <property name="title">
            <list>
                    <value>Sr.</value>
                    <value>Jr.</value>
                    <value>Ms.</value>
                    <value>Mrs.</value>
            </list>
      </property>
      <property name="gender">
            <map>
                    <entry key="male" value="Hi"/>
                    <entry key="female" value="Hello"/>
            </map>
      </property>
</bean>
```

If a bean has a constructor, then they need to be after the class definition.

```
beanId (class, contructor-param1 [, constructor-param-n])
```

Example:

```
  beans {
        helloWorldService ( com.mycompany.service.MyService, "Hello World")

        myGreeting ( com.mycompany.service.CustomGreeting, ref("defaultLanguage"))

        defaultLanguage( com.mycompany.i18n.Language, "english")
  }
```

```
//Equivalent to:
<bean id="helloWorldService" class="com.mycompany.service.MyService">
        <constructor-arg value="Hello World"/>
</bean>
<bean id=" myGreeting" class=" com.mycompany.service.CustomGreeting">
        <constructor-arg ref=" defaultLanguage"/>
</bean>
<bean id=" defaultLanguage" class=" com.mycompany.i18n.Language">
        <constructor-arg value=" english"/>
</bean>
```

It is necessary to add a defined namespace, and if a bean uses some attributes, then the name must be after the class definition, followed by a colon and the value; if the attribute contains a hyphen, it must be enclosed between single quotes. The namespace must be first on the line of the beans, separated by a space and the URL between double quotes and after a colon.

```
xmlns name:"URL"
beanId ( class, attribute : value [, attibute : value, 'attribute-xy': value ])
```

Example:

```
beans {

        xmlns rabbit:"http://www.springframework.org/schema/rabbit"
        rabbit.'connection-factory'(id:"rabbitConnectionFactory", host:"localhost")
}
```

```
//Equivalent to:
<beans xmlns="http://www.springframework.org/schema/beans"
        xmlns:xsi="http://www.w3.org/2001/XMLSchema-instance"
        xmlns:rabbit="http://www.springframework.org/schema/rabbit"
        xsi:schemaLocation="http://www.springframework.org/schema/beans
http://www.springframework.org/schema/beans/spring-beans.xsd
                http://www.springframework.org/schema/rabbit
http://www.springframework.org/schema/rabbit/spring-rabbit-1.2.xsd">

<rabbit:connection-factory id="rabbitConnectionFactory"
                        host="localhost"/>

        </beans>
```

As you can see, you can simplify your bean definitions by using the Spring DSL and you can remove all the verbosity from the XML. Of course, you can still use the XML together with this new Spring DSL. Imagine that you have a library already that contains an XML configuration and you want it to be part of the Spring DSL. How can you include it? Very easily; just use the importBeans and that's it. See Listing 18-8.

Listing 18-8. Spring DSL and XML Configurations: sampleBeans.groovy

```
beans {

        importBeans('classpath:/mydocuments-context.xml')

        //More beans
        //More beans

}
```

Listing 18-7 shows how to use existing XML configurations in the new Spring DSL.

Summary

In this chapter, you saw how the Spring Framework interacts regardless of the main programming language, Java or Groovy. You can use the new Spring DSL, which offers a more readable syntax and is easy to use. You can get rid of all of the XML verbosity and use a more dynamic way to define your beans.

You saw how to import more beans scripts, either using Groovy or via XML with the `importBeans` keyword. You learned the basic syntax of the Spring DSL and how to define any bean by translating the XML to the new Spring DSL.

In the next chapter, you will create a new Spring project, Spring Boot. Spring Boot simplifies enterprise development by using Java or Groovy to create micro-services.

CHAPTER 19

Spring Boot, Simplifying Everything

In Chapter 1, I showed a sneak peek of Spring Boot, a new technology by the Spring Framework team. In this chapter, you are going to translate your **My Documents** application into a Spring Boot application.

You can think of Spring Boot as a bootstrap engine that helps to create stand-alone and production-ready Spring applications with minimal effort—just code, and you don't have to worry about any extra configuration. Spring Boot gives you the flexibility to use Java or even Groovy scripts to create applications without any configuration files. In previous chapters, you depended on XML configuration files. Spring Boot eliminates all that!

Spring Boot

Let's start coding. Your first Spring Boot application will be in Java and you will still use Gradle as your building and testing tool. Listing 19-1 shows the build.gradle file and all the necessary dependencies.

Listing 19-1. build.gradle

```
buildscript {
        repositories {
                jcenter()
                mavenCentral()
                maven {
                        url "http://repo.spring.io/libs-snapshot"
                        url 'http://repo.spring.io/milestone'
                        url 'http://repo.spring.io/libs-release'
                }
                mavenLocal()
        }
        dependencies {
                classpath (group: 'org.springframework.boot', name:'spring-boot-gradle-plugin',
version: '1.1.1.RELEASE')
        }
}

apply plugin: 'java'
apply plugin: 'eclipse'
apply plugin: 'idea'
apply plugin: 'spring-boot'
```

```
jar {
        baseName = 'ch19-spring-boot'
        version =  '0.1.0'
}

repositories {
        mavenCentral()
        maven {
                        url "http://repo.spring.io/libs-snapshot"
                        url 'http://repo.spring.io/milestone'
                        url 'http://repo.spring.io/libs-release'
        }
}

dependencies {

        compile("org.springframework.boot:spring-boot-starter-web") {
                exclude module: "spring-boot-starter-tomcat"
        }
        compile("org.springframework.boot:spring-boot-starter-jetty")
        compile("org.springframework.boot:spring-boot-starter-actuator")
        compile("org.springframework.boot:spring-boot-starter-jdbc")

        runtime 'hsqldb:hsqldb:1.8.0.10'
        testCompile("junit:junit")
}
```

Listing 19-1 shows the build.gradle file. The important part of this file is where you describe the buildscript because you are going to use a **spring-boot** plug-in. The spring-boot plug-in has several tasks, one of which is the bootRun task. Don't worry too much about these tasks; you are going to use them very soon.

Remember that you still have all the **My Documents** classes from previous chapters. So let's reuse them, including some persistence like the JDBC. And because Spring Boot promotes zero configuration files, you are going to use some Java Config classes, as shown in Listing 19-2.

Listing 19-2. JDBCConfig.java

```
package com.apress.isf.spring.boot;

import javax.sql.DataSource;

import org.springframework.context.annotation.Bean;
import org.springframework.context.annotation.Configuration;
import org.springframework.context.annotation.ImportResource;
import org.springframework.jdbc.datasource.embedded.EmbeddedDatabase;
import org.springframework.jdbc.datasource.embedded.EmbeddedDatabaseBuilder;
import org.springframework.jdbc.datasource.embedded.EmbeddedDatabaseType;

@Configuration
@ImportResource("classpath:META-INF/spring/jdbc-context.xml")
public class JDBCConfig {
```

```
    @Bean
public DataSource dataSource() {
    EmbeddedDatabaseBuilder builder = new EmbeddedDatabaseBuilder();
    EmbeddedDatabase db = builder.setType(EmbeddedDatabaseType.HSQL).
        addScript("META-INF/data/schema.sql").
        addScript("META-INF/data/data.sql").build();
    return db;
}

}
```

Listing 19-2 shows the JDBC Config, which you will need at some point because you are using an in-memory database, and you are showing that you can still use XML files from other projects. In this case, you are going to use only one, the jdbc-context.xml that only contains the SQL statements. Listing 19-3 shows this file.

Listing 19-3. jdbc-context.xml

```xml
<?xml version="1.0" encoding="UTF-8"?>
<beans xmlns="http://www.springframework.org/schema/beans"
       xmlns:xsi="http://www.w3.org/2001/XMLSchema-instance"
       xsi:schemaLocation="http://www.springframework.org/schema/beans
http://www.springframework.org/schema/beans/spring-beans.xsd">

  <bean id="sql" class="java.util.HashMap">
    <constructor-arg>
      <map>
        <entry key="query">
          <value>
            select d.documentId, d.name, d.location, d.description as doc_desc,
            d.typeId, d.created, d.modified,
            t.name as type_name, t.description as type_desc, t.extension from
            documents d
            join types t
            on d.typeId = t.typeId
          </value>
        </entry>
        <entry key="find">
          <value>
            select d.documentId, d.name, d.location, d.description as doc_desc,
            d.typeId, d.created, d.modified,
            t.name as type_name, t.description as type_desc, t.extension from
            documents d
            join types t
            on d.typeId = t.typeId
            where d.documentId = ?
          </value>
        </entry>
        <entry key="type-name">
          <value>
            select d.documentId, d.name, d.location, d.description as doc_desc,
            d.typeId, d.created, d.modified,
```

```
            t.name as type_name, t.description as type_desc, t.extension from
            documents d
            join types t
            on d.typeId = t.typeId
            where t.name = ?
          </value>
        </entry>
        <entry key="insert">
          <value>
            insert into documents (documentId,name,location,description, typeId,
            created, modified)
            values (?,?,?,?,?,?,?)
          </value>
        </entry>
        <entry key="update">
          <value>
            update documents set name = ?, location = ?, description = ?, typeId =
            ?,modified = ?
            where documentId = ?
          </value>
        </entry>
        <entry key="delete">
          <value>
            delete from documents
            where documentId = ?
          </value>
        </entry>
      </map>
    </constructor-arg>
  </bean>

</beans>
```

Now, let's create the main Spring Boot application that will bootstrap everything and run the application in an embedded web server, as shown in Listing 19-4.

Listing 19-4. MyDocumentsApp.java

```java
package com.apress.isf.spring.boot;

import javax.sql.DataSource;

import org.springframework.boot.SpringApplication;
import org.springframework.boot.autoconfigure.EnableAutoConfiguration;
import org.springframework.context.annotation.Bean;
import org.springframework.context.annotation.ComponentScan;
import org.springframework.context.annotation.Configuration;
import org.springframework.jdbc.datasource.embedded.EmbeddedDatabase;
import org.springframework.jdbc.datasource.embedded.EmbeddedDatabaseBuilder;
import org.springframework.jdbc.datasource.embedded.EmbeddedDatabaseType;
```

```
@Configuration
@EnableAutoConfiguration
@ComponentScan("com.apress.isf.spring")
public class MyDocumentsApp {

    @Bean
    public DataSource dataSource() {
        EmbeddedDatabaseBuilder builder = new EmbeddedDatabaseBuilder();
        EmbeddedDatabase db = builder.setType(EmbeddedDatabaseType.HSQL).
            addScript("META-INF/data/schema.sql").
            addScript("META-INF/data/data.sql").build();
        return db;
    }

    public static void main(String[] args) {
        SpringApplication.run(MyDocumentsApp.class,args);
    }

}
```

Listing 19-4 shows the Spring Boot application. The main method executes the SpringApplication.run method and Spring Boot will take care of the rest. Now, open a terminal and run the following command:

```
gradle :ch19:bootRun
```

You should get the output shown in Figure 19-1. When you run the above command for the first time, the spring-boot plug-in will download all the necessary libraries needed to run the application. Because you are scanning all the components, services, and repositories that belong to the com.apress.isf.spring package, it will automatically create a web context, so it will open port 8080 for incoming HTTP requests and you will be able to do all the RESTful calls.

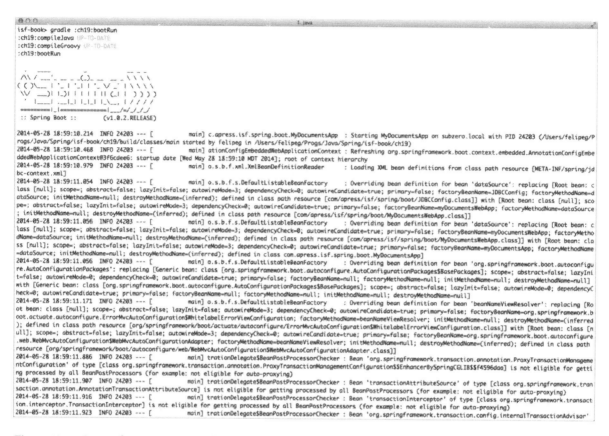

Figure 19-1. *Output from Running Gradle :ch19:bootRun*

Figure 19-2 shows your initial web page, `http://localhost:8080/documents`.

Figure 19-2. `http://localhost:8080/documents` *Exposes the RESTful Calls*

Deploying MyDocuments

You saw how Spring Boot downloads the dependencies and how it will trigger the correct context depending on the annotated classes. But what happens if you want to give this application to a friend, and this friend does not have an Internet connection? Do you still need to add all of the dependencies? Fortunately, the spring-boot plug-in has inherited some of the other plug-in tasks defined in the build.gradle and will take care of the dependencies.

Creating an Executable Jar

Let's create a stand-alone application, an executable jar. Go to the book's companion source code folder, and enter the following command:

```
gradle :ch19:build
```

The above command will jar up all the dependencies needed in one big jar. The jar will be created in the `build/libs` folder and it will be named according to the `jar` definition in the `build.gradle` (see Listing 19-1). Now you can run the Spring Boot application with

```
java -jar ch19-spring-boot-0.1.0.jar
```

and you should get the same output as shown in Figure 19-1 with the RESTful features.

Creating a WAR File

What happens if you need to create a WAR file because maybe you already have an application server like tcServer or Tomcat? You will need to make some small modifications. Let's start first with the `build.gradle` file. You just need to add the **war** plug-in, replace the jar section for the `war` section, and add the **configurations** section. Listing 19-5 shows the new `build.gradle` for creating a WAR file.

Listing 19-5. build.gradle

```
buildscript {
        repositories {
                jcenter()
                mavenCentral()
                maven {
                        url "http://repo.spring.io/libs-snapshot"
                        url 'http://repo.spring.io/milestone'
                        url 'http://repo.spring.io/libs-release'
                }
                mavenLocal()
        }
        dependencies {
                classpath (group: 'org.springframework.boot', name:'spring-boot-gradle-plugin',
version: '1.1.1.RELEASE')
        }
}

apply plugin: 'java'
apply plugin: 'eclipse'
apply plugin: 'idea'
apply plugin: 'war'
apply plugin: 'spring-boot'

war {
        baseName = 'ch19-spring-boot'
        version =  '0.1.0'
}

repositories {
        mavenCentral()
        maven {
                        url "http://repo.spring.io/libs-snapshot"
                        url 'http://repo.spring.io/milestone'
                        url 'http://repo.spring.io/libs-release'
        }
}
```

```
configurations {
    providedRuntime
}

dependencies {

        compile("org.springframework.boot:spring-boot-starter-web") {
                exclude module: "spring-boot-starter-tomcat"
        }
        compile("org.springframework.boot:spring-boot-starter-jetty")
        compile("org.springframework.boot:spring-boot-starter-actuator")
        compile("org.springframework.boot:spring-boot-starter-jdbc")

        runtime 'hsqldb:hsqldb:1.8.0.10'
        testCompile("junit:junit")
}
```

Listing 19-5 shows how to create a WAR file that can run on any application server. As you can see, there are several sections: apply plugin: 'war', war, and configurations. In the war section, you provided the base name and the version of the **WAR** file; in the configurations section, you added the providedRuntime keyword. This keyword tells the gradle not to package jars that are already part of the application server.

Next, you are going to create a new class that will be the entry point for Spring Boot. This call will know how to add dependencies and how to wire everything up for the WAR application. See Listing 19-6.

Listing 19-6. MyDocumentsWebApp.java

```
package com.apress.isf.spring.boot;

import javax.sql.DataSource;

import org.springframework.boot.SpringApplication;
import org.springframework.boot.autoconfigure.EnableAutoConfiguration;
import org.springframework.context.annotation.Bean;
import org.springframework.context.annotation.ComponentScan;
import org.springframework.context.annotation.Configuration;
import org.springframework.jdbc.datasource.embedded.EmbeddedDatabase;
import org.springframework.jdbc.datasource.embedded.EmbeddedDatabaseBuilder;
import org.springframework.jdbc.datasource.embedded.EmbeddedDatabaseType;
import org.springframework.boot.builder.SpringApplicationBuilder;
import org.springframework.boot.context.web.SpringBootServletInitializer;

@Configuration
@EnableAutoConfiguration
@ComponentScan("com.apress.isf.spring")
public class MyDocumentsWebApp extends SpringBootServletInitializer{

        @Bean
    public DataSource dataSource() {
        EmbeddedDatabaseBuilder builder = new EmbeddedDatabaseBuilder();
        EmbeddedDatabase db = builder.setType(EmbeddedDatabaseType.HSQL).
            addScript("META-INF/data/schema.sql").
            addScript("META-INF/data/data.sql").build();
        return db;
    }
```

```
    @Override
    protected SpringApplicationBuilder configure(SpringApplicationBuilder application) {
    return application.sources(MyDocumentsWebApp.class);
    }
}
```

Listing 19-6 shows the new class. You are now extending from the SpringBootServletInitializer class and you are overriding a configure method. In this method, you are returning an application that will tell Spring Boot how to initialize all web-related files. Also, note that you are using the @Configuration, @EnableAutoConfiguration, and @ComponentScan annotations. These annotations are essential for Spring Boot; they're the way it looks for all of the necessary components for the web application.

Before in the JAR application (Listing 19-4), Spring Boot recognized that it would be a JAR application because it had a main method and it was executing the SpringApplication.run method. This time, Spring Boot will identify this application as a web app because you are extending from the SpringBootServletInitializer class and overriding the configure method, and it will wire everything up so it can run on any Java web container.

The following command will create the WAR file in the build/libs folder:

```
gradle clean :ch19:build
```

Now you can deploy the WAR file on any application server or Java web container. If you are deploying in a Tomcat-like server, you need to remember that the context by default is the name of the WAR, so the URL will be http://localhost:8080/ch19-spring-boot-0.1.0/documents.

Spring Boot À La Groovy

Spring Boot also plays well with Groovy, so you are going to create just a subset of the **My Documents** Spring application, based on Groovy scripts—only the access to the in-memory database. See Listing 19-7 for the model.groovy file.

Listing 19-7. model.groovy

```
class Document {
        String documentId
        String name
        Type type
        String location
        String description
        Date created
        Date modified
}

class Type {
        String typeId
        String name
        String desc
        String extension
}
```

Listing 19-7 shows the `model.groovy` script that contains the definition of the two classes, the Document class and the Type class. Next, see Listing 19-8 for the `repo.groovy` script.

Listing 19-8. repo.groovy

```groovy
import groovy.sql.Sql
import org.springframework.core.io.Resource
import javax.annotation.Resource as R

@Repository
class MyDocumentsRepo  {
        def sqlEngine = Sql.newInstance("jdbc:hsqldb:mem:testdb", "sa", "", "org.hsqldb.jdbcDriver")

        @Autowired
        Resource schema

        @Autowired
        Resource data

        @R
        Map<String,String> sql

        @PostConstruct
        def init(){
                schema.inputStream.eachLine{
                        sqlEngine.execute(it)
                }
                data.inputStream.eachLine{
                        sqlEngine.execute(it)
                }
        }

        def getAllDocuments(){
                def result = []
                def type, document
                sqlEngine.rows(sql.query).each { row ->

                        type = new Type(
                                typeId:row.typeId,
                                 name:row.type_name,
                                 desc:row.type_desc,
                           extension:row.extension)

                        document = new Document(
                                documentId:row.documentId,
                                     name:row.name,
                                 location:row.location,
                                  created:row.created,
                                 modified:row.modified,
                              description:row.doc_desc,
                                     type:type)
```

```
                    result << document

            }
            result
    }

}
```

Listing 19-8 shows the repository class with less code. Don't worry too much about what is in this file, as I'll explain it in the next sections. Next, the service script is shown in Listing 19-9.

Listing 19-9. service.groovy

```
@Service
class MyDocumentsService {

        @Autowired
        MyDocumentsRepo repo

        def getDocs(){
                repo.allDocuments
        }
}
```

Listing 19-9 shows the service that will only retrieve all the documents from the database by calling the getDocs() method. Next, the controller script is shown in Listing 19-10.

Listing 19-10. controller.groovy

```
@Controller
@RequestMapping("/documents")
class MyDocumentsController {

        @Autowired
        private MyDocumentsService myService;

        @RequestMapping(method=RequestMethod.GET)
        @ResponseBody
        public def documents() {
                myService.docs
        }

}
```

Let's analyze the Groovy scripts. Listing 19-7 shows the model, the Document and Type classes. Because you're using Groovy, it's not necessary to use any setters or getters; you get them for free.

Listing 19-8 shows the MyDocumentsRepo class that will be the data access object. You are loading into the constructor the resources schema.sql and data.sql, which provide the table creation and data. And you are using some of the nice features that Groovy provides, like the alias on the class imports.

Listing 19-9 shows the MyDocumentService class that will call the repository to access all of the data from the in-memory database. For now, you are only implementing it to retrieve the document records.

Listing 19-10 shows the MyDocumentsController class, which is the RESTful calls entry class. You are implementing a single method just to prove that with Groovy it is even easier to create enterprise-ready applications.

Now you need to create the main class that will be the bootstrap of the application. See Listing 19-11.

Listing 19-11. app.groovy

```
@Grab("org.hsqldb:hsqldb:2.2.9")
@Grab("org.codehaus.groovy:groovy-sql:2.0.1")

@Configuration
class MyDocuments  {
    //Extra configuration
}

beans {
        importBeans("jdbc.xml")

}
```

Listing 19-11 shows the MyDocuments class, which is the bootstrap for the Spring Boot application. The new Spring 4 provides support for a Spring DSL context, so in this script you are including it just to prove that you can actually use external configurations. The book's companion source code contains all the scripts used in this section.

Now how do you run it? You need to have Spring Boot installed. (For more information about how to install Spring Boot, see Appendix A.) From the command line, just execute the following command:

```
spring run *.groovy
```

This command will execute Spring Boot and it will automatically recognize what to do. Figure 19-3 shows the output of this command.

Figure 19-3. *Spring Boot with Groovy*

Now you can go to any browser and enter the `http://localhost:8080/documents` URL and you should get the same as shown in Figure 19-2.

So how can you deploy the Spring Boot based on Groovy? It's as simple as executing the following command:

```
spring jar mydocuments.jar *.groovy
```

This command will create an executable JAR that you can use with this command:

```
java -jar mydocuments.jar
```

Summary

In this chapter you saw how to reuse the Java code and how Spring Boot can run this Spring application effortlessly. You saw how to deploy the application either creating an executable JAR or creating a WAR for deploying it to any Java web container. Also, you saw how it is even easier to create Spring applications with Groovy.

In the next chapter, I'll introduce to you to a new technology created by the Spring Framework team called Spring XD.

CHAPTER 20

Your First Spring XD Application

The last quarter of 2013 saw the release of the first milestone of Spring XD. The Spring Framework and Spring XD team have been working very hard to include more features into this new Spring module. But what exactly is Spring XD?

Spring XD is based on enterprise integration patterns and is based on the Spring Integration and Spring Batch modules. They play very nicely not only with Java but also with Groovy and Spring Boot. Spring XD is a service for real-time analytics, data ingestions, batch processing, and data export, and it provides a DSL (domain-specific language) for easy interaction. Also, it can work in single or distribute mode, making it more robust and extensible. It can also be used along with several technologies, like Hadoop, GemFire XD, RabbitMQ, Redis, etc.

Installing Spring XD

Let's start by installing Spring XD. There are different ways to install Spring XD. One of the most common way is just to download the distribution and unzip it in any directory, set some environment variables, and that's it. You will need to make sure that you have at least JDK 6 installed, but JDK 7 is recommended.

Using the Spring XD Distribution

Download the distribution from `http://repo.spring.io/simple/libs-milestone-local/org/springframework/xd/spring-xd/1.0.0.M7/spring-xd-1.0.0.M7-dist.zip` (this is the latest at the time of writing). Unzip it and set the XD_HOME variable to point to `<spring-xd-install-dir>\spring-xd\xd`. This installation can be Windows or any UNIX flavor.

Using OSX Homebrew Installation

Homebrew is one of the best package managers for the OSX (you can find it and install it from `http://brew.sh/`) and is recommended because you can run several versions without disrupting others. The following commands will install spring-xd:

```
$ brew tap pivotal/tap
$ brew install sprinxd
```

These commands will install Spring XD at `/usr/local/Cellar/springxd/1.0.0.M7` and the executable will be linked to `/usr/local/bin`.

Now you are ready to start the Spring XD service, but first you need to know some useful features that Spring XD supports.

Spring XD

Spring XD can work in two different modes, single and multi-mode. The single mode can be used for all processing and administration. The multi-mode is a distributed mode that can spread some jobs and tasks across a cluster of multiple nodes.

Spring XD has some key components, the XD Admin and the XD Container Servers, where the XD Admin will take a DSL command task and send it over to the XD container servers for processing using different types of transports (that can be specified at start time) such as in-memory (default), Redis, and RabbitMQ. Figure 20-1 shows a general Spring XD architecture.

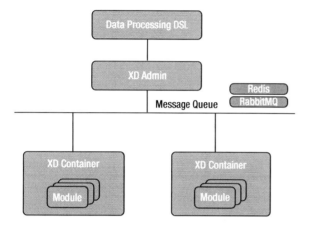

Figure 20-1. *Spring XD Runtime Architecture (DIRT – Distributed Integration Runtime)*

Modules

Spring XD supports three types of modules:

- **Source:** This module polls from an external resource or can be triggered by an event and only provides an output. This module is always a stream. Out of the box, Spring XD provides several sources: `file`, `gemfire`, `rabbit`, `http`, `mail`, `jms`, etc. You can see the complete list by executing the command `module list` on the XD shell (that you run later).

- **Processor:** This module provides some processing (business logic) or transforming; by providing an input and one or more outputs. Out of the box, Spring XD provides several processors such as `aggregator`, `http-client`, `bridge`, `filter`, `json-field-extractor`, `json-field-value-filter`, `object-to-json`, `script`, `splitter`, `transform`, etc.

- **Sink:** This module only provides one input and outputs the data to an external resource to terminate the stream. Out of the box, Spring XD provides several sinks such as `hdfs` (Hadoop), `file`, `gemfire-json-server`, `jdbc`, `mail`, `splunk`, `tcp`, `aggregatecounter`, `counter gauge`, `rabbit`, etc.

Taps

Spring XD provides taps that listen to data while it is being processed by a stream. This is the implementation of the WireTap pattern (enterprise integration patterns) on the Spring Integration module and it is one of the features you are going to use in your Spring application.

Using Spring XD with My Documents

Enough about concepts! Let's start playing around with Spring XD. The main idea of using Spring XD within your **My Documents** Spring application is to get some metrics on the number of PDF documents you are receiving from RabbitMQ. See Figure 20-2 for a general overview of what you need to accomplish.

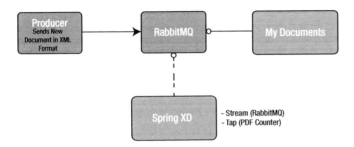

Figure 20-2. *Using Spring XD with the My Documents Application*

Figure 20-2 shows a basic architecture where you are going to use Spring XD along with the **My Documents** application. Because you are going to use RabbitMQ, you need to make sure it is up and running. After that, let's start Spring XD. The following command will start the Spring XD runtime:

```
xd-singlenode --transport rabbit
```

Figure 20-3 shows the output of executing the Spring XD runtime that will use RabbitMQ as messaging queue transport mechanism.

Figure 20-3. *Running xd-singlenode –transport Rabbit Will Use RabbitMQ as a Messaging Queue Mechanism*

Now let's start the Spring XD shell. This tool will be used to create the stream and tap that you are going to use to count how many PDFs the **My Documents** Spring application receives. The Spring XD shell uses a high-level DSL to define all the tasks needed.

You can open a new terminal and run the following command to start the Spring XD shell tool, as shown in Figure 20-4:

```
xd-shell
```

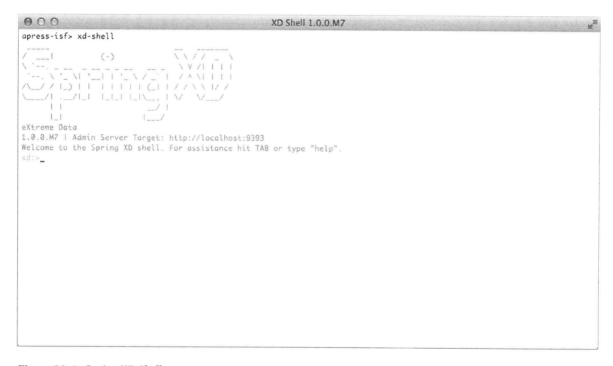

Figure 20-4. *Spring XD Shell*

Figure 20-4 shows the Spring XD shell, a tool that will interact with the Spring XD itself. Next, you are going to create the stream that will be listening from the RabbitMQ on one of your queues, in this case the docs-pdf. The following command will create the stream you need:

```
xd:> stream create --name docs-pdf --definition "rabbit | log"
```

The above command will create a rabbit stream and it will log all the incoming messages into the console. It is important to note that the name parameter is key and is related to the name of a queue. So the name "docs-pdf" is the name of the queue in RabbitMQ; if this name does not exist in RabbitMQ, it will be created.

Next, let's create the tap that will end in a sink (counter) that will have the number of the PDFs. The following command in the Spring shell will create the tap (see Figure 20-5):

```
xd:> stream create --name pdftap --definition "tap:stream:docs-pdf > counter --name=pdfcount"
```

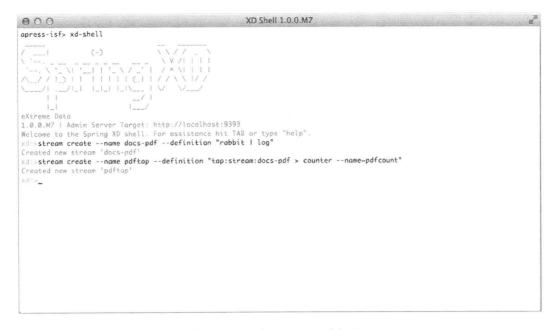

Figure 20-5. *The Spring XD Shell After Creating the Stream and the Tap*

Figure 20-5 shows the xd-shell and the commands you just typed. Spring XD has a notion of deployed/ undeployed streams, so by default (in version 1.0.0.M7) the streams are undeployed. One way to see this is to list the streams created and review their status. Execute the following command in the Spring XD shell:

xd:> stream list

After executing the above command, you should see something similar to Figure 20-6.

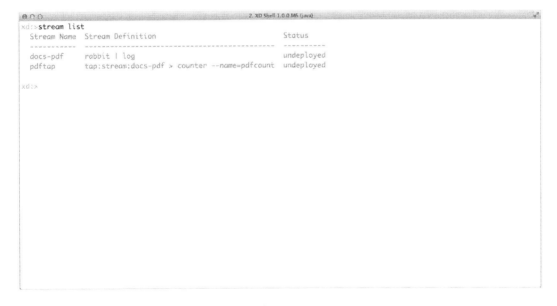

Figure 20-6. *Executing the Stream List Command*

As you can see in Figure 20-6, the two streams are undeployed. So let's deploy each stream by executing the following commands in the Spring XD shell:

```
xd:> stream deploy --name docs-pdf
```

```
xd:> stream deploy --name pdftap
```

After executing the above commands, you should have the streams deployed as shown in Figure 20-7.

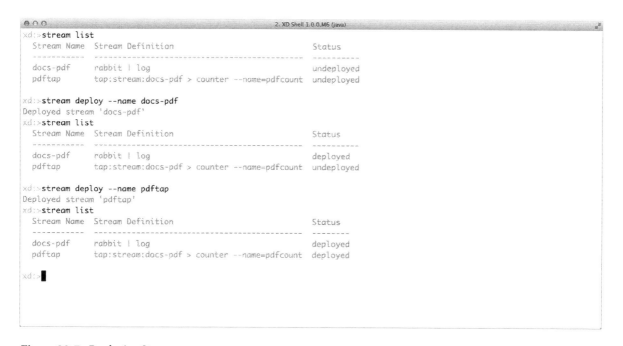

Figure 20-7. *Deploying Streams*

Figure 20-7 shows the result of deploying the streams. Now if you take a look into the RabbitMQ web console in the queues, you should see something similar to Figure 20-8.

Figure 20-8. *RabbitMQ Web Console*

Figure 20-8 shows the RabbitMQ web console and the queues. Take a closer look and you will find that Spring XD has just created a particular queue with an ID as its name and a **docs-pdf.0** queue that will be used for your counter.

Let's Do Analytics

Now you are ready to start sending documents through RabbitMQ and see another Spring XD feature: analytics! Spring XD provides analytics to support real-time analysis using metrics such as counters and gauges. For your Spring application you are going to use the counter that was declared on the tap. The name of your counter is "pdfcount".

You can open any browser and go to `http://localhost:9393/metrics`. This will show you JSON data, as shown in Figure 20-9.

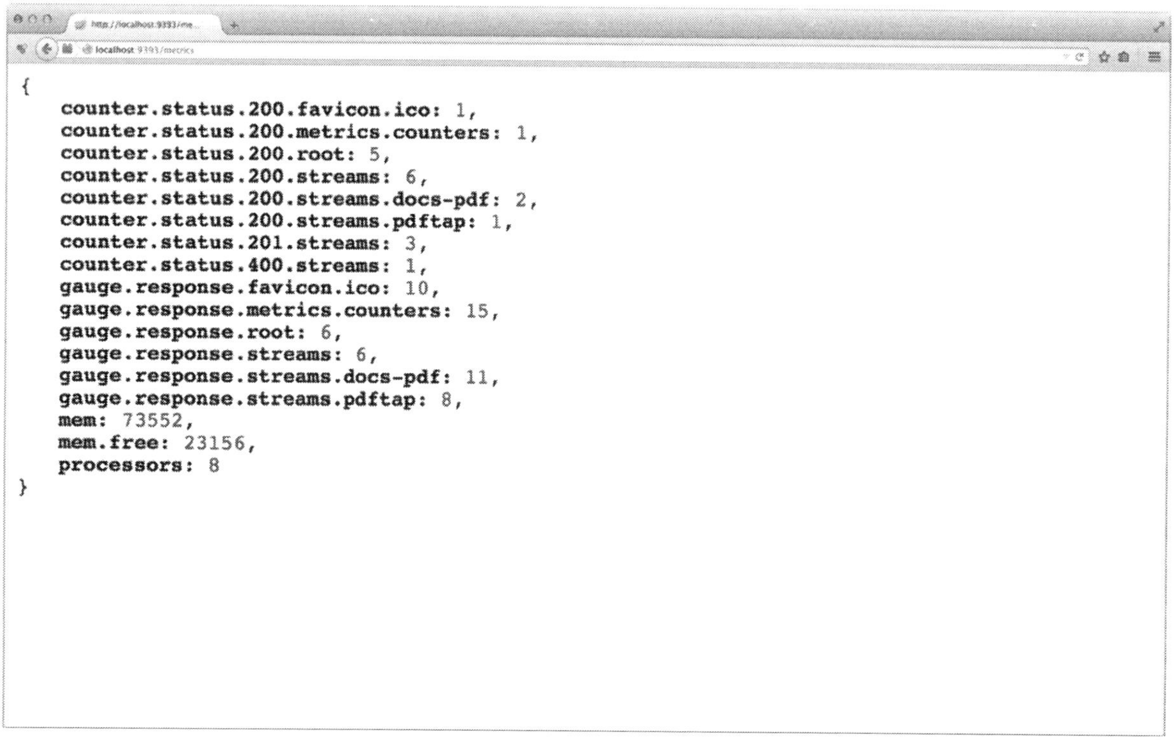

```
{
    counter.status.200.favicon.ico: 1,
    counter.status.200.metrics.counters: 1,
    counter.status.200.root: 5,
    counter.status.200.streams: 6,
    counter.status.200.streams.docs-pdf: 2,
    counter.status.200.streams.pdftap: 1,
    counter.status.201.streams: 3,
    counter.status.400.streams: 1,
    gauge.response.favicon.ico: 10,
    gauge.response.metrics.counters: 15,
    gauge.response.root: 6,
    gauge.response.streams: 6,
    gauge.response.streams.docs-pdf: 11,
    gauge.response.streams.pdftap: 8,
    mem: 73552,
    mem.free: 23156,
    processors: 8
}
```

Figure 20-9. *Spring XD's Metrics at* `http://localhost:9393/metrics`

Figure 20-9 shows the Spring XD's metrics; the counter you care about is **counter.status.200.streams.docs-pdf**. Also, you can go to `http://localhost:9393/metrics/counters` and see the name of the actual counter. In your case, it's "**pdfcount**".

Next, you are going to start by sending a few documents to the RabbitMQ. (You can use the RabbitMQ web console under the queues and select docs-pdf > Publish Message section.) Look at the metric reported by Spring XD; you should have the number of messages sent. Also, you can send document messages using one of the producers from other chapters. After sending the PDF document messages, you can open any browser and go to `http://localhost:9393/metrics/counters/pdfcount` (see Figure 20-10).

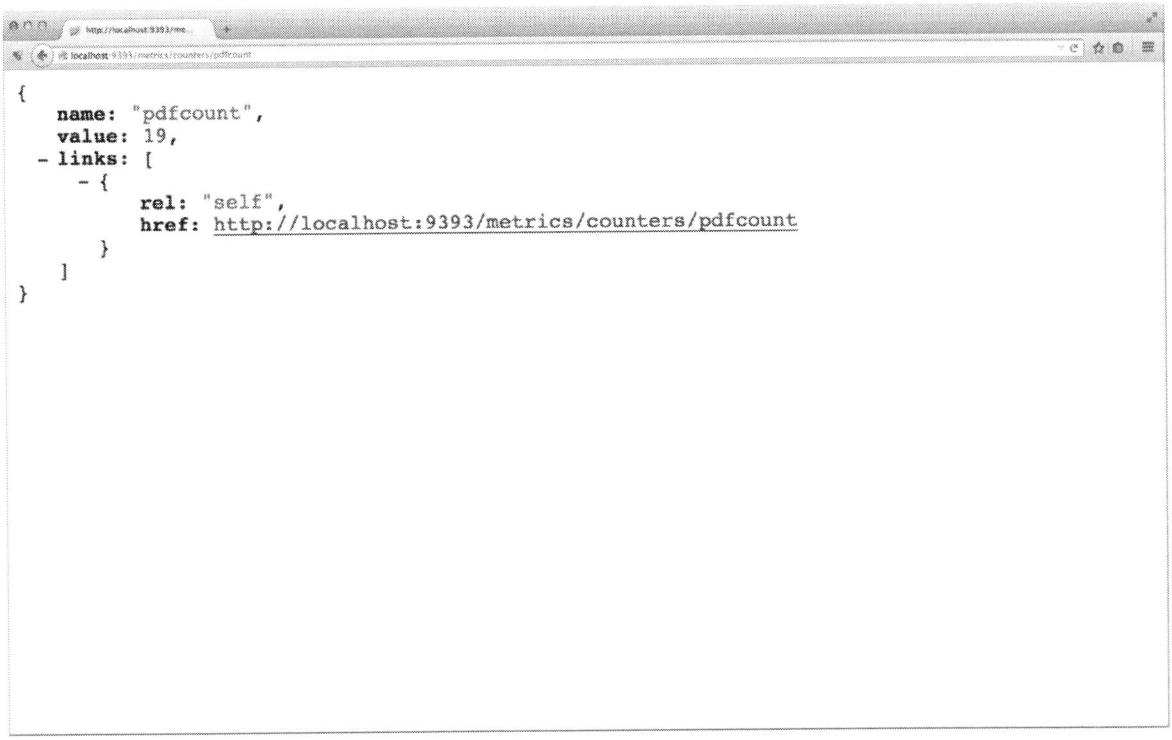

Figure 20-10. *Spring XD Counter at* `http://localhost:9393/metrics/counters/pdfcount`

Figure 20-10 shows the result of sending the PDF messages. In this case, the counter's value is 19.

Now you can start sending as many documents as you want. Listing 20-1 shows a Spring Boot client that uses rabbitmq and uses a consumer, just to see how it will interact with your Spring application and the Spring XD.

Listing 20-1. rabbitmqStream.groovy

```groovy
@Log
@Configuration
@EnableRabbitMessaging
class MyDocumentsRabbitMQStream implements CommandLineRunner {

        @Autowired
        RabbitTemplate rabbitTemplate

        private String queueName = "docs-pdf"
        private String exchangeName = "mydocuments"
        private String routingKey = ".pdf"

        @Bean
        Queue queue() {
                new Queue(queueName, false)
        }
```

```groovy
        @Bean
        DirectExchange exchange() {
                new DirectExchange("mydocuments")
        }

        @Bean
        Binding binding(Queue queue, DirectExchange exchange) {
                BindingBuilder
                                .bind(queue)
                                .to(exchange)
                                .with("docs-pdf")
        }

        @Bean
        SimpleMessageListenerContainer container(CachingConnectionFactory connectionFactory) {
                return new SimpleMessageListenerContainer(
                connectionFactory: connectionFactory,
                queueNames: [queueName],
                messageListener: new MessageListenerAdapter(new Receiver(latch:latch), "receive")
                )
        }

        void run(String... args) {
                log.info "Sending Documents..."
                500.times {
                        rabbitTemplate.convertAndSend(exchangeName, routingKey, "Document(id: ${it},
created: ${new Date().format('yyyy-MM-dd HH:mm:ss') })")
                        sleep 1000
                }
        }
}

@Log
class MyDocumentsConsumer {

        def receive(String message) {
                log.info "Document Received: ${message}"
        }
}
```

Listing 20-1 shows a Spring Boot rabbitmq example that you can use. Take a look at the new annotation called @EnableRabbitMessaging that will enable the Spring AMQP module into your Spring Boot application, and the CommandLineRunner interface. This interface has the run method that you need to override; it will be the entry point for your Spring Boot application. You can run this Spring Boot application by executing

`spring run rabbitmqStream.groovy`

After executing the above command, the application will send 500 messages (of course, you can change this number to 1,000,0000 messages) and it will use a PDF as a routing key. The purpose of this example is just to experience the power of Spring XD. Don't forget while you are running this example to take a look at `http://localhost:9393/metrics/counters/pdfcount` for the pdfcount value.

Summary

In this chapter, you saw how to use Spring XD to get some metrics on how many documents you are receiving, but this is just a small example of the power of Spring XD. You can do more analysis using other streams like GemFire, Hadoop, etc. The best part is that you can extend Spring XD by creating custom modules that are suitable for your needs.

I hope you enjoyed reading this book. Now you know what the Spring Framework is all about. And you learned some of the modules that the Spring Framework offers and how to use them to create enterprise ready applications.

I encourage you to keep learning about Spring by reading more exciting titles from Apress and of course by keeping up with the developments from the Spring Framework web site: `https://spring.io/` and its blog: `https://spring.io/blog`.

Installing Tools

In this appendix, you will learn how to install all the tools necessary to follow along with the examples in this book. Since all of the examples use these tools, you will need them all.

The following is the list of tools that you will be using in all chapters:

1. Java 7 or Java 8 (JVM – Java virtual machine)

2. Gradle—a tool for compiling, testing, and building Java and Groovy projects

3. Groovy—a dynamic programming language based on JVM

The following is the list of tools that you will be using in Parts II, III, and IV of the book:

1. MongoDB—a NoSQL database

2. ActiveMQ—a JMS (Java Message Service) messaging broker

3. RabbitMQ—a AMQP messaging broker

4. Spring Boot—a new Spring technology that simplifies development, favoring convention over configuration and designed to get you up and running as quickly as possible

5. Spring XD—is a unified, distributed, and extensible system for data ingestion, real-time analytics, batch processing, and data export

Depending of what operating system you are using it will be necessary to set up some environment variables, but don't worry because I'll explain the process of installing each and every one of these tools. So, get ready; you are going to start with Java.

Installing Java

Java is the primary tool that you are going to be using. Even though the book has some Groovy examples, the Groovy programing language is based on the JVM (Java virtual machine). So to install Java, you need to install the JDK (Java Development Kit). Open any browser and go to www.oracle.com/technetwork/java/javase/downloads/jdk8-downloads-2133151.html. There you need to accept the License Agreement and then choose the version of your OS you are using (See Figure A-1).

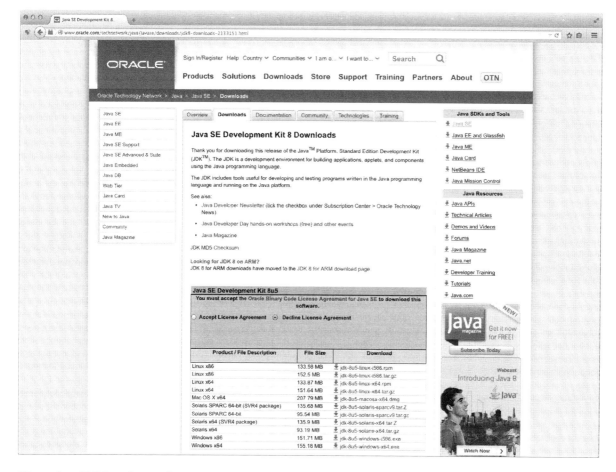

Figure A-1. *JDK Java SE Development Kit Download Page*

Installing Java for Windows OS

Since Windows XP through Windows 8.1 versions offer a similar installation process, follow the next steps. After you download your Windows version of Java, install it. I'll use Windows 7 64-bit version as an example (I downloaded the version Java SE 8 64bit - `jdk-8u5-windows-x64.exe`).

1. Double-click the `jdk-8u5-windows-x64.exe` file and follow the instructions. By default, most browsers will save the file in the `Downloads` folder, as shown in Figure A-2.

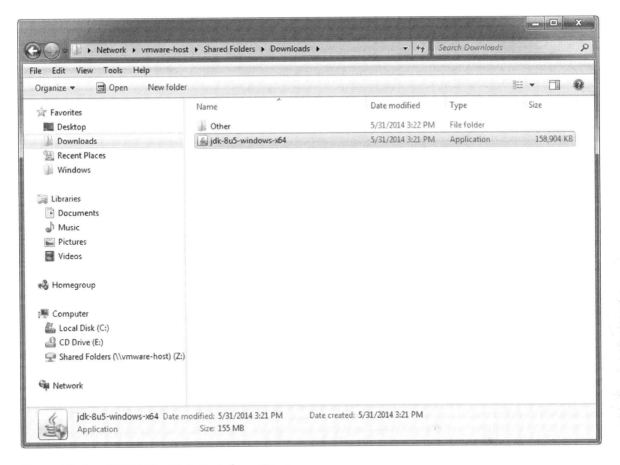

Figure A-2. Java SE JDK File: jdk-8u5-windows-x64.exe

2. After double-clicking the exe, Windows will show a User Account Control window asking for your permission to install Java. Click Yes and the install will continue, as shown in Figure A-3.

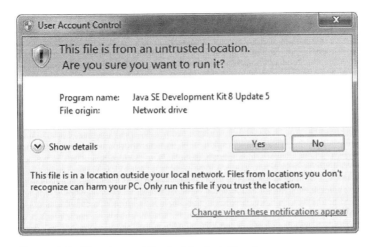

Figure A-3. User Account Control for Installing Java

3. You should see the initial installation dialog; click Next, as shown in Figure A-4.

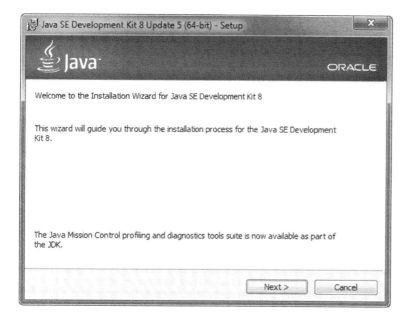

Figure A-4. *Initial Setup for Java SE 8*

4. This dialog will ask where you want to install Java; you are going to use the default settings (see Figure A-5). Click Next (it will ask you where to install the JRE; also leave the default settings, and click Next) and let the installer finish.

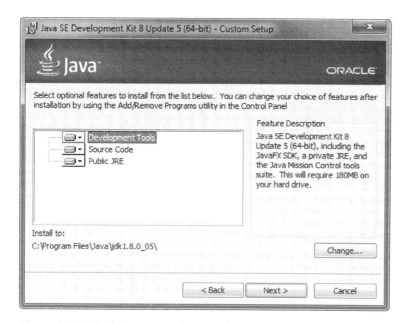

Figure A-5. *Default Features and Settings for Java SE 8*

Setting Environment Variables

This book's companion source code will be executed most of the time in a command line, and it needs to find the JVM, so is necessary to add two variables that will help to find it.

1. First, go to the Control Panel shown in Figure A-6 (Start Button ➤ Control Panel) and click System and Security.

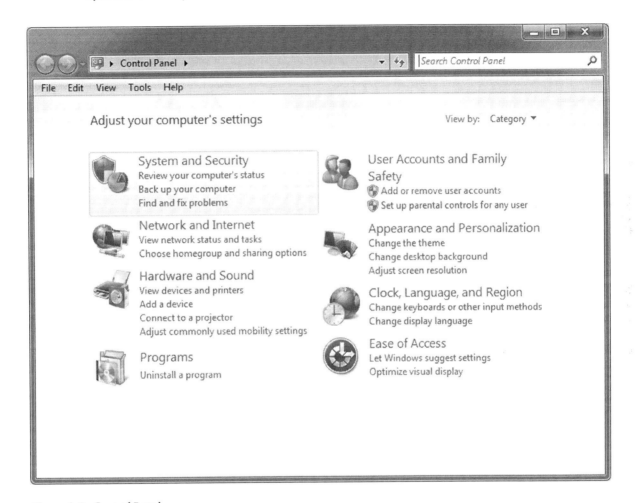

Figure A-6. *Control Panel*

2. From System and Security, click System (see Figure A-7).

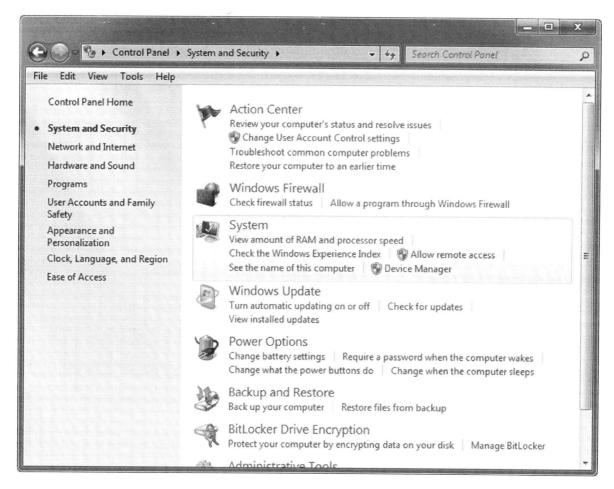

Figure A-7. *System and Security*

3. From System (See Figure A-8) click the left menu, Advanced system settings.

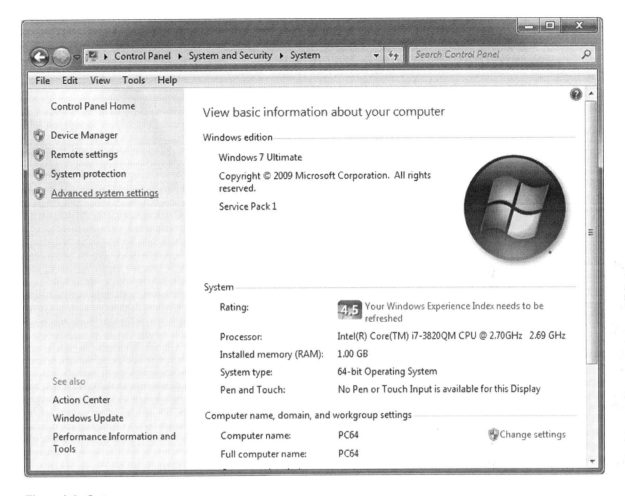

Figure A-8. *System*

4. After clicked Advanced system settings, it will display a System Properties dialog as shown in Figure A-9.

Figure A-9. *System Properties*

5. Click Environment Variables. Next, you are going to add one variable called JAVA_HOME that will be set to the Java installation path. (If you choose the Java's default path, it should install it in C:\Program Files\Java\jdk1.8.0_05, as shown in Figure A-10.)

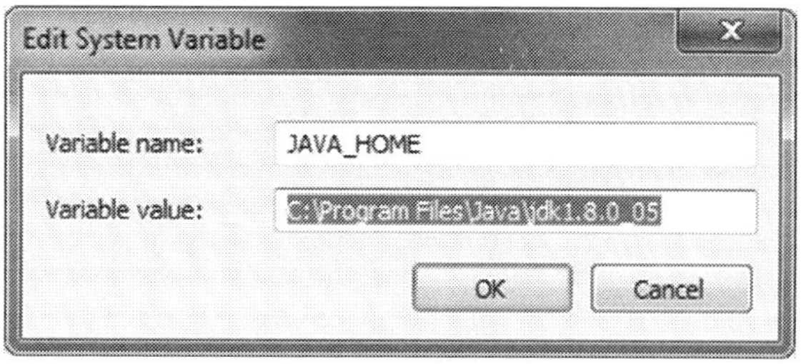

Figure A-10. *JAVA_HOME Variable*

6. Next, you are going to modify the `Path` variable, where you will be adding the binary path of the Java installation (`C:\Program Files\Java\jdk1.8.0_05\bin`) at the front of the existing value. In other words, this path should be at the beginning of any value of the `Path` variable. It's important to enclose the path with double quotes and end it with a semicolon. This is important because if there are spaces in the `Program Files` folder, and if you don't enclose it within quotes the Windows OS will truncate it and it won't able to find the executables. Figure A-11 shows that the path value will be "`C:\Program Files\Java\jdk1.8.0_05\bin`";.

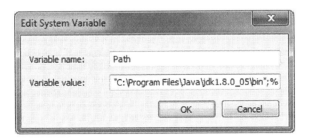

Figure A-11. *Path Variable*

7. Last, you need to test that the installation and the environment variables are correct. Open a DOS command window and execute the following commands:

```
C:\> echo %JAVA_HOME%
C:\> java -version
```

After executing the above commands you should not get an error and you should see something similar to Figure A-12.

Figure A-12. *Executing the echo and java Commands*

Installing Java for OS X

By default, OS X has the JDK preinstalled and the recent OS X Mavericks has Java 7 installed. You should be fine with this release, but if you want to you can install JDK 8. The advantage of installing JDK 8 is to get the new features that come with it, like lambdas and invoke dynamic.

1. If you want to install JDK 8, go to www.oracle.com/technetwork/java/javase/downloads/jdk8-downloads-2133151.html and click the Mac OS X version for the download. Once you download the jdk-8u5-macosx-x64.dmg file, double-click it, and a dialog will show something similar to Figure A-13.

Figure A-13. *jdk-8u5-macosx-x64.dmg File*

2. Double-click the JDK 8 Update 05.pkg file. It should show the next dialog (see Figure A-14).

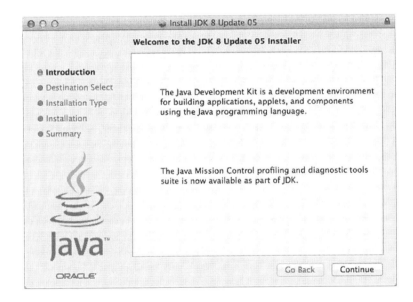

Figure A-14. *Installer Dialog*

3. Click Continue. And then click Install; after that the installer will prompt you for your password to continue with the installation (see Figure A-15).

Figure A-15. *Name and Password Dialog for the Installer*

After installing, it is necessary to make sure the JVM is accessible in the command line. So it is necessary to set some environment variables, and you can set them in your .bash_profile or .bash_rc files in your home directory. By default, the installer puts the JDK in the /Library/Java/JavaVirtualMachines path.

So, the values will be

```
export JAVA_HOME=/Library/Java/JavaVirtualMachines/jdk1.8.0_05.jdk/Contents/Home
export PATH=$JAVA_HOME/bin:$PATH
```

Then you can open a terminal and test Java by executing the following:

```
$ echo $JAVA_HOME
/Library/Java/JavaVirtualMachines/jdk1.8.0_05.jdk/Contents/Home

$ java -version
java version "1.8.0_05"
Java(TM) SE Runtime Environment (build 1.8.0_05-b13)
Java HotSpot(TM) 64-Bit Server VM (build 25.5-b02, mixed mode)
```

Figure A-16 shows the result of executing the above commands. Now you are ready to use Java, either a Windows or Mac OS X version. If you have a Linux box, you can download the Linux version and install it on /usr/lib/jvm or even in your home folder; just make sure to set up the JAVA_HOME and PATH environment variables.

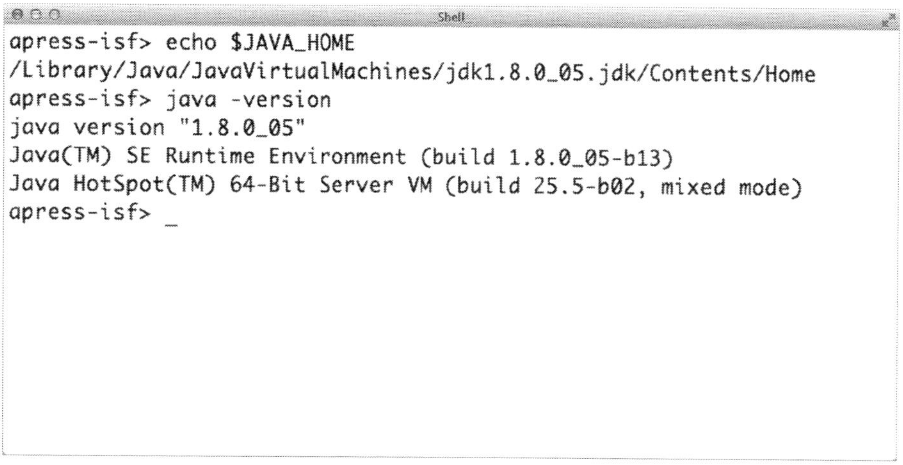

Figure A-16. *Mac OSX Terminal*

Tools for Mac OS X

This section covers the installation of two important tools and you should read it if you use Mac OS X. If you have a Mac, you will need to install these tools: Homebrew and GVM. I have a Mac and I've been working with these tools for several years now and I haven't had any problems so far.

Installing Homebrew

Homebrew is a package manager for Mac OS X that contains a lot of Linux packages that you can run in OS X as well. You will need Homebrew in order to install the rest of the tools described in this appendix, such as MongoDB, ActiveMQ, RabbitMQ, and Spring XD.

So, let's start. Go to the Homebrew web page at `http://brew.sh`, as shown in Figure A-17, and then go to the bottom of the main page and copy the code to install Homebrew.

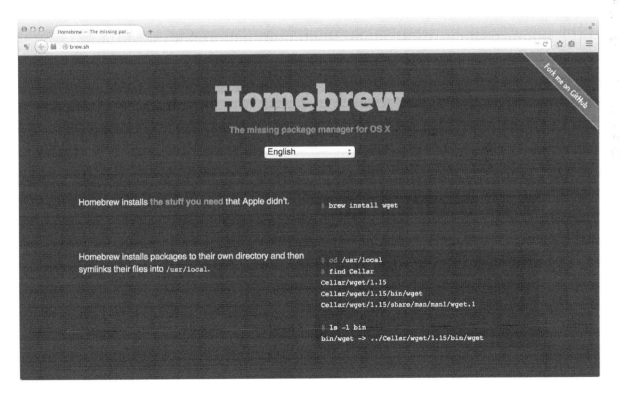

Figure A-17. *Homebrew Web Page*

Open a terminal and execute the following command to install Homebrew on your Mac:

```
$ ruby -e "$(curl -fsSL https://raw.github.com/Homebrew/homebrew/go/install)"
```

▓ **Note**   As you can see, you need the Ruby programming language to run Homebrew. By default, Mac OS X comes with it. If not, you can install Xcode from the App Store. Another alternative is to use the rvm (Ruby Version Manager) from https://rvm.io/.

After you install Homebrew, you need to execute the following command in order to update any new versions of the tools you will use:

```
$ brew update
```

▓ **Note**   There is no version for Windows or Linux. For Linux, you will need to install either a ZIP file or a rpm/deb package, depending on what version of Linux version you are running.

Installing GVM

GVM, the Groovy enVironment Manager, is a tool that can be installed either on Mac OS X or Linux without any problems. It will help you to install Gradle, Groovy, and Spring Boot. Remember that before using these tools it is necessary to have created JAVA_HOME and PATH environment variables; if you don't have them, the GVM installer will fail too.

To install GVM, go to http://gvmtool.net/, as shown in Figure A-18, and then copy the instructions in a terminal window.

Figure A-18. *GVM Web Page*

To install GVM in your Mac or Linux, execute the following command:

```
$ curl -s get.gvmtool.net | bash
```

After you execute the above command, you must either open a new terminal or in the same terminal execute the following command:

```
$ source ~/.gvm/bin/gvm-init.sh
```

■ **Note Using GVM on Windows** So far GVM only works on Unix OS, but there is one way to make it work on Windows. You can either install Git (another great tool for code version control; `http://git-scm.com/download/win`) or cygwin (a Unix/Linux environment for Windows; `www.cygwin.com/`).

Installing Gradle

Gradle is the primary tool that you will be using for building, testing, and deploying your Spring application. You can find Gradle at `www.gradle.org` (see Figure A-19).

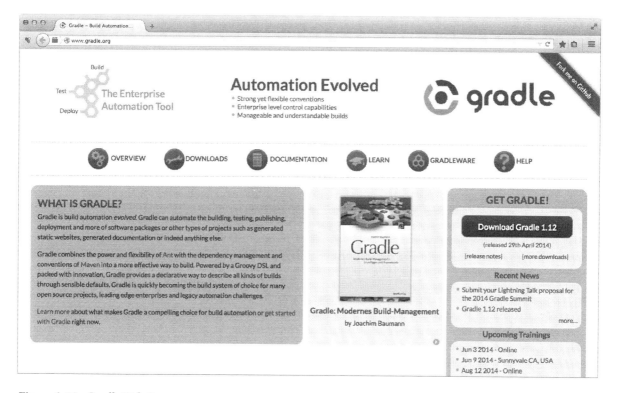

Figure A-19. *Gradle Web Page*

Installing Gradle on Windows

To install Gradle on Windows, first you need to go to `www.gradle.org/downloads` and download the `gradle-1.12-all.zip` file. After you download it, you can uncompress it and put it in the `C:\Tools\` folder.

Next, you need to add a new environment variable, `GRADLE_HOME`, and add the `GRADLE_HOME\bin` to the `Path` variable as well. Remember how you added the `JAVA_HOME` variable? This is the same, so go to `Control Panel ➤ System and Security ➤ System ➤ Advanced system settings ➤ Environment Variables`. See Figure A-20 that shows the Environment variables dialog for `GRADLE_HOME`.

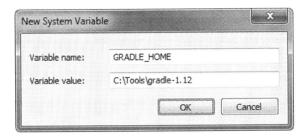

Figure A-20. *GRADLE_HOME Environment Variable Setting*

Next, you need to modify the Path variable; add this at the beginning: %GRADLE_HOME\bin;. See Figure A-21.

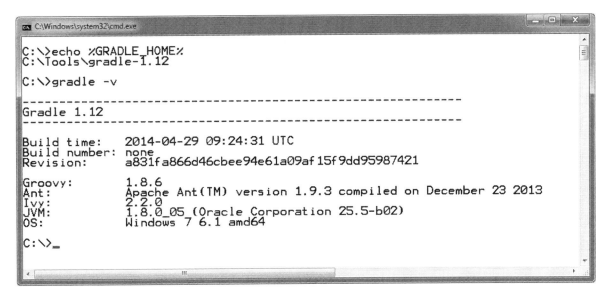

Figure A-21. *Path Variable Setting*

To verify that Gradle is correctly installed, open a DOS terminal and type the following:

```
C:\> echo %GRADLE_HOME%
C:\> gradle -v
```

After you run the above commands, you should have something similar to Figure A-22.

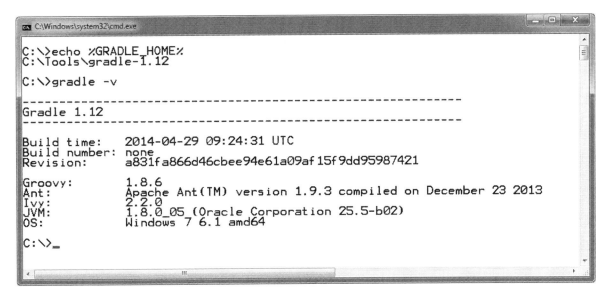

Figure A-22. *MS DOS Terminal*

Installing Gradle on a Mac OS X or Linux

Remember that you need to have the GVM installed already, and this is because Gradle depends on it. So, to install Gradle on a Mac or a Linux computer, just execute the next command:

```
$ gvm install gradle
```

You can test your Gradle tool by executing

```
$ gradle -v
```

```
------------------------------------------------------------
Gradle 1.12
------------------------------------------------------------

Build time:   2014-04-29 09:24:31 UTC
Build number: none
Revision:     a831fa866d46cbee94e61a09af15f9dd95987421

Groovy:       1.8.6
Ant:          Apache Ant(TM) version 1.9.3 compiled on December 23 2013
Ivy:          2.2.0
JVM:          1.8.0_05 (Oracle Corporation 25.5-b02)
OS:           Linux 3.13.0-24-generic amd64
```

Installing Groovy

Groovy is another programming language that you will need to use from the start of the book. Groovy has become one of the most important dynamic languages in the JVM ecosystem, providing many features that other languages have borrowed, even the new JDK 8—features like closures!

For information about Groovy news and latest releases, go to http://groovy.codehaus.org (as shown in Figure A-23).

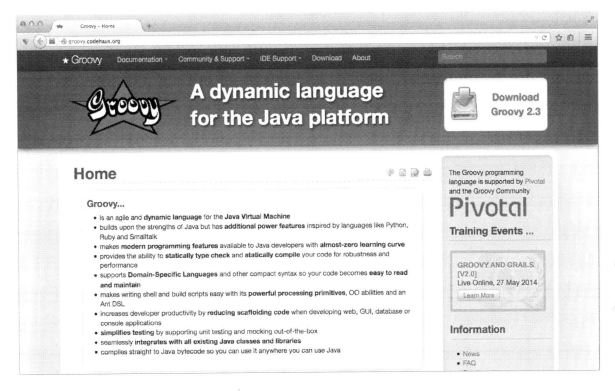

Figure A-23. *Groovy Web Page*

Installing Groovy on Windows

To install Groovy on Windows, go to `http://groovy.codehaus.org/Download` and choose the Windows installer. It will be something similar to the Java installer. Choose all the default settings. Even though the installer sets all the environment variables, you need to make sure the `GROOVY_HOME\bin` is at the beginning of the `Path` variable, as shown in Figure A-24.

Figure A-24. *Path Environment Variable Dialog*

Next, make sure that Groovy is working by opening a DOS terminal and executing the following command (see Figure A-25):

```
C:\> groovy -v
```

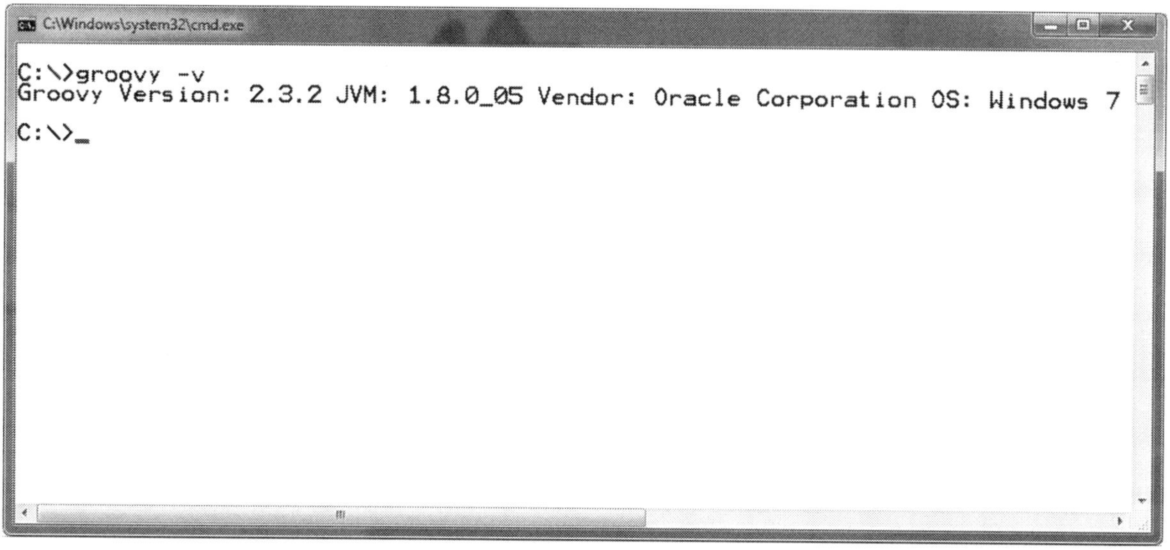

```
C:\>groovy -v
Groovy Version: 2.3.2 JVM: 1.8.0_05 Vendor: Oracle Corporation OS: Windows 7

C:\>_
```

Figure A-25. *MS DOS Terminal Running Groovy*

Installing Groovy on a Mac OS X or Linux

Remember that you need to have the GVM installed already; this is because the GVM tools make it easy install Groovy! So, to install the Groovy programming language on a Mac or a Linux computer, just execute the next command:

```
$ gvm install groovy
```

You can test the Groovy programming language by executing

```
$ groovy -    version
Groovy Version: 2.3.2 JVM: 1.8.0_05 Vendor: Oracle Corporation OS: Linux
```

Installing MongoDB

MongoDB is an open source document database that you are going to use in several chapters. Remember that this is a NoSQL database server, as shown in Figure A-26. The URL for the MongoDB is www.mongodb.org/.

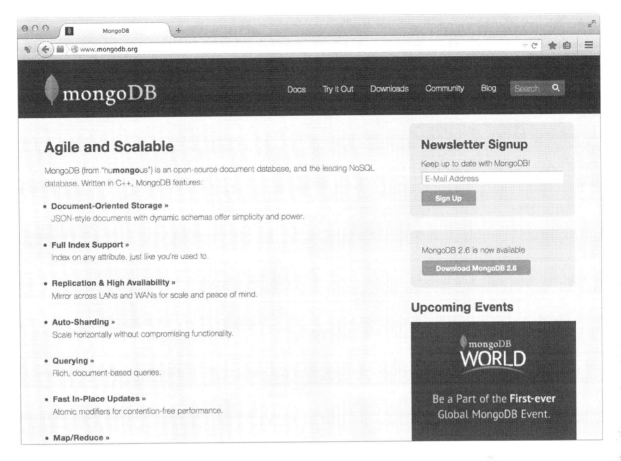

Figure A-26. *MongoDB Web Page*

Installing MongoDB on Windows

To install MongoDB on Windows, go to `www.mongodb.org/downloads` and choose the msi package, either the 64-bit or 32-bit version depending on your Windows OS.

Install MongoDB by double-clicking the `mongodb-win32-x86_64-2008plus-2.6.1.msi` file. Choose the default settings. The installer will put MongoDB in `C:\Program Files\MongoDB 2.6 Standard\bin`. You need to add path to your `Path` environment variable. You can do the same thing as with the previous tools and, even though it is not necessary, you can define a `MONGODB_HOME` and add the `%MONGODB_HOME%\bin` to your path (see Figure A-27). You need this in order to execute some mongo commands in a DOS terminal window. This happens when you start the server or when you need to query a collection in Mongo.

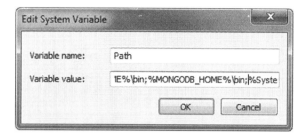

Figure A-27. *Path Environment Variable with the MONGODB_HOME/bin*

The MongoDB server also needs a storage path where it will allocate all the data for your collections (these collections will hold all the documents and types that you will be using in several chapters). So every time you start the server you need to add this path with the --dbpath parameter.

Start MongoDB server

To start the MongoDB server, execute the following command (also see Figure A-28). It is important that the DATA path exists:

```
C:\> mongod --dbpath C:\Data\mongodb
```

```
C:\>mongod --dbpath C:\Data\mongodb
2014-06-06T23:49:09.764-0600 [initandlisten] MongoDB starting : pid=2900 port=27017 dbpath=C:\Dat
2014-06-06T23:49:09.780-0600 [initandlisten] targetMinOS: Windows 7/Windows Server 2008 R2
2014-06-06T23:49:09.780-0600 [initandlisten] db version v2.6.1
2014-06-06T23:49:09.780-0600 [initandlisten] git version: 4b95b086d2374bdcfcdf2249272fb552c9c726e
2014-06-06T23:49:09.780-0600 [initandlisten] build info: windows sys.getwindowsversion(major=6, m
e_pack='Service Pack 1') BOOST_LIB_VERSION=1_49
2014-06-06T23:49:09.780-0600 [initandlisten] allocator: system
2014-06-06T23:49:09.780-0600 [initandlisten] options: { storage: { dbPath: "C:\Data\mongodb" } }
2014-06-06T23:49:09.780-0600 [initandlisten] journal dir=C:\Data\mongodb\journal
2014-06-06T23:49:09.780-0600 [initandlisten] recover : no journal files present, no recovery need
2014-06-06T23:49:09.827-0600 [initandlisten] waiting for connections on port 27017
```

Figure A-28. *Running MongoDB*

Stop MongoDB Server

To stop the MongoDB server, just press Ctrl+C from the window where it is running and it will close all connections and shut down the server.

▓ **Note**　If you need to run MongoDB as a service, you can follow the steps from MongoDB's web site: `http://docs.mongodb.org/manual/tutorial/install-mongodb-on-windows/`.

Installing MongoDB on a Mac OS X

You need to install the Homebrew tool first (remember, Homebrew makes it easy to install any tool or library). To install MongoDB, just execute the following commands:

```
$ brew update
$ brew install mongodb
```

After installing MongoDB, make sure everything is installed correctly by executing

```
$ mongo -version
MongoDB shell version: 2.6.1
```

Start MongoDB server

To start the MongoDB server on your Mac, just execute the following command:

```
$ brew services start mongodb
==> Successfully started `mongodb` (label: homebrew.mxcl.mongodb)
```

Stop MongoDB server

To stop the MongoDB server, just execute the following command:

```
$ brew services stop mongodb
Stopping `mongodb`… (might take a while)
==> Successfully stopped `mongodb` (label: homebrew.mxcl.mongodb)
```

Start MongoDB at Login

If you want to have MongoDB started every time you login into your Mac, the following command will do the trick:

```
$ ln -sfv /usr/local/opt/mongodb/*.plist ~/Library/LaunchAgents
```

▓ **Note**　How you install MongoDB on a Linux computer will depend on your version of Linux, either RPM (for RedHat-based distributions) or .deb (for Debian-based distributions). Usually you can find the installation package at the MongoDB site (`www.mongodb.org/downloads`).

Installing Apache Active MQ

Apache Active MQ is one of the brokers you will use in several chapters, and it will take care of the JMS (Java Message Service) messages. The Apache ActiveMQ URL is http://activemq.apache.org (see Figure A-29); there you can find more information about it.

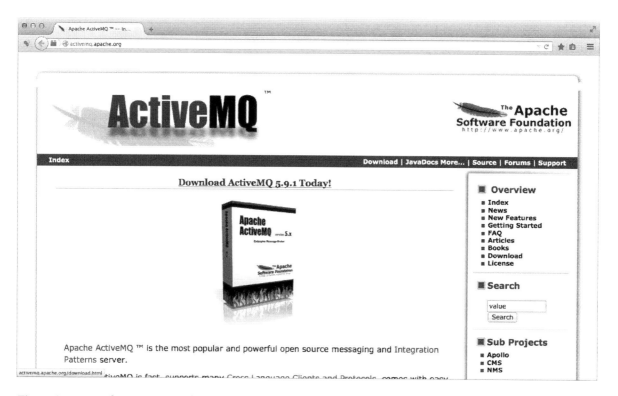

Figure A-29. *Apache ActiveMQ Web Page*

Installing Apache ActiveMQ on Windows

Installing Apache ActiveMQ in Windows is very straightforward. Navigate to http://activemq.apache.org and then go to the download section and download the binary file in a ZIP format: apache-activemq-5.9.0-bin.zip.

After downloading the ZIP file, you can uncompress it to the C:\Tools\ folder.

Start ActiveMQ

To start ActiveMQ, you need to go directly to the bin folder. So, open a DOS terminal and execute the following command:

```
C:\> cd "C:\Tools\apache-activemq-5.9.0\bin\win64"
C:\Tools\apache-activemq-5.9.0\bin\win64> activemq start
```

Stop ActiveMQ

To stop ActiveMQ, press Ctrl+C on the DOS terminal where the ActiveMQ is running or you can execute the following command in another DOS terminal:

```
C:\> cd "C:\Tools\apache-activemq-5.9.0\bin\win64"
C:\Tools\apache-activemq-5.9.0\bin\win64> activemq stop
```

▓ **Note**   You can add the ActiveMQ as a service; just execute the `InstallService.bat` in the `C:\Tools\apache-activemq-5.9.0\bin\win64` path. For more information, take a look at `http://activemq.apache.org`.

Accessing the ActiveMQ Web Console Hawtio

To access hawtio, you need the ActiveMQ running. Open a browser and go to `http://localhost:8161/hawtio`. It will prompt you for some credentials, such as username and password. The username and password are admin/admin. This console will be needed in some chapters, so you must have it ready.

▓ **Note**   It is important to note that version activemq-5.9.1 doesn't include the HAWTIO web console, which you will be using in Chapter 11. So it's important to use this version: 5.9.0.

Installing Apache ActiveMQ on a Mac OS X

Remember that you need to have Homebrew installed. To install Apache ActiveMQ, execute the following command:

```
$ brew update
$ brew install activemq
```

To verify that the installation was successful, execute the following command:

```
$ activemq --version
INFO: Using default configuration
ACTIVEMQ_HOME: /usr/local/Cellar/activemq/5.9.1/libexec
ACTIVEMQ_BASE: /usr/local/Cellar/activemq/5.9.1/libexec
ACTIVEMQ_CONF: /usr/local/Cellar/activemq/5.9.1/libexec/conf
ACTIVEMQ_DATA: /usr/local/Cellar/activemq/5.9.1/libexec/data

ActiveMQ 5.9.1
For help or more information please see http://activemq.apache.org.
```

Start ActiveMQ

To start ActiveMQ broker, execute the following command:

```
$ activemq start
```

Stop ActiveMQ

To start ActiveMQ broker, execute the following command:

```
$ activemq stop
```

■ **Note** For Linux computers, just download the `.tar.gz` file from `http://activemq.apache.org/download.html` and uncompress it in your favorite path. For starting or stopping the activemq, usually the scripts are in the `bin/` folder.

Installing RabbitMQ

RabbitMQ is a message broker that knows AMQP. You will be using it in some chapters. For more information about RabbitMQ, go to `www.rabbitmq.com` (as shown in Figure A-30).

Figure A-30. *RabbitMQ Web Page*

Installing RabbitMQ on Windows

RabbitMQ is based on the Erlang VM, so you need to install Erlang first. To install Erlang, go to www.erlang.org/download.html. Install version otp_win64_17.0.exe (remember to check your Windows OS version, either 32-bit or 64-bit). During the installation, choose the default settings. Also, you need to add the ERLANG_HOME environment variable and set it to C:\Program Files\erl6.0.

To install RabbitMQ, go to www.rabbitmq.com/install-windows.html and download the rabbitmq-server-3.3.1.exe file. Double-click the file and choose the default settings. By default, the installer will set the RabbitMQ as a service, and it will start after you install it.

You can start and stop RabbitMQ by going to Control Panel ➤ System and Security ➤ Administrative Tools ➤ Services and looking for RabbitMQ.

Installing the RabbitMQ Web Console

By default, RabbitMQ doesn't have the web console enable, so you need to enable it by executing the following commands:

```
C:\> cd "C:\Program Files (x86)\RabbitMQ Server\rabbitmq_server-3.3.1\sbin"
C:\Program Files (x86)\RabbitMQ Server\rabbitmq_server-3.3.1\sbin> rabbitmq-plugins.bat enable
    rabbitmq_management
```

After you execute the above commands, you need to restart RabbitMQ, and then you can go to http://localhost:15672/. The username and password are guest/guest.

Installing RabbitMQ on a Mac OS X

Remember to install Homebrew before you install RabbitMQ; if you haven't installed it yet, you can take a look at the "Installing Homebrew" section of this appendix. To install RabbitMQ, execute the following commands:

```
$ brew update
$ brew install rabbitmq
```

The above commands will install RabbitMQ and its dependency, the Erlang VM.

RabbitMQ Useful Commands

RabbitMQ has different commands that can be executed in the command line to start, stop, or check out the status of RabbitMQ.

Start RabbitMQ

To start RabbitMQ, execute the following command:

```
$ brew services start rabbitmq
==> Successfully started `rabbitmq` (label: homebrew.mxcl.rabbitmq)
```

Stop RabbitMQ

To stop RabbitMQ, execute the following command:

```
$ brew services stop rabbitmq
Stopping `rabbitmq`… (might take a while)
==> Successfully stopped `rabbitmq` (label: homebrew.mxcl.rabbitmq)
```

RabbitMQ Status

To get the status of RabbitMQ, execute the following command:

```
$ rabbitmqctl status
```

Installing the RabbitMQ Web Console

By default, RabbitMQ doesn't have the web console enabled, so you need to enable it by executing the following commands:

```
$ rabbitmq-plugins enable rabbitmq_management
$ brew services restart rabbitmq
```

After you execute the above commands, you need to restart RabbitMQ, and then you can go to http://localhost:15672/. The username and password are guest/guest.

Start RabbitMQ at Login

If you want to have RabbitMQ started every time you login into your Mac, the following command will do the trick:

```
$ ln -sfv /usr/local/opt/rabbitmq/*.plist ~/Library/LaunchAgents
```

■ **Note** For Linux computers, just download the correct package distribution from www.rabbitmq.com/download.html.

Installing Spring Boot

Spring Boot is a new technology for creating enterprise and production-ready Spring applications (see Figure A-31). To get more information about this project, go to http://projects.spring.io/spring-boot/.

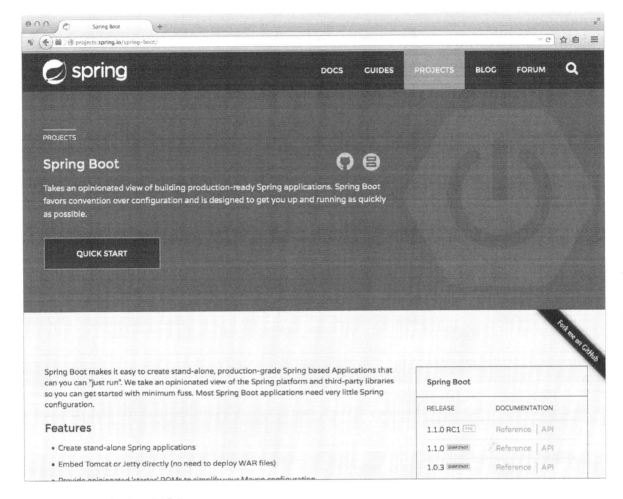

Figure A-31. *Spring Boot Web Page*

Installing Spring Boot on Windows

To install Spring Boot on Windows, you need to download and install the Spring CLI (command-line interface) from `http://repo.spring.io/snapshot/org/springframework/boot/spring-boot-cli/`. From the previous URL, you can choose the latest version of the CLI. In this example, I'm using `spring-boot-cli-1.1.2.BUILD.XXX-bin.zip`; once you download it, you can uncompress it into the `C:\Tools` folder.

Next, you need to add the `bin` path to the `Path` environment variable, and even though is not required, I suggest you add the `SPRINGBOOT_HOME` environment variable that points to `C:\Tools\spring-1.1.2.BUILD-SNAPSHOT` and then modify the `Path` environment variable by putting this at the beginning of the existing value: `%SPRING_HOME%\bin;`.

%SPRINGBOOT_HOME

Installing Spring Boot on a Mac OS X or Linux

Remember to have the GVm tool installed. To install Spring Boot on your Mac or Linux, execute the following command:

```
$ gvm install springboot
```

To make sure that Spring Boot was successfully installed, execute the following command:

```
$ spring --version
Spring CLI v1.1.1.RELEASE
```

Installing Spring XD

Spring XD is part of the last chapter of the book, and even though it tells you how to install it, I'm putting more detailed instructions for Windows and Unix users here. The Spring XD web page URL is http://projects.spring.io/spring-xd/ (see Figure A-32); it's where to go for more information.

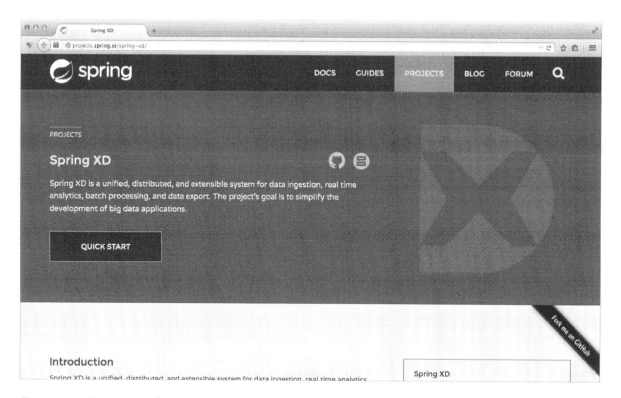

Figure A-32. *Spring XD Web Page*

Installing Spring XD on Windows

To install Spring XD on Windows, you need to do a manual install (the same as Spring Boot). Go to `http://projects.spring.io/spring-xd/` and go to the manual installation part and download the latest version shown there. In my examples, I use the `spring-xd-1.0.0.M7-dist.zip` file. Download it and uncompress it into the `C:\Tools` folder.

Next, you need to add the `XD_HOME` variable and add the `bin` folder to the `Path` environment variable. So the `XD_HOME` can point to `C:\Tools\spring-xd-1.0.0.M7\xd`; also, add the following to the beginning of the `Path` environment variable: `%XD_HOME%\bin;`.

Installing Spring XD on a Mac OS X

Remember that you need to have Homebrew installed (if you haven't installed it yet, go to the "Installing Homebrew" section of this appendix). To install Spring XD, execute the following commands:

```
$ brew update
$ brew tap pivotal/tap
$ brew install springxd
```

Summary

Now you have all the tools necessary to compile, test, and run all the examples of this book. You can also download the book's companion source code from the Apress web site. Now you have all the tools and code you need for this book!

Index

Get the eBook for only $10!

Now you can take the weightless companion with you anywhere, anytime. Your purchase of this book entitles you to 3 electronic versions for only $10.

This Apress title will prove so indispensible that you'll want to carry it with you everywhere, which is why we are offering the eBook in 3 formats for only $10 if you have already purchased the print book.

Convenient and fully searchable, the PDF version enables you to easily find and copy code—or perform examples by quickly toggling between instructions and applications. The MOBI format is ideal for your Kindle, while the ePUB can be utilized on a variety of mobile devices.

Go to www.apress.com/promo/tendollars to purchase your companion eBook.

Apress®
THE EXPERT'S VOICE™

45761947R00195

Made in the USA
Lexington, KY
08 October 2015